The Social Organization
of Mental Illness

The Social Organization of Mental Illness

Lindsay Prior

SAGE Publications
London • Newbury Park • New Delhi

First published 1993

 SAGE Publications Ltd
6 Bonhill Street
London EC2A 4PU

SAGE Publications Inc
2455 Teller Road
Newbury Park, California 91320

SAGE Publications India Pvt Ltd
32, M-Block Market
Great Kailash – I
New Delhi 110 048

British Library Cataloguing in Publication data

Prior, Lindsay
    Social Organization of Mental Illness
    I. Title
    362.2

    ISBN 0–8039–8499–5
    ISBN 0–8039–8500–2 (pbk)

Library of Congress catalog card number 93–084109

Typeset by The Word Shop
Printed in Great Britain by Biddles Ltd, Guildford, Surrey

In memory of Frank Prior,
who loved books

Contents

List of Figures

List of Tables

Preface

The origins of this book lie in a piece of empirical research which was carried out at various periods between the summer of 1988 and February 1991. The research programme in itself was somewhat limited in scope and primarily evaluative in intention. It involved a comparison of the social worlds of a number of psychiatric hospital in-patients with those of patients who had left the hospital up to five years previously and who were, by that stage, 'living in the community'. Naturally enough, the people who had sanctioned the research wanted some specific answers to their very general questions (such as whether the resettlement programme was working, what improvements could be made in the living arrangements of ex-patients and so on). Whether they approved of the answers which they eventually got is something I never discovered.

One thing which I did discover, however, was that by concentrating on the technical issues at hand, evaluation research tends inevitably to squeeze out broader sociological questions concerning the context in which research is being undertaken in the first place. And very often, whilst my empirical programme was being directed towards the accumulation of data on such things as measures of activity and inactivity, patient satisfaction and the range and nature of social contacts, a large number of basic sociological questions lay round and about the research setting – untouched. In my case two broad sets of questions intrigued me from the outset. The first concerned the reasons as to why there were so many people in the hospital to begin with (and why they had been living there for such a long time). And the second concerned the reasons as to why those same residents were now being encouraged to leave the hospital for homes in the community.

At first sight, of course, it seemed as if answers to such questions were in plentiful supply. And those answers made reference to such things as social policy changes, new drugs, economic theories and oh so many more features of the 1980s. Some explanations even cited mental illness itself as the source of both the puzzles and their answers. Yet to my mind at least, the problems remained unresolved. For to suggest, for example, that the patients had been in hospital because they suffered from serious mental illnesses begged the question as to how their illnesses had been sufficiently alleviated to enable them to live in the community. To suggest that they were not really ill in the first place but merely 'deviant', begged the question as to why organizational reactions to such deviance had changed. In a similar way, to suggest that the patients had been hospitalized (and were now being dehospitalized) for their 'own good', begged the question as to why that 'good' had been so radically reinterpreted. And this perpetual question begging did not come to a halt when I considered the kinds of explanations which referred to alterations in political policy; the anti-institutional ethos which emerged in social policy discussions of the 1950s and 1960s (and which found its sociological expression in such works as Goffman's *Asylums*); the changing nature of economic interests; or the capacity of modern pharmacology to control the wilder excesses of the schizophrenic personality. In fact, it seemed to me that what all these explanations omitted was any substantial reference to movements within the world of psychiatry itself, and in particular to the ways in which psychiatric professionals (by whom I mean nurses, social workers, occupational therapists and psychologists as well as medically trained psychiatrists), had essentially redefined the concept of mental illness. What that redefinition involved, how it occurred and how it was represented through the work of psychiatric professionals themselves is, quite naturally, a matter which I leave until later.

In many ways, of course, the ideologies of the professionals just referred to ultimately display their effects in the lives and activities of the hundreds of thousands of human beings who are said to be suffering from one or other form of mental illness. And professional representations of such illness often become evident only in so far as psychiatric workers describe, discuss and organize real live 'patients' and 'clients' in real circumstances. Consequently, and as well as examining various forms of texts, vignettes, visual images and numerous other forms of social representation, this book also makes reference to the lives and everyday experiences of patients who were living in (or who had recently lived within) the study hospital at the time of the original research. Exactly how psychiatric ideology impinged on their lives is, as one might expect, a matter dealt with in the remainder of the book. At this point I would merely like to record my gratitude for the goodwill which the patients showed towards the research – for whatever merits this book may have is in large part a direct product of their generosity.

Although I found this a very difficult book to write I can honestly say that at almost every stage of the research and the writing process I was given more help and assistance than I had the right to expect, though, naturally enough, the sources of such assistance varied according to the nature of the work being undertaken. The empirical research was mainly financed by a grant from the Joseph Rowntree Memorial Trust, and I would like to thank the Trustees and their administrators for their generous help and support during 1989. The very first source of support, however, was the Health and Health Care Research Unit of Queen's University Belfast, and I would especially like to thank its first Director, Dr Charles Normand, for his early and unequivocal vote of confidence in the research plan. Once into the enquiry, I was of course assisted and encouraged in many different ways by a large number of people who, unfortunately, are too numerous to mention individually. I would, however, like to single out Dr Philip McGarry and Dr Michael Donnelly for both their practical help and for their timely discussions – discussions which invariably served to sharpen up what would have otherwise been a somewhat hazy comprehension of the data at hand. When the time arrived to begin writing the book, I was very generously helped by a small grant from the Nuffield Foundation which enabled me to work in the Library of the Royal College of Medicine (which proved to be a lovely experience in itself), and the British Library. The curators of the Galerie Nationale de Prague gave permission to reproduce the painting by Josef Čapek which is used on the cover of the book. Karen Phillips, the commissioning editor at Sage, was patient beyond reason in waiting for the manuscript. And last but not least I must, for the sake of my own conscience if nothing else, thank my wife and best friend Pip, for help and encouragement which never faded from beginning to end.

1

Introduction: Social Representations and Social Worlds

The Aims of the Book

Social life is made up of representations.

Emile Durkheim (1952: 312)

The primary aim of this book is to examine the fundamental principles in terms of which medical and social services for people with serious psychiatric disorders have been organized. The essential focus of the book is on the most important and far-reaching of all the organizational changes which have affected twentieth century psychiatry, namely the transition from the provision of hospital centred to community centred services. The book seeks to trace the rationales which lay behind that, as well as other transformations, and to examine their consequences for both the mentally ill and the professionals who organize their care and treatment.

The basic sociological argument of the book involves an elaboration of the claim that the ways in which we organize care and treatment for psychiatric disorders serves both to reflect and constitute what such disorders actually are. In that sense psychiatric illnesses are not simply seen as being 'in' patients, but are rather viewed as phenomena nestled within the whole gamut of socio-medical relationships and socio-medical arrangements which ordinarily surround them. (Though the presentation of this argument is not meant to detract in any way from the very real personal agonies which are routinely experienced by people who are clients of psychiatric services.) In particular, it will be contended that it is by studying what people do and say about what is commonly called mental illness, that we may best come to understand what it is. And the utilization of such a principle has an immediate sociological pay-off in so far as it incites us to study and analyse not merely the activities and beliefs of people who are said to suffer from such illness, but also the activities and beliefs of those who surround them. Though given the fact that most of the describing, explaining, treating and managing of psychiatric disorder is carried out by members of professional or quasi-professional groupings, this book involves in large part the study of essentially professional knowledge and practice in the realm of the psychiatric. To that extent it is a study of what is professionally known and practised in relation to the various maladies which fall under the rubric of mental illness rather than a study of such things as lay interpretations of mental illness, or family reactions to it.

What people do and say, of course, is always circumscribed by time, place and socio-historical context. And in reporting on what people do, the sociologist is constrained by these same parameters. So despite the fact that there are various dimensions to the scope of the study contained herein, there are also strict limits as to its nature – limits which serve both to focus it and to structure it. The first set of limits arises out of the fact that the author has used the experiences of a specific group of adult psychiatric patients as a touchstone for examining how psychiatric practice is currently organized. In fact, the later part of the book deliberately examines the social worlds of a group of patients who, during the late 1980s, lived and worked in a variety of hospital and community based facilities. Needless to say, their worlds were peculiar and singular to them, but in studying how those worlds were organized we cannot help but gain insights into the complex nature of social and medical practices as they unfold in concrete empirical circumstances. And they are insights which cannot be obtained simply from the study of what we might call vade mecum knowledge – as might be gained from manuals, textbooks or other prescriptive and descriptive accounts concerning the organization of professional practice. This is so partly because the concepts and ideas which are enveloped in and expressed through literature are never detailed enough to capture the multifarious nature of reality, and partly because it is only in and through empirical action that theories and assumptions come to exist as relevant domains of experience. In that sense, the detailed technical descriptions and explanations of psychiatric disorder and its organization which one finds in psychiatry, nursing and other related texts offer little more than abbreviations of the practical processes through which such disorder is confronted in routine affairs. In this context one is reminded of that much quoted aphorism of Charcot's which was both directed at and quoted by Freud with approval, namely, 'La théorie c'est bon, mais ca n'empêche pas d'exister' (Freud, 1966b: 13). In other words medical, social work, and nursing theories are all well and good, but they are always subject to some form of encounter with the world as it is experienced. And it is a statement which can serve as a salutary reminder of the fact that whatever professionals may officially say and write about the people and activities that fall within their domain of influence, there is usually a gap between grand theoretical statements and the nature of things as they are ordinarily confronted in everyday life. It is for these kinds of reasons that we need to examine how the assumptions and beliefs of professionals are actually reflected in, and impinge on the lives of real patients in specific circumstances.

The lives and worlds of the patients and ex-patients who are referred to in this book were, of course, structured both in terms of the practical contingencies of everyday interaction, and in terms of a system of concepts, ideas and theoretical frameworks – much of which had been 'in place' long before any of the patients had been born. Thus, both the concept of the psychiatric hospital and the actual physical structure in which patients were treated and cared for had come into existence during the first decade of the present century. In addition the official diagnostic system by means of which most of the patients' disorders were recognized and described had been emerging since 1911, whilst the forms of therapy to which patients were and had been subject – occupational therapy, shock therapy, drug therapy, and in some cases, surgical intervention – had been woven into psychiatric theory and practice at quite diverse points of the twentieth century. And when one reflects on such facts it becomes evident that just as abstract theory requires reference to essential detail, so the study of personal biography and social worlds requires cognizance of larger conceptual and ideational contexts. Indeed, it is plain that such personal detail cannot be fully understood by restricting oneself to the immediate empirical contexts of action in which patients commonly find themselves. Thus, when a social worker talks to a 'schizophrenic patient' in a hospital ward about how that patient would consider the possibility of living in the community, we can legitimately ask a whole series of sociological questions about the entities and processes which underpin the entire conversational transaction. Why, for example, are the interactional roles structured in terms of social worker and patient in a hospital environment? Why is it only during the latter quarter of the twentieth century that the question of living 'in the community' adopts a new meaning and a new significance? And what in any case is a schizophrenic patient? This is not, of course, the point at which to answer such questions, and at this stage I merely wish to indicate how personal biography is forever related to aspects of big structural arrangements and cultural systems, such that we cannot begin to comprehend the one without being aware of the other. Consequently, and in order to look at the larger context in which mental illness is organized, we have to look far beyond the limits of time bound interactions.

There are, of course, numerous routes through which one might study the structural arrangements and conceptual frameworks by means of which personal histories are shaped and moulded. In this book, however, I intend to tackle the problem mainly by examining the ways in which psychiatric disorder has been represented in the literature and activities of specific professional groups during the twentieth century. Representations of disease and illness are, of course, numerous, emanating as they do from lay, medical, paramedical and even religious sources (to say little of the specific pharmacological, psychoanalytic or social psychiatric representations which may be found within clinical psychiatry itself). Inevitably some representations are more accessible for study than are others – yet it is only through the sum total of its representations that any given phenomenon comes to be fully known. In terms of mental illnesses, for example, this means that we can only truly get to know what the phenomena are by studying, among other things, the ways in which they are represented through classificatory tables and descriptive vignettes – as may, for example, be found in textbook discussions and official psychiatric nosologies. Or by studying the ways in which such illnesses are represented through aspects of architectural design; the ways in which they are reflected and represented through the organization of the professional division of labour; and perhaps even the ways in which they are represented through sociological and epidemiological descriptions of incidence, as well as the ways in which they are represented in and through the petty bureaucratic paraphernalia of nurses, social workers, psychiatrists and paramedical therapists. Naturally, these various representations tend to exist in systems of mutual support and so any given (and fundamental) belief in, say, the organic basis of illness is represented again and again many times over in many different ways and many different contexts. In that respect professional understandings of a single illness are diffused over numerous sites and through a variety of activities. It is to the study of such interlinking forms of representation that the first six chapters of this book are devoted, though I should add that I neither wish nor feel capable of producing a definitive twentieth century history of such representations. Instead I merely wish to use the social environment and biographies of the members of the study group as a set of boundary markers for my analysis. Thus, to cite just one example, I wish only to discuss the theoretical basis of shock therapies, or of occupational therapy because they were therapies which were administered to members of the study population. In other parts of the world perhaps other therapies and other practices reigned, and a definitive vision of psychiatric disorder in the twentieth century would have to take such things into account.

Social Representations of Mental Illness

> **Represent**: 1. To bring into presence. 2. To bring clearly and distinctly before the mind, esp. by description. 3. To give out, assert, or declare to be of a certain kind. 4. To show, exhibit, or display to the eye; to make visible or manifest. 5. To exhibit or reproduce in action. 6. To symbolize. 7. To stand for or in place of (a person or thing). 8. To take or fill the place of (another). 9. To serve as a specimen or example.
>
> *Shorter Oxford English Dictionary* (1986)

As I have stated already, this is a study of the ways in which mental illness is socially organized in the modern world. It does not, however, seek to describe and analyse such illness merely by examining the isolated miseries or behaviours of individuals in private circumstances, but instead to analyse mental illness in terms of the framework of public and collective categories through which such private troubles are organized. In short, it seeks to comprehend mental illness by examining the *social representations* in terms of which it is described, organized and explained.

The social representations of which I speak are in the everyday nature of the world, carried by concepts and circulated through descriptions and images. Very often they become crystallized in forms of social practice and spatial organization. And frequently they coalesce into institutionalized patterns of action. Naturally, and as one might expect, my understanding of social representations has its origins in Durkheimian sociology, though in this book I do not wish to presuppose anything about collective sentiments (or a *l'âme collective*), a 'conscience collective', or collective forces. Nor do I wish to focus solely on the process of cognition as has been fashionable in the works of such people as Herzlich (1973), Jodelet (1989), or Moscovici (1984, 1988), and which tend to reduce the concept of representation to that of a personal 'image', idea or interpretation. (Though as these latter works serve to show, Durkheim's use of the term *representations* was certainly multiplex.) Indeed, in Durkheim's hands the concept of representation was one which was both ambiguous and confusing (see Lukes, 1973). Above all it was one which was necessarily linked in to many of the metaphysical speculations about the nature of 'society' which Durkheim felt forced to make. Stripped of Durkheimian metaphysics, however, it is a term which immediately directs our attention to those aspects of daily life which lie above and beyond the behaviours, beliefs and actions of mere individuals so as to focus on the collective frameworks within which people organize and report upon their social existence. This, it seems to me, is its most valuable property. Though there is, of course, no call to assume that such collective frameworks rest on a consensual social basis – especially as they are so commonly imposed and presented to people as *faits accomplis* by the various social groups whose ideas, beliefs and material interests they usually express. Nevertheless, the Durkheimian claim (1964: 45) that when 'the sociologist undertakes the investigation of some order of social facts, he must endeavour to consider them from an aspect that is independent of their individual manifestations', is accepted here as a fundamental rule of procedure. This, of course still leaves aside the question as to what these collective entities may be.

For Durkheim (1964: 7), it was 'the collective aspects of the *beliefs, tendencies, and practices* of a group that characterize truly social phenomena' (my emphasis). In effect, however, Durkheim placed particular stress on cognition (and it is on the basis of that stress that modern social psychologists have picked up the concept and developed it as a tool for analysing patterns of belief). Some of his earliest proposals were offered in the 1903 publication *Primitive Classification*, in which he and Mauss argued that 'The first logical categories were social categories' (1963: 82) – thus anchoring thought in the intricateness of social structure. And these preliminary Durkheimian notions were then developed in *The Elementary Forms of the Religious Life* in which Durkheim made his most insightful claim namely, '[C]oncepts are collective representations . . . they belong to the whole social group' (1915: 435). Thus locating the problem of cognition in an extra-personal domain – far beyond the reach of isolated, individual subjects. In fact, this insight combined with the concept of *mentalité* as introduced by another of Durkheim's colleagues, Lévy-Bruhl (1985), began to point towards entirely new objects of analysis – objects which could not be dealt with adequately by studying the 'subject' of psychology.

The focus on forms of thought, on mentalities, is in some ways equally central to this study, though it is ultimately the study of the *products* of thought and social practice which is of primary interest here. These products, as I have mentioned previously, are to be found in such things as the physical structures in which mental illness is observed and treated; the organizational arrangements through which it is analysed and monitored; and the forms of professional practice which surround the ever changing objects of psychiatric disorder. Indeed, it is only by means of such products that specific diseases, illnesses, and forms of sickness, come to have a definite shape, come to be located in specific categories, come to be named, come to be allocated specific kinds of therapies and thereby come to be visible. But in order to establish my argument further, it may be as well at this stage to cite a few elementary examples of the kinds of representations with which we shall be concerned.

Table 1.1   *All admissions to mental illness hospitals and units in Scotland by diagnostic category and sex of patient, per 100,000 population, 1990*

Diagnosis	Rates per 100,000 Male	Female	Excess % Female/Male
All diagnoses	567	611	8
Schizophrenia, paranoia	89	55	(−38)
Affective psychoses	65	117	80
Senile and pre-senile dementia	79	140	77
Alcoholic psychoses and alcoholic dependence syndrome	120	45	(−63)
Other psychoses	37	46	24
Neurotic disorders	11	17	55
Personality and behaviour disorders	18	18	—
Mental retardation	20	10	(−50)
Depressive disorders: non-psychotic	55	103	87
Mental illness, diagnosis unknown	38	42	11

Source: Scottish Health Statistics 1991, Edinburgh: HMSO, 1991.

The nature of the 'visibility', shape, and location of psychiatric illness is evident, for example, in my first representation – which is Table 1.1. It is a table which in part exhibits the nosological mesh through which psychiatric illness is currently categorized and classified. Reflected herein, for example, are concepts of schizophrenia and depression, of neuroses and psychoses, of behaviour and affect, as well as of mental illness and mental retardation. They are, in fact, concepts and terms which point towards theories of illness as well as towards our notions of what mental (as distinct from physical) illness might be. (Indeed, as Wing *et al.* (1981: 2) put it, diseases *are* names for theories rather than the names of 'things'.) In that sense they are the words used both to explain and to describe what illness is. In addition, of course, we can also note that woven within the diagnostic mesh provided by the table is another scheme – written in terms of the characteristics of age, sex and standardized ratios, and to which one could very easily append (in theory at least) further dimensions; such as, the distribution of illness by ethnicity and social class, occupation or marital status.

Indeed by looking at such a table, a sociologist might be tempted, even at this early point, to ponder about the causes of the distributions which are represented therein. That is, to wonder about the propensity of females to depression or anxiety, or the propensity of males towards alcoholism. But our task will not be to explain the 'causes' of such patterns. Instead we shall seek to examine what it is that is represented here, and how what is represented is interpreted. In this sense, the analysis of the different rates at which males and females are classified as being psychotic or neurotic, demented or alcoholic, is not a precursor to an examination of what causes neurotic depression in women, or why males are more prone to alcoholism than are females. Rather, it is a precursor to an analysis of such things as the assumptions and frameworks surrounding the concepts of neuroses and dementia themselves, and the changing significance and interpretation of 'sex' in twentieth century psychiatric epidemiology. We are interested in the data contained in such tables then, not so much because the data mirror an independent distribution of disease and illness within the world, but because the tables mirror something about our cultural understandings of illness behaviour among males and females, old and young, married and unmarried, employed and unemployed – as well as our understandings of the causes of such illness. Thus, if women are twice as likely to be classified as having a neurotic or depressive disorder as compared to men, this tells us as much about how our culture uses the concepts of neurosis as it does about the causes of depressive disorder.

Take as another example of a representation, the plan of the ward for the 'colored' patients at the Jackson Memorial Hospital, Dade County, Florida (*c.* 1950) in which images of mental illness are overlapped with images of the social structure of the American South (Figure 1.1). This single ward for coloured patients had to accommodate people of all classifications (whereas whites were placed in wards according to a main diagnosis), and consequently within the racist strictures of Florida we can see at a glance the important nursing categories of psychiatric disorder during the early 1950s. Note how men are segregated from women, how the disturbed are separated from the quiet, the suicidal from the depressed. Note also how isolation, insulin shock therapy and hydrotherapy figure among the spatial representations – and thereby reflect the physicalist ideology in terms of which white and coloured bodies were managed. And, of course, underneath each one of these divisions lies a series of further categories concerning Western notions of psychiatric health and illness and its differentia-

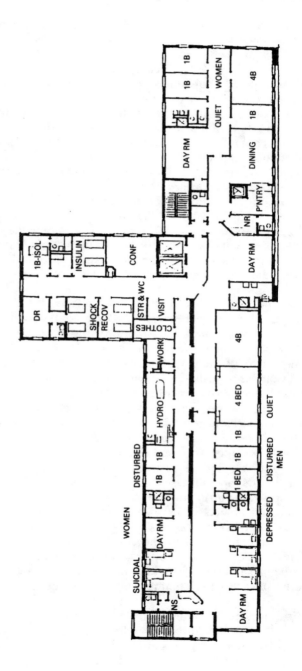

Figure 1.1   *Jackson Memorial Hospital, Dade County, Florida* (c. 1950)

tion from physical health and illness. More importantly, perhaps, we can see how we are dealing with what are essentially social categories which are reflected in a social area, and which as a consequence are incapable of being reduced to the lives and behaviours of isolated individuals. For the concepts of mental disorder, of depression and psychoses – together with the accompanying assumptions and theories about the management of such disorders – are not to be found at the level of the singular individual. It is in this respect that the psychiatric order is one which demands a sociological analysis of appropriate phenomena – an analysis which, as the Durkheimians showed, cannot be reduced solely to matters of psyche and personal consciousness.

My third example of a representation is to be found on the first floor of the Y-shaped psychiatric block of Kings County Hospital, New York (*c.* 1938 – see Figure 1.2). As well as inscribing the stages through which patients were actually admitted into hospital, namely, preparation, examination, history taking (in rooms 23–25), it also encapsulates something of the system of occupational divisions in terms of which mental illness was professionally organized. For here are included offices for the Chief Psychologist, Nurses and Social Services Personnel, whilst on the third floor (among other things) are included offices for the Psychiatrists and Psychoanalysts. It is impossible to pin down with any accuracy the world debut of most of these professions, but it is reasonably clear that even 38 years previously few, if any, would have had provision made for them under those precise titles. Attendants, yes; doctors certainly, even alienists perhaps, but psychoanalysts and psychologists – most unlikely. Note too that there is no specific mention of psychiatric social workers or occupational therapists or physiotherapists. And yet the appearance and disappearance of these various occupational groupings tells us as much about the organization and understanding of mental illness as do the layouts of psychiatric hospitals themselves. For in and through the division of labour are reflected changing objects of psychiatric practice and psychiatric therapy. They are, however, objects of practice and therapy which, once again, cannot be found in the conscious life of psychiatric subjects. On the contrary, for they are woven into and fabricated through a wide mesh of social activities and medical theories, and it is only in terms of such a mesh that the subject of modern psychiatry emerges.

On the Frontispiece of Cannon and Hayes's *The Principles and Practice of Psychiatry* (1932) are printed four photographs – the first is of a Mongolian idiot, the second is of a chrondric-dystrophic dwarf, next comes the stigmata of degeneration, and finally the

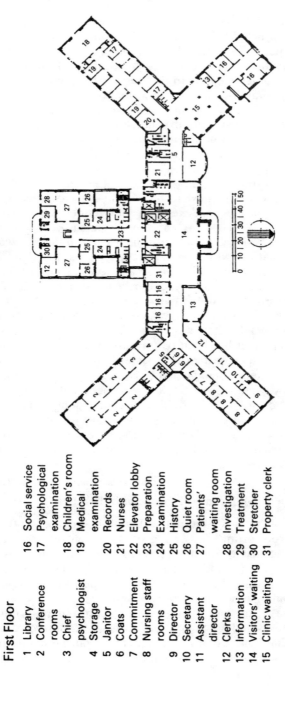

First Floor

1 Library
2 Conference rooms
3 Chief psychologist
4 Storage
5 Janitor
6 Coats
7 Commitment
8 Nursing staff rooms
9 Director
10 Secretary
11 Assistant director
12 Clerks
13 Information
14 Visitors' waiting
15 Clinic waiting
16 Social service
17 Psychological examination
18 Children's room
19 Medical examination
20 Records
21 Nurses
22 Elevator lobby
23 Preparation
24 Examination
25 History
26 Quiet room
27 Patients' waiting room
28 Investigation
29 Treatment
30 Stretcher
31 Property clerk

Figure 1.2 *King's County Hospital, New York* (c. 1938)

microcephalic idiot. And the photographs reflect not simply the sad faces of the afflicted, but also representations of bodily defect as forms of mental defect. Indeed, they represent a strongly held belief that inner mental abnormalities express themselves in outward appearance and demeanour. In that respect the pictures instruct us to look for mental disorder and abnormality in the physical frame. Similarly, and for exactly the same reason, one finds in the casebooks of the early twentieth century asylum, photographs of the demented and melancholic, of the earliest schizophrenics and of the mournful looking paranoiacs. Indeed, from the nineteenth century drawings of Theodore Géricault to the writings of Kretschmer (1925), we see represented not just faces of madness, but the claim that mental disorder is inextricably woven into corporeality. And this claim has also been developed and refined throughout the current century – to the extent that even casual psychological distinctions are believed to manifest themselves in the physicality of the body. That is why Cyril Burt peppered his *The Young Delinquent* (1925), and his *The Backward Child* (1937), with photographs of selected adolescents whose assumed psychological symptoms were supposedly visible in their physiques. And it is why the modern psychiatric nurse feels justified in assessing his or her patients with the aid of behavioural instruments. (In fact, during the twentieth century, it has been behaviourism rather than photography which has been primarily responsible for welding outward physical appearance to judgements concerning inner mental disorder.) In any event, it is clear that what people think and believe about mental disorder is invariably reflected in some manner in the conceptual, material and bureaucratic tools which they use to organize such conditions. Consequently, by examining those tools one inevitably comes to understand the nature of the raw materials which they shape.

The Sociological Significance of Professional Practice

I opened this chapter by stating that the basic sociological theme of the book involved 'an elaboration of the claim that the ways in which we organize care and treatment for psychiatric disorders serves both to reflect and constitute what such disorders actually are'. And in talking of representations I hope to have gone some way to explaining how aspects of care and treatment (including the associated forms of description, classification and reporting) can reflect an understanding of psychiatric disorder. But however that may be, in what sense can it be said that the organization of care and treatment serve to constitute psychiatric disorders? For is it not the case that forms of social, and especially of professional, practice merely respond to the pre-given material (organic and physical) realities of the world? And does not medical and paramedical practice mirror disease and illness in the same way that science mirrors nature? And if that is so, then is it not also the case that whilst medical practices might reflect something about psychiatric reality, they can never be said to be responsible for constituting it?

In the empiricist view of the world, of course, objects of study such as schizophrenia and depression are not only believed to exist entirely independently of human action, but also to be capable of directly shaping forms of professional practice. Crudely put, the empirical world presents itself to observers (or perhaps merely 'exists') and they respond to it appropriately. In the case of diseases, for example, the empiricist is likely to hold that such things occur as natural kinds – untainted by human will and action – and thus remain to be discovered, observed, defined, treated and possibly cured through human intervention (see, for example, Reznek, 1987). It also follows from such a view that if observers come to make a 'correct' analysis of a disease, then certain correct forms of medical action are likely to follow in train. So syphilis ought, for example, to be treated with antibiotics rather than with mercury or magic (notwithstanding the fact that *Spirochete pallida* was cited as a causative agent of syphilis some 30 or so years before the provision of antibiotics). An advocate of such a line of thought may happily concede that nosography and diagnosis can take different forms in different historical or social circumstances, but they would also assert that such variations as might exist are nothing but a response to a gradually emerging truth, and that once the object world has been correctly and rationally understood and described, then correct and rational responses to a disease become possible. In this context, therefore, professional practice is seen as nothing but a necessary reflection of, and reaction to the objectively given nature of specific disease entities. (Prefrontal lobotomy, for example, was thus viewed as a necessary correction to a pathology which existed in the frontal lobes and which, left 'untreated' gave rise to and sustained schizophrenic reactions.)

The empiricist vision of disease and its treatment (as we shall see) dominated medical, and especially hospital psychiatric ideology for most of the present century. And, more importantly, it also dominated many historical and pseudo-sociological accounts of psychiatric practice. So much so that some historians (such as Hunter and Macalpine, 1974), tended to see changes in psychiatric policy and practice as nothing but a direct response to the growth and development of medical knowledge. These enlightenment visions of the world, however, have been very forcefully challenged during the last 30 years or so, and since the 1970s especially, the once imposing edifice of empiricism has shown signs of considerable weakness. Indeed, the study of its rather shaky foundations has been executed in numerous fields of scientific activity – and not least within medicine itself. In fact, among the very earliest critiques of empiricist epistemology in the field of science was that advanced by Ludwig Fleck (1935) whose work was concerned with the discovery of the Wasserman reaction and the diagnosis of syphilis (translated as *Genesis and Development of a Scientific Fact*, 1979). Fleck, predating Kuhn by many decades, sought to show that, 'A fact always occurs in the context of the history of thought and is always the result of definite thought styles [*Denkskollectiv*]' (1979: 95). In other words, scientific facts are not so much discovered as created and invented. And as we now know, this basic principle was later taken up and developed extensively in the broad sweep of Kuhnian historical studies of science – and not least by Kuhn (1970) himself. Indeed, and to a large degree, it has been further developed in what is sometimes referred to as the strong programme of the sociology of knowledge (see for example, Bloor, 1991).

This attack upon empiricism has also (and more recently) been advanced through various Foucauldian and other postmodernist frameworks. And the use of the latter has even encouraged some authors to argue that diseases as independent objects of scientific knowledge simply do not exist. Thus Delaporte, for example, states very early on in his study of cholera, that 'Disease does not exist. . . . What does exist is not disease but practices' (1986: 6). And one assumes that in this tradition of analysis the numerous objects of medical attention and therapy are believed to be constructed objects which are devoid of stable, objective character- istics (that is, independent of their discovery and analysis by human agents). Something akin to this line of thought, though denuded of its idealist garb, has also been freely adopted in studies of mental illness. Szasz's (1960) work providing one example, and Sedgwick's claim that 'there are no illnesses or diseases in nature' (1982: 30), seems to point towards another. By implication, it is clear that idealist interpretations lay a heavy burden on medical (and especially psychiatric) practice – because it is supposedly only in and through such practice that the primary objects of medical therapy come into existence. It is not, perhaps, the most satisfactory of positions to adopt – though it is beyond the bounds of this introduction to discuss the weaknesses of such idealist claims or the nature of the postmodernist flight from 'facts' in general. Instead, it will prove more useful to elaborate upon the critical stance towards the nature of professional practice which is adopted in this book.

In his work on a realist theory of science Bhaskar (1975, 1989), argues that there are always and forever two sides to knowledge. The first lies in the existence of 'things' which exist independently of human will and action – which Bhaskar refers to as intransitive objects of knowledge. The second lies in a socially conditioned knowledge – which he refers to as the transitive dimension of knowledge. Things exist, but as Bhaskar puts it, 'In science humans come to know human-independent nature, fallibly and variously' (1989: 25). Thus, our knowledge of the intransitive always takes specific social and historical forms such that things can never be known in some pure state untainted by human action. In Bhaskar's framework, then, we have no need to deny that specific psychiatric diseases and disorders exist, but we can deny that professional psychiatric practice is nothing more than a pure reflection of those disorders. And it is in the context of Bhaskar's distinctions that we can both investigate the nature of mental illness sociologically, and point towards the significance of professional practice for its construction without in any way denying the possibility of such illnesses constituting what J.S. Mill would have called 'natural kinds'.

Such a realist position, then, lays a steady emphasis on the role of social practice and ideology in the manufacture of the world, without falling into the idealist traps of relativism and the postmodernist trap of nihilism. More importantly, from a sociological standpoint, it throws a research focus on those who are responsible for responding to and understanding phenomena, as much as it does on the phenomena themselves. Thus, in the context of this book, it suggests that an important and significant way in which we can come to know insanity, mental diseases, psychiatric disorders, and mental illnesses, is through the study of the activities and practices of psychiatric professionals themselves. At the same time, one does not need to deny the existence of organic (or other) processes in sustaining the nature of psychiatric objects, or to argue for the 'myth' of mental illness (Szasz, 1960). Consequently, we may say that professional practice is significant for at least two reasons. First, because much of what we know about the object world is reflected through such practice, and secondly, because practice forever moulds and remoulds the intransitive objects of knowledge in culturally and historically specific ways. It is, if you like, practice which holds the objects of psychiatry together.

It should be clear then that I have no wish to query the existence of mental illnesses as natural kinds, though I believe that there are good grounds for so doing. And I certainly have no wish to belittle the experiences of those who are assumed to be afflicted with serious psychiatric disorders by assuming that there are nothing more than social processes at work in their condition. Instead, I wish to examine something about how psychiatric disorders come to be known, managed and understood in routine practical circumstances – simply because the ways in which such disorders are professionally recognized and managed are central and significant features of what they *are*. As I hope to demonstrate, visions of mental illness can differ quite markedly between different groups of professional practitioners (and even within a single professional group), yet it is only by studying the sum total of these visions and their practical effects that we can come to truly comprehend the social and medical circumstances in which people with chronic psychiatric disorders are routinely found.

The Social Worlds of the Mentally Ill

> The sociological imagination enables us to grasp history and biography and the relations between the two within society. That is its task and its promise.
>
> C. Wright Mills (1970: 12)

Mental illness is then, organized, explained, described and reported on through collective frameworks and activities of the types which I have so far been discussing. Indeed, these frameworks and activities provide the grid in terms of which we come to understand the nature of such illness. In that respect we may say that representations of mental illness are nothing less than theories realized. Hospital architecture, for example, expresses and realizes specific theories of psychiatric disorder. Diagnostic instruments make plain and visible the essential characteristics of the maladies to which they are addressed. As such they are directly comparable to the 'instruments' of physics which Bachelard (1984) understood to be the expression of what he called the new scientific spirit. Yet, a study of mental illness which restricted itself to such instruments and frameworks would probably omit the examination of the most important and significant elements of the entire system, namely, the social worlds of mentally ill people themselves.

The emergence and elaboration of theories and frameworks, designs and practical rules are essential components of mental disorder. But tracing the rise and establishment of such phenomena tells us little or nothing about how these elements are woven into everyday practice in the here and now, and how such things actually touch upon the lives of people with a psychiatric disorder. As I have previously stated, this is so because the study of conceptual, theoretical or ideological systems in themselves reveals only a limited portion of 'lived' reality. In many ways, they merely provide what Oakeshott (1962) once called an abbreviation of concrete activity, and as such are incapable of reflecting adequately the detail of commonplace reality. What has to be studied claimed Oakeshott (speaking of political rather than social life), are not just abstract ideas and rules, but the empirical features and arrangements of everyday life 'in all of its intricateness' (1962: 129). For ultimately it is real live human beings who are discussed, described, treated, organized and cared for in terms of the big frameworks, concepts and ideational systems out of which the modern psychiatric order is constructed. It is, equally, real live human beings who do the discussing, treating and organizing. There is an important sense, therefore, in which it is in the interaction between the grand frameworks of understanding and description, and the minute details of everyday psychiatric practice that the nature of psychiatric disorder is made real and palpable. And a study which failed to move beyond psychiatric texts and research monographs would in that respect emerge as nothing more than a summary of summaries. It is therefore in social worlds that concepts and theories are put into play and it is through social worlds that the objects of modern psychiatry are effectively constituted. What is required, therefore, is an analysis of the ways in which big concepts and fussy detail interweave so as to create and fashion the realm of the psychiatric.

It is for this reason that throughout the text I shall make reference to the experiences of a group of psychiatric patients whose social worlds formed the focus of a specific research project during the late 1980s (Prior, 1991a). Their lives and their experiences will serve as both the origin and the touchstone for many of the issues which we shall examine. And it will be through their lives and their experiences that we will be able to recognize many of the abstract terms and concepts of psychiatry as a living reality. The patients concerned all had a history of chronic psychiatric illness (most were diagnosed as being schizophrenic) and they either were, or had been, long-term in-patients in a psychiatric hospital (some having spent the best part of 40 years in the same hospital). By the very nature of things, these patients and ex-patients were tied to a specific spatio–temporal location (in this case a Northern Irish city of some 300,000 people). From a sociological standpoint, however, we shall see that in many ways their spatio–temporal location is of only marginal significance to their individual fates. For their lives, rather like our own lives, were organized in terms of cultural categories and structural arrangements which recognized no parochial political boundaries or geographical frontiers. In this sense the nature of the 'chronic schizophrenic' or of the chronic depressive is described and understood in similar terms wherever he or she may live in the Western world. That is to say, most of the commonly diagnosed chronic psychiatric illnesses are subject to a common array of medical, nursing, social work and therapeutic practices no matter where they may be found. Naturally the quality and range of the services which different individuals receive in different countries, and the detailed and specific circumstances in which people live varies extensively (and therein lie the limits of empirical social research), but the big structures – the organization of illness in terms of psychiatric hospitals, day centres, and facilities for community care – and the ideological systems which define the natures of disease, illness and sickness have a striking commonality across the Western world.

It is in the desire to examine the interface between individual fates and aspects of structural change; between personal biography and social forces; between what C. Wright Mills (1970) referred to as private troubles and public issues, that the latter portion of this book turns towards an examination of what is done to and for psychiatric 'patients' and social services 'clients' in hospital and community settings. As well as taking an interest in psychiatric subjects, however, we will also focus upon the ways in which nurses, psychiatrists, social workers and associated professionals understood, described and organized those subjects. We will examine the everyday nature of patient worlds and something about how patients structured their worlds. We will examine what happened to patients when they left hospital and how the rearrangements of their worlds impinged on their status as 'ex-mental patients'. We will also examine the nature of the communities into which they were discharged and in which they had to structure their identities. Yet, whatever detailed facet of daily life we do eventually examine we will forever find ourselves in the shadow of the assumptions, concepts, terms and theories of Western psychiatric discourse. In that sense it matters little whether the empirical investigation had been based in central Germany, southern England, the American mid-west or a medium sized city on a small island on the edge of the Northern Atlantic. For wherever we started we would have been able to say with some certainty – just as Marx said to a German readership pondering on the relevance of English capitalism to their own particular circumstances – *De te fabula narratur* (this story is about you).

The Scope of this Book

It is perhaps clear then, that as a consequence of my standpoint I do not wish to focus first and foremost on psychiatric 'subjects' and their personal disorders, but seek instead to link our comprehension of such disorders to the socially structured and socially organized responses which they generate. In Chapters 2 to 6, my strategy will be to concentrate on some major sites of psychiatric practice. The sites which I have selected for study are the psychiatric hospital, the diseased and disordered patient, the community and the family. These are not, of course, the only sites in which psychiatric practice has operated or does operate, but in one way or another they have all been central to the nature of the twentieth century psychiatric enterprise.

Broadly speaking, and as I have already explained, I shall use the experiences of people in the study group as a starting point for the analyses which are to follow. And taking each site of practice in turn (hospital, patient, community and family), I will attempt to examine how these sites have been variously understood and represented through professional practice. I shall also seek to discover how changes in such representations have reflected changes in the nature of the various objects to which psychiatric practice has been addressed. Chapter 2, for example, takes as its starting point the psychiatric hospital and analyses the ways in which images of the hospital have changed between the second decade of the current century, when the study hospital was planned and built, and the present day. That is to say, it will examine images of the specialized psychiatric hospital as asylum, as a place of treatment, as a therapeutic community, and more recently as a damaging and perhaps perverse 'total institution'. In fact, the essential focus in Chapter 2 will be on the marginalization of the specialized psychiatric hospital, and the associated processes of deinstitutionalization and dehospitalization. This, as I have previously stated, constitutes the single most important organizational change in the provision of care and treatment for the mentally ill and it therefore demands explanation. Some of the more common accounts of the transition will be reviewed in Chapter 2, but the essential argument advanced therein is that the move away from hospitalization policies and towards care in the community programmes expresses and represents a fundamental alteration in the ways in which professional groupings have analysed and understood the nature of psychiatric disorder. In other words, the moves towards community care will be seen first and foremost as an expression of new psychiatric ideologies rather than as a response to various forms of extra-

professional economic interests, technological (and especially pharmacological) advances, or simple policy changes.

These latter ideas will be further developed in Chapters 3 and 4,
both of which focus on the diseased and disordered patient. The
first of these two chapters outlines some of the dominant theoretical
and practical strategies in terms of which hospital based psychiatrists have viewed psychiatric disorder during the present century.
As such, we will see how an early twentieth century concentration
on brain and 'nerves' translated itself into a series of physical
therapies ranging from malarial therapy to various forms of
psycho-surgery. Our entry point into such matters lies in the fact
that a number of the study group patients had undergone surgical
treatment, as well as various forms of shock and convulsive therapy,
for their psychotic disorders. In that sense the abstract theories of
somatic psychiatry had literally left their mark on the study group
patients – some of the patients, for example, suffered from speech
defects and epileptic seizures as a direct result of old surgical
practices. It would be quite wrong to suggest, however, that
psychiatry was ever monopolized by such physical therapies and
physicalist interpretations of causation and disease. For we know
that from the very opening of the century there had been close
consideration of the role of 'mind' as well as of brain in the
generation of psychiatric illness – considerations which were above
all evident in the work of Freudian and other psychologically
inclined practitioners. An analysis of psychiatric representations
must therefore take account of relevant conceptualizations of mind
and personality as well as of conceptualizations of the more recent
objects of psychiatric focus such as behaviour and social relations.
Furthermore, because theorizations of disease and illness usually
march hand in hand with ideas about therapy, we will also be
required to examine the logic of therapy (and its associated
instrumentation), as much as the world of psychiatric theory itself.
Therapies and instruments tend to be as varied as the theories which
support their use. Yet whatever form they may take, they invariably
constitute a concrete and very practical expression of culturally
generated assumptions about the nature of mental illness and/or
psychiatric disorder. In this respect, the existence of the leucotome
(the surgical instrument used in lobotomy) serves to underline the
significance of brain to neuropsychiatry every bit as much as the
abreaction session underlines the significance of the psyche for the
psychogenesist.

Chapter 4 also has its notional focal point in the diseased patient,
but here the patient is used to mirror the multifarious and changing
representations of mental illness which are to be found in the

professional accounts of nurses, social workers, occupational therapists and clinical psychologists. In part this means that we are called to examine how the assumed needs of psychiatric patients have been divided and redivided among the various personnel who enter into the psychiatric ward, and how the consequent division of labour in itself reflects important and significant features of what mental illness is considered to be at any one time. Equally we will be called to examine the ways in which the central objects of nursing, social work and psychological attention have altered during the period under review so as to reflect the changing nature of psychiatric disorder. So, for example, as well as noting how the psychiatric nurse has emerged from being a custodial attendant of diseased bodies, to a multiskilled therapist of patients entangled in social and family networks, we will also study how diverse concepts of community have entered into nursing practice and how these interlink with the big structural changes evident in the overall transition from asylum to community care. Or, to take another example, we shall note how the switch of focus from casework to social networks and informal care, which is so evident in the theory and practice of social work, informs us about changed policy goals and changing interpretations of what the mentally ill supposedly 'need'. And in like manner, we shall see how equivalent shifts in the attentions of occupational therapists and clinical psychologists reveal not just variable self-images of paramedical professionals, but also essential features of how mental illnesses are understood, described and acted upon.

Psychiatric professionals are increasingly encouraged to address their activities to non-institutional settings, and (in the case of social work) even to reorientate themselves away from individuals as the primary objects of practice and towards broader community groupings. Yet community is an ill-defined term and a poorly theorized concept. More importantly, the history of sociological research provides evidence enough that one cannot counterpoise community with institution and argue as if the two orders are mutually exclusive. Yet the strange thing is, that this is precisely what occurred within the language of social policy during the 1970s and 1980s. As a result, it became increasingly difficult for practitioners to speak, or even to think, of community care as being provided in anything other than non-institutional settings. It was not always so, of course, and one of the central tasks of Chapter 5 is to document the different ways in which an interest in community has manifested itself in psychiatric theory and practice during the last 50 or so years. In that process of documentation it should become increasingly clear that 'community' managed to enter into psychiatric discourse by at least four different routes. The first such route involved a recognition that community acted as a repository for large pockets of previously unrecognized psychiatric morbidity. (And it was probably this discovery which went some way to breaking down the once rigid barrier that was believed to exist between sanity and madness.) The second such route involved a recognition of community organization as a factor in the origins of morbidity patterns themselves. That is to say, a recognition that factors such as social (community) disorganization, and the unequal distribution of material and cultural resources had some relationship to the incidence of psychiatric disorder. The third route involved a recognition that small, rationally constructed communities could be regarded as valuable therapeutic instruments *per se* – and it was in this context that psychiatrists such as Maxwell Jones believed it possible to develop therapeutic communities within the asylum grounds. Whilst the fourth, final and most recent route has involved a recognition of community as the true and proper place to care for and to treat most cases of serious psychiatric disorder. It is, of course, only during this last phase that community has been redefined entirely in terms of a privatized and non-institutional existence. The implications of that redefinition for the members of the study group will be examined in Chapters 7 and 8.

Chapter 6 will concentrate on the family and its relation to psychiatric illness. The family has, understandably, always been central to the comprehension of mental disorder, but the ways in which it has entered into the explanatory score have altered dramatically during the current century. When the century opened, for example, the family was related to the patient almost entirely through hereditary connections. That is to say, the family was viewed in terms of a genetic pool from which 'bad stock' could emanate – and therein lay the source of many of the policy proposals which were once advanced by interest groups such as the eugenicists and racial theorists. Their physicalist interpretation of family influence was, however, paralleled by other interpretations – interpretations which focused in the main upon the social contacts and emotional relationships of family members. The primary impetus for these latter visions probably sprang out of the work and theories of psychoanalysts and child psychologists, but whatever their origin, it is clear that they served to shift the domestic arrangements of psychiatric patients out of the shadows of psychiatric discourse and into the theoretical limelight. On some occasions, of course, the family emerged as a source of stress and social pathology, at other times as a source of social support, and lately as a source of care and control. There were even occasions when, as we shall see, it was argued that the only viable unit of psychiatric examination and treatment was the family itself, (rather than simply the patient within it). But whichever image of family life prevailed it was at least clear that neither the theory nor the practice of modern psychiatry could ignore the links which existed between the family as a social and emotional unit and its individual members. Our task, of course, is not to discuss or to disentangle any of the causal relationships which were seen to exist between psychiatric symptoms and the nature of family arrangements, but rather to examine how intra-family relationships were and are represented in the broad corpus of modern psychiatric knowledge.

General principles and broad abstraction of the type so far referred to are, of course, rarely sufficient to explore the endless detail of the empirical world, and so as I have previously explained, in the later part of the book the focus will be on how the broad principles examined in the earlier chapters find expression in everyday detail. Chapters 7 and 8 therefore examine how much of the language, concepts and principles of modern professional practice are applied in routine circumstances. Chapter 7 concentrates on the social world of the hospital in-patient, and examines how psychiatrists, nurses, social workers and psychologists interpret the nature of mental illness and patienthood in institutional contexts. It will examine the ways in which notions of psychiatric disorder and illness are related to patient life and how psychiatric discourse is used to underpin the existence of the psychiatric hospital as a medical institution. In addition to examining professional representations of the psychiatric hospital, however, Chapter 7 will also seek to analyse in-patient images of hospital life. Among other things, it will demonstrate that rather than being viewed by in-patients as some nightmarish medical institution designed to mortify the persona, the long-stay hospital was more commonly seen as a place of refuge and often as a place of friendship in which a sense of community still existed. And it is, above all, through this clash of interpretations between professionals and patients, between the representations of the hospital as a site of 'treatment' and the hospital as asylum that the diverse social worlds of patients and staff are structured.

Through Chapter 8 we will follow ex-patients into the community and examine how big policy changes for community care work themselves out in routine detail. In essence we will see how the move from psychiatric hospital to the community is in large part related to a structural transfer of care from health to social services, and we will examine what is entailed by that transfer. We will also analyse patient destinations and note the extent to which policies for deinstitutionalization should more properly be viewed as a policy of institutional substitution. But perhaps most important of all, we will see how the discourse of care in the community re-presents the patient and his or her illness in terms of a new conceptual mesh. It is, above all, a mesh which serves to subordinate aspects of sickness and personal disorder to the (socio-political) characteristics of independence and normality. Though, in practice, the ex-patient in everyday life tends to remain as firmly lodged as ever in a sub-world of disability and handicap. Indeed, it is a world composed of other ex-patients, psychiatric professionals and care assistants – and it is one which touches upon mainstream community life only fleetingly and superficially. As such, people with serious psychiatric disorders increasingly find themselves 'in the community' but rarely as members of a community.

The book concludes with a consideration of the concept of social representations and its value for a sociological understanding of disease and illness. It argues that by emphasizing the supra-individual dimension of human affairs the concept serves to displace the 'subject' as the focal point for the study of psychiatric disorders in favour of truly social phenomena. In consequence and by concentrating on such things as the organization of psychiatric services, and the ways in which psychiatric phenomena are reflected through diverse forms of professional practice, it frees sociological analysis from the dominance of a discourse which, at best, has only ever permitted its practitioners to serve as under labourers to the master craftsmen of medical psychiatry.

2

Changing Images of the Psychiatric Hospital

A pawn *is* the sum of the rules according to which it moves (a square is a piece too).

Wittgenstein (1979: 134)

Planning for Madness

The hospital which housed the study group patients had been designed during the first decade of the present century and built, for the most part, during the second decade. In keeping with the style and ideas of the age, it was sited on the outskirts of the city which it primarily served, and it was organized (both physically and socially) according to the principles of the colony system. As with many similar asylums elsewhere it was deliberately planned so as to divorce its inmates from the everyday demands of mainstream metropolitan life – its outer walls and its gate lodge, in particular, functioning to emphasize a boundary which at that time was believed to exist between sanity and madness. The plans for the study hospital were incorporated in the *Report of the Royal Commissioners on the Care and Control of the Feeble Minded* (1908) – a report which was delivered to the UK Parliament in the same year, and which recommended the establishment of a Board of Control to oversee the affairs of the insane and the mentally defective. It is noteworthy that 32 years later, the (English) Board of Control (1940: 4), was still recommending that mental hospitals should be situated in rural surroundings beyond the 'zone likely to be developed for housing or other building purposes'; and preferably on an elevated site which was not intersected by roads or rights of way. In other words, on sites which were entirely isolated from the broader communities which they overlooked.

Building plans, in general, invariably reveal something about both the intentions and concerns of their makers, as well as the cultural precepts of the social groups for whom the designs are drawn up – and this is no less so with plans for asylums and hospitals than it is for other public buildings. Ideas about insanity are in that sense reflected in physical structures. In particular, they are reflected both in boundary features (which relate the asylum as a unit to the outside world) and in internal structural arrangements. In fact, with these claims in mind, it is interesting to note exactly the kinds of building features to which the Board of Control addressed itself in its 1940 document (cited above). For example, the Board suggested that the modern hospital should cover nearly 90 acres of ground, with adequate area for outdoor employment and recreation. It suggested that there should be detached villas for the housing and care of patients (and to facilitate the classification of patients into discrete groups – male and female, child and adult, idiots and maniacs); and that such villas should surround an administration and treatment block (containing facilities for hydrotherapy, electric therapy and occupational therapy). It also suggested that there should be a hospital for treating (physically) sick patients, a nurses home, a sports pavilion, farm buildings, a mortuary, a church, a canteen and a shop, a library and lecture room. In other words all the items necessary for the establishment of a self-contained community.

This siting of colonies in the countryside was essentially believed to fulfil a double function. First, it ensured the existence of an adequate barrier between what were assumed to be the insane and degenerate bodies within, and the healthy stock which was presumed to live without. And second, it enabled a safe and positively structured therapeutic environment (fresh air, tranquillity, productive activity) to be provided to those who required asylum in the more traditional sense of that word. (Interestingly, some of the older patients in the study hospital still make reference to 'the colony' even though that term has long since disappeared from official descriptions and documents.) In the UK, this fascination with self-contained and medically dominated communities had actually arisen directly out of the work of the 1908 Commissioners who had gathered a great deal of evidence about the management of lunatics and the feeble minded from North American sources. In particular, they had noted how the US authorities had successfully harnessed madness to the principles of scientific management by placing mental disorder under medical control. And as a result of their observations, the members of the Commission proposed not only that UK institutions adopt the medical principles of their US counterparts, but that the word asylum be replaced by the word hospital – thereby emphasizing the extent to which insanity could truly and properly be regarded as a medical problem.

These requirements and demands for self-contained extra-metropolitan and relatively enclosed asylums were consistently advanced throughout the first half of the twentieth century. Thus, in addition to the sources already mentioned, they were also advocated in the *Report of the Mental Deficiency Committee* (1929) and the *Report of the Departmental Committee on the Construction of Colonies* (1931a). The latter arguing that as far as housing of mental defectives was concerned, 'the colony method holds the field' (1931a: 4). Indeed, in the advanced industrial world as a whole, it was not until the 1950s that consistent criticism of the isolated colony system as a method of psychiatric hospital building began to appear. Thus Goshen and Keenan, in a 1959 US publication, *Psychiatric Architecture*, were among the first to criticize interwar hospitals for being constructed as 'human warehouses', as well as for being too large, too isolated, too lacking in privacy and entirely absent of commonplace activities such as traffic and shopping. And a similar critical edge is also present in a 1959 World Health Organization (WHO) publication on psychiatric architecture in which is described an imaginary composite of a psychiatric hospital, namely:

> [B]uildings partly hidden by high walls and screens of trees, tall gates and a prominent porter's lodge to check arrivals. The buildings usually massive and only comparable with prisons or barracks, most commonly the former, are usually hideous. . . . It is common for the hospital to be approached by a stately drive which culminates in a direct approach to the centre of an enormous block of buildings. This block often has a central tower, and the entire character of the architecture derives from a style of which the implicit purpose was to impress and overawe . . . . Such buildings make the visitor feel small, powerless and insignificant. (Baker *et al.*, 1959: 44)

Yet despite these early critiques, the basic concept of a specialized psychiatric hospital was retained, and it was mostly matters of hospital size and isolation which were viewed in a negative light. Consequently, proposals for the building of self-contained and dedicated psychiatric hospitals (on a reduced scale) were still being advanced until the early 1960s. Thus, Figure 2.1, taken from the 1959 WHO publication on the design of psychiatric hospitals, reflects all of the main features of early twentieth century thinking about the building requirements for people suffering from chronic mental illnesses – their need for isolation in a rural (village) atmosphere, the enclosure of both inmates and staff in the same institution, and the provision of all social, therapeutic and other facilities on one site. Nineteen fifty-nine, in all probability, marks one of the very last points at which such suggestions could have been seriously considered as a basis for the design of a metropolitan psychiatric service. And the reasons why such a proposal would not be seriously considered in the 1990s are central to an understanding of the fates of people with chronic psychiatric disorders.

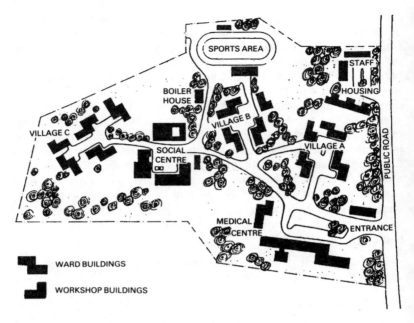

Figure 2.1   *WHO block plan for a psychiatric hospital of 280 beds (c. 1959)*

The existence, design and siting of asylums, then, reveals a great deal about our understanding of psychiatric disorder in the Western world, and a number of implications concerning the organization of madness can be extrapolated from our analysis so far. First, we should note how the construction of asylums (and later of mental hospitals), marks out an important cultural boundary between diseases and illnesses with purely physical symptoms – organized in terms of hospitals for physical ailments – and a different kind of illness called mental illness which presumably involves the identi-fication of symptoms other than physical ones. (Notwithstanding the fact that the exact form which these 'other' symptoms might take seems to vary from time to time – here pertaining to the nervous system, there to psychological impairment, then again to behavioural impairment and sometimes to social impairment.) Secondly and relatedly, we should note how the presence of an external boundary between psychiatric and non-psychiatric hospit-als, serves to emphasize an assumed unity of the intramural disorders. In other words, the presence of psychiatric hospitals underlines the ways in which, within Western culture, there is a belief that the activities of the 'insane' (no matter how varied and complex these may be) exist as a reality in their own right. And if madness is viewed as a *sui generis* reality, then it cannot be entirely reduced to, or confused with, other forms of pathology – such as physical, or social pathology – and for which other institutional arrangements are made. Whilst the third and final implication which we can extrapolate from the discussion so far concerns the fact that the existence of psychiatric hospitals marks out a boundary not just between the physical and the mental, but also between the normal and the abnormal. In this respect the deliberate isolation of the psychiatric hospital from the wider community reflected a firmly held belief that one could actually draw a dividing line between sanity and madness. By implication, the demise of such hospitals and the integration of psychiatric illness into the community suggests that belief in this latter distinction has diminished.

From Asylum to Hospital

The recommendation of a change of name from asylum to hospital referred to in the previous section hints at a series of fundamental alterations, many of which were evidenced in numerous parts of Europe during the first five decades of the present century. In the UK the name change had been suggested in 1908, but it was not until the 1930s that the suggestion was acted upon. Indeed, and as far as Great Britain was concerned, 1926–30 marks the period in which a whole new vocabulary of madness was officially introduced into the world, and in this respect the 1930 Mental Treatment Act is of considerable interest. This is so, first because in matters concerning the definition and organization of mental disorders it gave an imprimatur to medical rather than legal interests (see Jones, 1991b), and secondly because it insisted upon the use of a new descriptive framework. Gone were the old concepts of insanity, asylum, lunatic and attendant, and in came the new terms of hospital, patient, doctor and nurse. (For, as the American psychiatrist Southard (1917: 567) had observed, 'Insanity [was] a legal concept; mental disease a medical concept'.) And from 1930 until the 1970s the new vocabulary provided the essential building blocks of psychiatric practice. Most of that vocabulary is, of course, still with us, though the semantic force of some of its elements has weakened considerably. Thus, references to patients have more likely been replaced by references to clients, and references to hospitals by references to units and centres. Yet in the altered terminology we are witness to something far more significant than a mere change of words. So, for example, the concept of a hospital is suggestive of treatment and eventual cure rather than simple custody and care, and (chronologically speaking) this change of terminology marched hand in hand with a significant change of practices – practices which in retrospect sometimes appear to have been ill-considered, but which were nevertheless directed towards the amelioration of personal disorder and the eventual reintegration of the psychiatric patient into the everyday world.

In fact, and aside from the revolution in psychotherapy brought about by Sigmund Freud and his associates and followers, we see from 1917 onwards growing confidence in the development of *materia medica* specifically aimed at cure rather than mere control. Among the therapies developed and increasingly used were malarial therapy for patients afflicted with General Paralysis of the Insane (GPI) (first used 1917), hydrotherapy (n.d.), electro-convulsive therapy (ECT) (1937), insulin coma therapy (1933), and psychosurgery (1936). We may also add to these the increasing use of phenothiazines (after 1952) and lithium salts (after 1956). I leave aside questions concerning the effectiveness of such treatment, and emphasize only that the emergence of such therapies was marked out in both psychiatric and nursing texts as standing in some kind of contrast to the regimes of moral treatment, custodial care and sedation which typified the nineteenth century and early twentieth century asylum. And there can be little argument about the fact that the mental hospital (also known during the earlier part of this century as the psychopathic hospital, the nerve hospital and the hospital for nervous diseases), increasingly came to be regarded by both psychiatrists and nurses as a place for treatment and as a place where cures could be executed. It is interesting to note in this context that some members of the study group had in fact received almost the entire gamut of such twentieth century therapies, and more than one patient in the group had been treated by means of insulin shock therapy, electro-convulsive therapy and leucotomy, as well as treatment with major tranquillizers (though none of these treatments seemed to have very much effect on the original symptomatology of the patients, and they certainly did not result in discharge from the hospital).

As one would expect, the adoption and application of these therapeutic developments were invariably reflected in the design of mental hospitals. Thus, as the twentieth century progressed the provision of ECT rooms, hydrotherapy pools, surgical facilities, abreaction rooms, psychotherapy suites, and occupational therapy facilities, were all built in the wake of diverse theoretical waves (and the presence of some of these features can be seen in Figures 1.1 and 1.2.). Of course, not all of these facilities appeared in the study hospital, though the latter did contain almost everything other than a hydrotherapy pool and an abreaction unit. More importantly, however, it is clear that many of the broader developments in professional psychiatry which were reflected in the design of the study hospital, also resurfaced in its detailed archives. So that if one were to examine the turn of the century case notes of the afflicted, for example, one would see quite clearly how the objects of therapy and care in the old mental hospital had actually changed in relation to the period under consideration. Thus, in the earlier case notes one reads not so much about the substantive detail of the manias and melancholias which disturbed the various inmates, and still less of the social circumstances which led to the onset of such disturbances, but of the bodily state of the patients. And whilst one would discover very little about the content of patients' delusions, imaginings, feelings and emotions, one would be swamped with detail concerning bodily features. Details of a patient's body weight, height, the shape of the nose, the head, the hands and the feet. Therein also one could read of the somatic controls to which inmates were subjected – of the bromides and cannabis, of the calomines and the sulphur, which were used either to sedate the overactive, or to purge the lethargic. Not surprisingly perhaps, there is no mention of psyche or of mind (and still less of social relations), in the case notes. In fact, whichever way one looks at such notes, it would be clear that the old asylum was primarily, if not entirely, directed towards bodily care and control rather than any positive attempt to cure, or even to reintegrate patients back into everyday life. Indeed, it is only during the 1930s that the case notes begin to reflect a regime which was truly directed towards active therapeutic measures – that is to say, a regime aimed at cure, rather than control. And it was, in all probability, at that stage that the hospital came to be regarded as a place where therapy could be legitimately imposed on patients 'for their own good'. It was at that stage also that the mental hospital turned itself into a professionally and medically managed instrument for the cure of mental disorders.

We shall return to examine the nature of the new therapies in the next chapter. For now it is only necessary to note their introduction, and that the very process of their discovery was hailed in many psychiatric textbooks as a 'revolution' – as signalling the threshold of a new order. Thus Sargant and Slater in their *An Introduction to Physical Methods of Treatment in Psychiatry* (1944), stated that, 'It is a remarkable fact that despite the popular notion that psychotherapy is the only method of treatment of psychological conditions, most of the big advances in psychiatric therapy have been along somatic lines' (1944: 1), and they went on to suggest that the nature of therapy had been truly made scientific by the advent of somatic treatments. Whilst Henderson and Gillespie in the fifth edition of their *A Textbook of Psychiatry* (1940) spoke of 'considerable advances' and the 'brilliant results' which could be obtained by means of the new therapies. Overlapping with these perceived revolutionary developments, however, were others which may well have had a longer lasting and far more profound effect on the organization of psychiatric care. And I refer here to those developments which rested on the belief that the social relations between patients, and between patients and staff were every bit as important to therapeutic outcomes as were the surgeons' leucotome or the psychiatrists' shock therapy techniques. That is to say, the recognition that psychiatric disorder had a social as well as an organic and a psychological base.

Interest in social relationships as a basis for psychiatric therapy cannot, unfortunately, be traced back to any single point of origin. Adolf Meyer (1866–1950) and H.S. Sullivan (1892–1949), had each in their different ways pointed towards the influence of social contexts on psychiatric health and illness, but they alone were not responsible for the creation of what was to be called social psychiatry (a term first used by Southard, 1917: 569). Indeed, there were numerous individuals who, through their efforts in the field of social work, occupational therapy and the like, had long concentrated on the social environment as a therapeutic agent. As far as social relationships within the hospital were concerned, however, one is drawn to locate an explicit and detailed concern with such matters mainly as a product of the 1940s and 1950s. Though one of the earliest displays of interest in the social relations and friendship patterns of hospital patients actually appears in the 1939 volume of *Psychiatry* (see Rowland, 1939) – a journal which had been founded by Sullivan the previous year. In that article the author had commented on the clear existence of patterns of interaction and friendship in asylums and its appearance marks, if nothing else, a recognition among social scientists that the in-patient world of the large asylums was not necessarily an isolated, passive and entirely negative world. Detailed studies of the social life of hospital in-patients, however, were not truly published until the following decade and later, and perhaps the most well known of these was contained in the work of Stanton and Schwartz (1954) which reported upon everyday life in a small private hospital in Maryland. The Maryland hospital was one which laid heavy emphasis on psychoanalytic therapies, and Stanton and Schwartz were keen to point out that social relations between staff, as well as those between staff and patients, had a significant and important impact on patient stability and development. They described how interactions among staff affected patients, and how careful planning of nursing and medical services could lead to improvements in patient life and symptomatology. Indeed, they argued that aspects of psychiatric pathology were frequently linked not so much to features of individual psychology but to the social circumstances in which the patient existed. For example, they noted how conflict between staff aims and practices often produced a personal tension in patients. Indeed, said Stanton and Schwartz, the hospital should be understood as a *social* system and the hospital ward as a social world in which events occurring in one part of the system could have a significant impact on personal processes in another part of the system. In many respects then, they tended to analyse the mental hospital as a community, and we should perhaps recall that their views had long been preceded by the activities of a number of hospital psychiatrists who, having recognized the community like qualities of hospital life, had made quite radical attempts to use the organization of the mental hospital as a therapeutic tool. Thus during the 1940s Tom Main together with other psychiatrists from the Tavistock Clinic had attempted to treat neuroses (at Northfield Military Hospital) by improving social relationships in the hospital. Indeed, the Northfield experiment, said Main, '[was] an attempt to use a hospital not as an organization run by doctors in the interests of their own greater technical efficiency, but as a community with the immediate aim of the full participation of all its members in its daily life' (Main, 1946: 67). His article on the Northfield experiment was entitled 'The hospital as a therapeutic institution', and it was here that the concept of a therapeutic community was introduced to the world. At roughly the same time Maxwell Jones at the Belmont Industrial Neurosis Unit was developing equivalent ideas about the role and power of social relationships in sustaining psychiatric health. (The work of this latter unit was later described by the anthropologist Robert Rapoport in his book *Community as Doctor* (1960), in which he referred to the therapeutic community as 'a form of social organization with healing properties' (1960: 10).) And in many respects the importance of these developments was underlined by a 1953 WHO report on mental health which recommended that psychiatric treatment ought to be redesigned in terms of hospital based therapeutic communities (rather than in terms of psychiatric units in general hospitals). In any event, the changes which occurred in hospital life during the early 1950s were neatly summed up in the title of Greenblatt et al.,'s *From Custodial to Therapeutic Patient Care in Mental Hospitals* (1955) – a work devoted not just to demonstrating how a therapeutic milieu could be constructed within the hospital walls, and how the hospital was in itself a therapeutic machine, but also one which was dedicated to underlining the ways in which the aims of hospital psychiatry had changed during the fifth and sixth decades of the twentieth century. In addition to the published work of Stanton and Schwartz (1954), Greenblatt *et al.* (1955), and the psychiatric practice of Main and Maxwell Jones, many other students of the psychiatric hospital also highlighted the significance of social interaction for symptomatology – though not always in the same positive fashion. Caudhill for example, published work on social relations in a small psychiatric hospital in 1958. The author had spent some time in the unit as a 'patient' and consequently reported how sick roles were both taught and learnt by inmates. He indicated how patients were socialized into specific interaction patterns with their doctors – taking on board information about what fantasies particular doctors liked to hear and so on. This emphasis on socialization into hospital culture was also a theme developed by Dunham and Weinberg (1960) in their 1940s study of Columbia State Hospital, Ohio. Once again the authors emphasized how the hospital world was essentially a social world of interaction, and how patterns of both friendship and domination could develop in ward culture. Furthermore, and in recognition of what Goffman was to refer to as the underlife of the asylum, Dunham and Weinberg recognized that 'patients are capable of developing a common collective social life within the hospital' (1960: 250). And many of the more positive characteristics of in-patient hospital life noted in these various studies also appeared in the work of Goffman himself. Thus in his essay on asylum 'underlife', Goffman (1961) noted various instances of solidarity and camaraderie among inmates, and painted a picture quite different from that suggested by the use of his more notorious terminology of mortification and total institutions. Finally, we should mention how Strauss and his colleagues in their 1964 study of a Chicago hospital pointed towards the importance of psychiatric ideologies in the treatment process and how different ideologies (the three most important being described as somatic, milieu and psychotherapeutic) were associated with different forms of therapeutic organization. For Strauss *et al.* (1981), an institution in itself was not necessarily a bad place for patients to be, for the quality of life and fates of in-patients primarily depended on the psychiatric ideologies of the professionals who surrounded them rather than on institutional care *per se*. And some closely related arguments to these were later echoed by Wing and Brown (1970) in their comparative study of three mental hospitals in England.

The notion of the hospital as a therapeutic community, then, tends to overlap with the vision of the hospital as a place of scientific treatment. And along with this vision of the hospital as a therapeutic instrument in itself there developed a recognition that hospital in-patient life was far more dynamic and complex than had previously been assumed. Crude beliefs and assertions about passive patients and directive and custodial staff were therefore not always matched by the findings of empirical researchers. And this awareness of the complexity of hospital in-patient culture is also evident in relatively recent work – such as in Alaszewski's (1986) study of a hospital for the mentally handicapped. On the basis of the kinds of studies referred to above, then, it seemed that hospital patients could construct a meaningful social world within the confines of the hospital and that it was possible to link that world with the demands and interests of a staff world so as to structure a community for therapy. If the sociological story of in-patient life was to stop at this point, however, we would be in danger of doing a gross disservice to both the history of the hospital movement and to a number of the studies which have just been cited. For virtually side by side with this relatively complex vision of the mental hospital as a therapeutic instrument was another which painted a rather negative and worrying portrait of the modern asylum.

It is an interesting sociological question in itself as to why, given the production of two somewhat opposing sets of claims concerning the benefits and efficacy of hospital life, it was anti-institutional claims that were the most influential in the long run. Naturally, critiques of hospital life are as old as the notion of hospital therapy itself and Rothman (1980) cites some early twentieth century criticisms of the asylum as an institution. Yet the difference between the critiques which existed in the first half of the century and those of the second half rest in the fact that the former rarely if ever questioned the belief that institutional life was the most appropriate form of care for people with psychiatric and other 'mental' problems. Indeed, it seems fair to say that it was only during the 1950s that we witnessed the emergence of a broad based and persistent critique of institutional care *per se*. In fact, from the late 1950s onwards it seems to become increasingly difficult for anyone to write a good word about psychiatric hospitals, and from then on it is mainly the negative side of hospital life which is emphasized. Belknap's *Human Problems of a State Mental Hospital* (1956), for example, presented an image of the state hospital as a dumping ground for the old, the sick and the poor, and he further illustrated how the state hospital was run by unqualified attendants rather than by medical professionals. The attendants, suggested Belknap, determined the treatment status of patients and the extent to which patients were distributed throughout the wards. Furthermore, patient labour was exploited through the operation of the attendant system and patients were frequently bullied (and sometimes ignored entirely). This conflict between a staff world and a patient world was an issue which also arose in Caudhill's work – though not quite so disparagingly. Caudhill emphasized the separate social worlds of patients and staff, the lack of adequate channels between the worlds and the development of separate cultures in the two groups. Equally, by the 1960s, Dunham and Weinberg had alighted on 'employee culture' and suggested that the central goal of this culture was 'the complete subjection and control of patients' (1960: 249). On top of this Goffman spoke of the processes of 'mortification' and systems of self-degradation which stripped inmates of mental hospitals, and other 'total institutions', of all defences, and left them prey to a domineering institutional culture. And in the UK too, an anti-institutional agenda developed throughout the 1950s and 1960s. Hospitals, far from being therapeutic agencies, were now being seen as carriers of a new disorder, increasingly referred to as 'institutionalism'. Thus, Martin (1955) pointed out how both staff and patients lost much of their individuality and initiative when in mental hospital, and became subject to rigid routines. Whilst Barton, in a 1959 booklet on institutional neurosis, sought 'to present in a systematic form the dreadful mental changes that may result from institutional life' (1959: Preface). The frontispiece carried photographs of the gait and posture which were supposedly characteristic of such neurosis which was a 'disease characterized by apathy . . . lack of interest . . . loss of individuality . . . a man made disease caused by lack of contact with the outside world' (1959: 12). And later Pauline Morris in her *Put Away* (a 1969 study of the hospitalization of mentally handicapped individuals) questioned the medical ideology in terms of which such hospitals were organized. More interestingly, however, the book carried a foreword by Peter Townsend in which he spoke of 'the isolation, cruelty and deprivation of the hospital organization' (1969: xxxii) – remarks which were not always justified in the light of the book's varied (and sometimes positive) findings. These anti-institutional stances resonated with a loud echo in a series of widely advertised scandals in British hospitals for the mentally handicapped which were reported upon during the late 1960s and early 1970s. Martin's *Hospitals in Trouble* (1984), reviewed the scandals and in so doing took a further opportunity to highlight the negativity and sense of hopelessness which supposedly characterized hospital culture.

As one might expect, and in addition to these directly targeted critiques, there were many other negative stances evident in a wide range of publications – some concerned with hospital architecture (to which I have already referred), others concerned with new ways of organizing care and treatment – such as those relating to the establishment of halfway houses, day hospitals, day centres and care in the community. And this anti-institutionalism was inevitably reflected in political policy. Thus in 1961, the British Minister of Health envisaged a world in which there would be a 50 per cent reduction in mental hospital beds in the space of the following 15 years and where the long-stay hospital population would eventually dwindle to zero (Ministry of Health, 1961). Two years later a National Plan for community care was published, (Ministry of Health, 1963).

All in all, then, and for reasons which we shall come to, it seems clear that the fate of the hospital was sealed somewhere in the 1950s. Indeed, Greenblatt *et al.*'s 1955 claim that 'the prognosis for the future of psychiatric hospitals is hopeful' (1955: 4242), looks positively foolish from the standpoint of the 1990s. But neither Greenblatt nor his colleagues were to know that much of the positive psychiatric work which had been carried out in hospitals, and many of the positive empirical findings concerning hospital life were to be increasingly overlooked and buried beneath the burgeoning claims for community care. Korman and Glennerster (1990) in their study of hospital closure cite this growing anti-institutional ethos as a causal factor in the trend towards care in the community policies. It seems more likely, however, that the attack on hospital life was a symptom rather than a cause of change, and that the reasons why the anti-institutional case was listened to so readily are to be located in a changing vision of what psychiatric disorder was all about. And that is a theme which we must necessarily explore in some detail throughout the remainder of this book.

Trends in Hospitalization of the Mentally Ill

The transition from hospital based care for the mentally ill to what is loosely termed 'community care', has been a fact of North American and European life for more than two decades. The characteristic features of this transition have been documented in both quantitative terms (as, for example, in DHSS, 1977b and 1985) and in more interesting and graphic terms (see, for example, Dear and Wolch, 1987; Jones, 1988; Mangen, 1985). Broadly speaking, it is a transition which exhibits three main trends. A decline in the in-patient populations of mental hospitals (though this is often associated with a massive increase in the number of admissions), a decline in the actual number of large mental hospitals, and an increase in the number of psychiatric units in general hospitals, together with an increase in the number of day hospitals, day centres and the like. And some of these trends are visible in the data for England and Wales contained in Figure 2.2. For example, it is evident from that figure that what amounts to an exponential rate of increase in hospital admissions has been paralleled by a more gradual decrease in the number of mental hospital residents as at 1 January of each year. (Though given the changing definitions of such basic concepts as hospital, institutional care, mental illness and its distinction from mental handicap, the construction of such a graph is no easy business and should itself be regarded as a late twentieth century representation of an apparent trend, rather than as an accurate reflection of independent events.) Naturally, on a European wide scale, the changes referred to are not always as simple as are sometimes claimed. Thus the percentage decrease in the number of mental hospitals is not necessarily as startling as one might expect because the trend has been towards smaller psychiatric hospitals rather than fewer psychiatric hospitals. But even so it is clear that big changes have occurred in countries as diverse as the UK, Ireland, Sweden and Spain (see Freeman *et al.*, 1985). In the context of the study group referred to herein, for example, the regional decline in in-patient psychiatric hospital beds during this period was 10 per cent, and the increase in beds in general hospital psychiatric units was 81 per cent – and in that sense the study context reflects quite strongly the trends which are evident in numerous other parts of Western Europe.

In the UK much of the current debate concerning the hospital to community transition, centres on whether or not sufficient and appropriate organizational and financial resources have been allocated to the relevant health and social services sectors. Little (if any) attention is devoted to understanding why such a transition occurred in the first place and why policies for such a fundamental change have found widespread cross-national support and expression. Nevertheless, explanations for the hospital–community transition do exist, and broadly speaking they tend to take one of a limited number of forms. The most frequently attested of these usually appears as a form of scientific or technological determinism in which it is argued that developments in pharmacology during the early 1950s, and especially the discovery of the 'neuroleptics' (sometimes called major tranquillizers), enabled many of the grosser aspects of psychotic behaviour to be stabilized or toned down, thus facilitating the move of psychotic patients from hospital custody to community care. Accounts of this nature first appeared in the writings of Brill and Patton (1957, 1959, 1962), and nowadays appear as a routine feature of a wide range of writings. They can, for example, be found in the UK Governments' 1975 White Paper on *Better Services for the Mentally Ill* (DHSS, 1975), and in many recent writings on the mental health services (see, for example, Jones, 1988). The second form of explanation usually appears in the guise of economic rather than scientific determinism and suggests (in different ways) that the transition from hospital to community care is little more than the organizational expression of some kind of monetary or cost cutting exercise or, more sophistically, an expression of some actual or impending fiscal crisis of the welfare state. This kind of explanation (as specifically applied to mental health policy making) is much favoured, for example, in the writings of Scull (1984, and 1989), and Warner (1985), but may also be found to a lesser extent in the writings of Dear and Wolch (1987) and, in a broader form, Offe (1984). Whilst the third kind of argument tends to confuse effects for their causes. It is what might be called the anti-institutional argument, and it points towards a growing disenchantment with institutional care in all of its forms, as a source of organizational change from the 1950s onwards. Korman and Glennerster (1990), for example, provide one particular instance of the error by arguing that a series of intellectual, legal and welfare movements during the 1960s in particular, encouraged a form of anti-institutionalism which eventually expressed itself in terms of care in the community policies.

Naturally all three kinds of argument generate numerous empirical and theoretical difficulties. Of these, the argument of the pharmacological determinists is perhaps the easiest to deal with. Indeed, there are two grounds on which we have cause to question pharmacological determinism. First, it is clear that no matter how powerful and effective the neuroleptics were in controlling the symptoms of the psychoses, their discovery and use entirely fails to explain why community care policies were applied to large groups of people for whom the neuroleptics had nothing to offer. Thus, care in the community, as we know, is a policy applied to the mentally handicapped, the young, the old, and even in certain circumstances the criminal – though of these we may look no further than the mentally handicapped. For despite the fact that the movement of the latter group from hospital to community care was, and is, carried out in tandem with the mentally ill, that transition has not been (and could not have been) dependent on the introduction of the neuroleptics (simply by virtue of the fact that the neuroleptics have no impact on people with learning difficulties). Secondly, and more damning perhaps, there are good grounds for suspecting that the move from hospital to community actually predates the use of

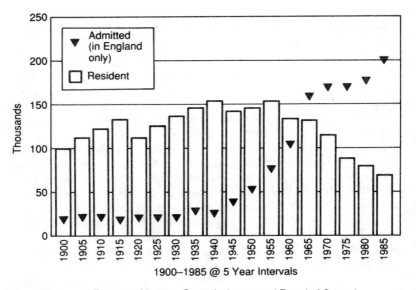

Figure 2.2   *Mental hospital statistics (England and Wales), admitted to, and resident in, institutions*

the neuroleptics by up to ten years. So there was, for example, a distinct fall in the number of hospital residents in England and Wales throughout the 1940s – a fall which is evident in Figure 2.2 – some years before the new chemical therapies were pressed into use. And Klerman (1961) reports on numerous American studies which indicated that there was a progressive rise in hospital discharge rates during the late 1940s in a number of eastern US hospitals. So Delaware State, Warren State (Pennsylvania) and Boston Psychopathic are all cited as examples of institutions which achieved discharge rates of 70–80 per cent during the critical period. In addition, one must also recall that there were already moves towards the creation of halfway hostels, therapeutic communities, and a recognition of community as a valid site for treatment at least a decade before the introduction of chlorpromazine and reserpine into psychiatric hospitals.

As with the pharmacological determinists, of course, the arguments of the economic determinists also fall down on a series of grounds. And not least because the available data demonstrate how the movement towards the integration of psychiatric treatment into general medicine and the community is common to countries with diverse ideological roots. So it matters little whether one examines social democratic, or ex-state socialist or overtly *laissez-faire* capitalist states, for one witnesses similar strategies for the dehospitalization of the mentally ill in all of them. This, at the very least, suggests that crude appeals to monetarist economics are insufficient to account for the policy trend. Equally significant, however, is the fact that examination of the policy data from individual countries exhibits little evidence that community care was ever intended to be a cost cutting exercise in itself. The British Government's 1975 policy statement on community care, for example, makes no mention of costs. Nor is there much evidence that the move from hospital to community results in actual cost savings. The data here are still somewhat sketchy of course, and assessment of cost can turn into a complex accounting exercise, yet detailed assessment by Korman and Glennerster (1990) of the costs involved in provision for the dehospitalized mentally handicapped suggested that the 'recurrent annual costs of reprovision were more than in the old large Victorian hospital' (1990: 156–7). Whilst Weissert *et al.* (1988) in a review of some 27 studies of costing for home and community based long-term care for the elderly concluded that, 'Home and community care as it has been practised during the last 30 years has not tended to produce cost savings in most studies' (1988: 345). What is clear is that in the movement from hospital to community care, costs are transferred from health to social services budgets – and that transfer has very significant organizational consequences, though cost savings are not necessarily associated with them.

Finally, to deal with the anti-institutional argument, we have already discussed how the evidence concerning the appropriateness or inappropriateness of institutional care for the mentally ill was never particularly clear cut. So for every study which painted a portrait of hospital life in dark colours, there was at least one other which painted a lighter and more positive picture. In that sense the arguments about the deficits of institutional life were never ones which were based on empirical evidence alone. In fact, the ideology of anti-institutionalism gained hold only after the trend towards dehospitalization began, and therefore one is drawn to view the anti-institutional movement more as a symptom of some deeper change rather than as a cause of change in itself.

Above all, however, and from the point of view adopted herein, it seems clear that the three kinds of explanation (in all of their variants) ignore the fact that innovation and change always occur in specific and detailed discursive contexts, and that the latter inevitably moulds and fashions the ways in which any particular set of interests are taken up and expressed. In other words, we must be aware that scientific advances and economic interests can never enter the world by some magic route unmediated by concrete and existing social practices. And given this, it is clear that any explanation of organizational change which appeals to the causal efficacy of extra-discursive interests not only tends to produce history with a hollow centre (that is, a form of stimulus–response history), but forever leaves us in ignorance as to what goes on in the black box which supposedly manages to translate known interests and forms of technological or scientific advance into *specific* forms of organizational change. In the context of this book, therefore, I am asserting that if we wish to understand the nature of the transition from hospital to community care for the mentally ill, it is first necessary to understand something about the ways in which psychiatric disorder is and has been structured and represented in the modern world. Indeed, my argument will be that the causes of large scale changes in patterns of psychiatric health care are to be truly located in the changing ways in which mental illness and other forms of 'mental' disability have been socially constituted during the twentieth century. And those changes (which I shall discuss throughout the rest of the book) have rendered long-term institutional care for the mentally ill inappropriate in most cases. Indeed, it will become clear that, for the most part, the castle (of institutionalism) was, so to speak, destroyed from within, rather than by attack from without. This is not to deny that members of various ideological, libertarian, or economic interest groups joined in the attack on hospitalization once it began, but it is to deny that hospital psychiatry was undermined by forces which were entirely external to it.

In summary then, we might say that during the late nineteenth and early twentieth centuries, insanity had a marked spatial distribution – contained as it was in extra-metropolitan asylums. The population of those asylums climbed steadily during the nineteenth century (see, for example, Finnane, 1981; Jones, 1972) and continued to climb roughly until the mid-point of the current century. However, somewhere near that mid-point there was a radical reassessment of what mental illness was, and where it should and could be located. That reassessment seems to have resulted in a dissolution of the asylum system, and once collapsed, new architectural representations of psychiatric disorder came into being.

The Architecture of Change

Whilst 1959 was probably the last point at which the building of a relatively isolated and specialized psychiatric hospital could have been advocated as an appropriate response to the need for organized psychiatric health care, it is clear that hospital care for psychiatric patients has not been abandoned. In fact the growing provision of psychiatric units in general hospitals has, if anything, served to underline the continuing existence of a specifically medical view of psychiatric impairment (Baruch and Treacher, 1978). Yet side by side with hospital care there has also arisen a new array of practices and facilities, and consequently the functions of care and treatment of the mentally ill are now dispersed and fragmented across numerous sites and numerous professional groupings, rather than concentrated on a single site. But at what point did this fragmentation and dispersal begin?

In later chapters we will spend some time plotting the points at which certain types of treatment and certain types of words and phrases appeared or disappeared in the historical record. The plotting of such points has its uses, but what really counts is not one isolated appearance (or disappearance) of this or that word, or this or that form of treatment, or this or that idea, but rather the emergence of a galaxy of concepts, services and institutions which hang together in some coherent structure, and which do so to such an extent that they present themselves as a distinct and alternative form of practice to the ones which prevail in any given age. For example, the philosophy and practice of community care in the UK can in some respects be traced back to what was probably the very first mention of the term in the *Seventeenth Annual Report of the Board of Control* (1931b). (And in that report it is not just the phrase which appears, but also the modern concept of community care – though its application was restricted to the lives of 'mental defectives' rather than the mentally ill.) The report claimed that, 'there has been a growing realisation that public care and protection of the majority of mentally-defective persons must be organized outside institutions and colonies' (1931b: 61), and suggested that through the 'thorough organization of community care', including the provision of day centres, the needs of mental defectives could be met. But despite this it would be wrong to claim that care in the community policies date back to 1931, for at that time there was no recognizable array of alternative services or physical facilities available for the hospitalized population. Indeed, the infrastructure of community care programmes – comprising as it does such things as social work, community nursing, day centre and occupational therapy facilities – was built up only slowly and gradually. That build up can in part be traced through the emergence of specific architectural forms. For in the same way that hospital psychiatry found its physical expression in asylum buildings, so too did community psychiatry eventually find its expression in physical spaces of a different (though still distinctive) kind.

It is, perhaps, in the provision of hospital out-patient departments that we find the first elements of the emergent structure. And during the second and third decades of the current century these departments were to be increasingly found in both psychiatric hospitals and in general hospitals. An early example of a specialized psychiatric hospital (with an out-patients' department), designed along the lines of the general hospital rather than along the lines of the asylum, was the Maudsley Hospital (London) which opened in 1923 (Allderidge, 1991). And the birth of the Maudsley was linked to that expansive vision of the psychiatric hospital as a site for therapy and cure of which I have already spoken. (The Maudsley, however, was not the first hospital of its kind – the Neurological Clinic of the Massachusetts General Hospital in Boston probably has better credentials for that claim.) The existence of an out-patients' building, of course, expressed a general theoretical recognition that there was a role for non-custodial treatment of the insane in the wider network of the therapeutic system. And such theoretical recognition appears, for example, in both the early American work of Adolf Meyer and of Southard (that is, roughly during the 1900–15 period). In England the fashion for out-patients' clinics and 'nerve clinics' in general hospitals developed increasingly after 1923, and by 1929 Lord was able to report the existence of a new concept of psychiatric treatment (the 'nerve hospital') in which psychologists, social services personnel and psychiatrists worked together at a common site dedicated to out-patient treatment and short-term care (Lord, 1929). Following on the provision of out-patients' clinics – which were given backing in the Mental Treatment Act of 1930 – came day centres (especially for the mentally defective), and I have already made mention of numerous Board of Control reports from the early 1930s which spoke of the need for such things as day care and occupational therapy facilities. Furthermore, and subsequent to the emergence of a distinct social psychiatry during the 1935–45 period, we eventually encounter such things as the day hospitals and therapeutic patient clubs. Thus, Bierer (1952), refers to the establishment of a day hospital in 1948 under the auspices of the Institute of Social Psychiatry in London. The day hospital utilized a range of therapies from individual and group psychotherapy, to ECT, social therapy, psychodrama and art therapy, all integrated, of course, in terms of the principles of social psychiatry. During roughly the same period Bierer (1948) was able to discuss the nature of therapeutic social clubs, formed in the wake of some principles of Adlerian psychotherapy – which laid primary emphasis on group processes. Their aim, stated Bierer, was to counter asociality and to integrate patients into social relationships – a goal which itself generated a need for 'social therapists'. Quite naturally, and side by side with these developments, were the much larger developments in therapeutic communities which gradually moved out of their hospital bases and into various spheres of non-psychiatric care (see, for example, Bloor *et al.*, 1988). Emergent, too, was the halfway house movement which according to Raush and Raush (1968) aimed to provide 'bridges between hospital and community' (1968: 6). (And though only three such houses existed in the USA before 1953, there were over 40 of them by the early 1960s.) So gradually, and in one way or another, psychiatry expanded into a wide range of organizational sites. (This to say little of the fact that in the UK at least, the overwhelming bulk of minor psychiatric disorders were increasingly dealt with in the community through the general practitioner service.)

Apart from the establishment of new sites for psychiatric practice, it was also clear by the late 1960s that it was the psychiatric team – composed of social worker, psychologist, nurse and psychiatrist – rather than the psychiatrist alone, which was laying claim to the patient. A WHO document on the role of the psychiatric hospital had spoken of the 'medico-social team' and its responsibilities for mental health in the community, as far back as 1957 (WHO, 1957). And this team, even when it was hospital based, was designed to move into and through the community as a matter of routine – mainly because the problems of its 'clients' (rather than its patients) were now believed to be linked to a diverse array of social and economic pressures as well as inner psychological or organic faults. In addition, and as we shall discover later on, psychiatric disorder was by this stage increasingly viewed as something widely distributed in the community at large, and therefore there was no good reason why it should not be dealt with *in situ*. Indeed, given these changing images of the causes and distribution of psychiatric disorder, it was perhaps inevitable that the wall which once divided the sane from the insane and the normal from the abnormal was destined for demolition.

Among the very first English mental hospitals earmarked for closure was Powick hospital in Worcestershire (eventually closed 1989). Its demise gave birth to the Worcester Development Project – a project aimed at the provision and evaluation of care in the community facilities. Among the buildings evaluated in the project were hospital wards, day centres, day hospitals and a community mental health centre (see Rooney and Mathews, 1982). The latter contained room for psychiatrists, social workers and a psychologist, all of whom were to 'share the initial referrals'. Naturally, consultation rooms and activity rooms are provided on site, but what marks this particular building out in the history of psychiatric provision is that 'the centre is a converted building on a side street off one of [the town's] main roads. It is not obviously different from the rest of the property on the street' (1982: 24). In other words, its distinctiveness rests in its normality, and in its capacity to be quietly absorbed into mainstream life. Its presence thus underlines the ways in which psychiatric illness is now regarded as an abnormality in only a quantitative rather than a qualitative sense – as something which differs from normality in degree, rather than in kind. In that respect, mental illness is no longer viewed as a master status which might dominate the entirety of a life. And just as the lunacy and madness of old demanded the construction of isolated asylums, so the modern forms of psychiatric disorder demand an architecture consonant with its special principles – which very often means an architecture domestic in its scale and appearance. Interestingly, it is also an architecture under the control of a new authority – namely that of the social services department – a fact which demonstrates how, hand in hand with the normalization of psychiatric disorder, has often gone a transfer of responsibility from medical to welfare agencies.

3
The Diverse Objects of Psychiatric Theory

> Azande think that witchcraft is a round thing in the small
> intestine.
>
> Evans-Pritchard (1937: 40)

Social Policy and Psychiatric Theory

It is often argued, and sometimes merely taken for granted, that changes in the organization of care for the mentally ill are a direct and conscious product of the wishes and activities of reformers and legislators. This line of reasoning is evident, for example, in the works of both historians and sociologists. Hence, Rothman (1985) can be found arguing that in order to comprehend the nature of asylum growth during the last century, 'one should turn first to the rhetoric of the reformers' (1985: 115). In a similar manner, Grob (1973), Jones (1972) and Scull (1989) also look towards the sentiments, motives and intentions of reformers for explanations of the major organizational changes which affected the lives of the mentally ill during the nineteenth and twentieth centuries. And in the same vein, much of the work which focuses on the most recent developments tends to view organizational change as a product of policy innovations consciously and deliberately pursued by the members of various political interest groups (see, for example, Korman and Glennerster, 1990). Though some, like Tomlinson (1991: 27), whilst noting the absence of detailed centralized plans for mental hospital closure, and the haphazard nature of policy developments in general, nevertheless argue as if the prime sources of organizational change must be sought outside of, rather than within, psychiatry.

This sidestepping of psychiatric interests usually fits in well with what we might call a policy oriented view of the world. That is to say, a view of the world which takes conscious human plans as the starting point of analysis and then seeks to reveal the manifest or latent reasons as to why such plans were adopted and pursued at different times by specific (political, economic or moral) interest groups. One weakness of this view is that it tends to ignore the possibility that innovations in the organization of social life often begin as the result of the unintended consequences of unplanned actions rather than of rationally calculated schemes of activity (Merton, 1967). In this respect the motives, reasons and intentions of planners can, at best, reveal only part of any evolutionary story. More importantly, however, the policy oriented view of social life also tends to overlook the fact that (as was stated in Chapter 2) innovation always occurs in some discursive context or other, and that human interests (whatever their source) always have to be translated into, and mediated through, the conceptual and theoretical structures of the age. In the context of changes in the field of psychiatry this implies that the ideas, concepts and theories of psychiatrists must actually count for something in our attempts to understand the move from asylum based to community based care. And they do so, in large part, because it is only in terms of shifting ideas about the nature of mental illness that policy innovators can express their plans about how the 'needs' of the mentally ill are to be met. It is on that basis that this chapter concerns itself with the varying ways in which mental illness has been represented in the work of professional psychiatrists. Inevitably, the aim is to demonstrate how changes in the provision of services for the mentally ill are linked to a changing vision of what mental illness might be, and how it should be treated.

Naturally enough, deciding what mental illness is and where exactly the origins and nature of psychiatric disorder are to be located continues to be fundamental to the entire psychiatric enterprise. Thus, a medicine which locates the essentials of disorder in the central nervous system is going to be organized a great deal differently from a medicine which believes that the core of psychiatric disorder is to be located in, say, social relationships. Similarly a medicine which endorses a belief in the ontological reality of disease is more likely to embrace policies of hospital treatment, than is a medicine which questions whether forms of psychiatric disorder are understandable as discrete disease processes in the first place. Unfortunately for us, however, the history of twentieth century psychiatry does not lend itself to the drawing of simple divisions, nor to the display of any easily readable trends away from one set of objects and locations and towards another. On the contrary, it is often difficult to see what exactly the objects of psychiatric study are. And this is so not only on the big screen of professional psychiatric theory, but also in the minute detail of empirical encounters – such as were found, for example, in the study hospital.

In this chapter we are going to examine what we might call vade mecum knowledge of mental illness. That is to say, representations of mental illness as they appear in psychiatric texts. In many ways these are the most powerful representations of their kind because they emanate from the most powerful professional group involved in psychiatric affairs. For many, it is these representations which reveal to us what psychiatric illnesses 'really are'. Unfortunately, these same representations are also ones which are constructed in a highly detailed and intricate technical form. Such a form is not, of course, appropriate to this book and for that reason we will have to restrict our focus to a study of the broad fields of action within which psychiatry has chosen to operate. Despite this apparent limitation, however, the following examination should nevertheless function to reveal to us exactly where the major objects of psychiatric practice have been located during the twentieth century, and how those locations have altered. As a corollary of this it ought also to become clear why therapeutic responses to psychiatric disorder have altered, and how those alterations have affected overall patterns of social and medical organization. Our starting point will lie in the earliest decades of the present century. This, in part, will enable us to see something of the conceptual and theoretical structure in terms of which the study hospital was originally planned, and it will also help us to assess the reasoning which lay behind the treatments to which patients in the study hospital had occasionally been subjected. (It may be as well to note here that, at the time of the empirical study, the longest staying patient in the study hospital had been resident there since 1921; seven other patients had also been based there since the mid-1920s.)

In the light of the forthcoming discussion, a number of observations will emerge. First, that the fields of activity and objects of study which appear in most of the older psychiatric texts (such as brain and central nervous system), are those which were particularly well suited to medical understandings and hospital based therapies. In contrast, many of the later objects of attention (such as social relations and behaviour) were not necessarily those which physical medicine could easily monopolize, and nor were they always well suited to somatic treatments. Secondly, that the numerous fields and objects of psychiatric study which are referenced in psychiatric texts often overlay one another in a complex matrix of ideas and practice – they do not present themselves individually, sequentially and discretely. Thus, in any one text (and this is especially so of the most recent texts) several objects of attention and fields of action appear in a single theoretical framework. Thirdly, that despite numerous changes and shifts in psychiatric theory, it is above all the soma of the isolated individual which holds pride of place in virtually all forms of clinical psychiatry. Finally, it should become increasingly clear that as the fields of action and objects of study have widened, psychiatrists (though they remain by far and away the most powerful professional group) have experienced difficulty claiming a monopoly over both the definition of psychiatric disorder, and over the specification and design of the therapeutic response to such disorder. In fact, these days, psychiatric disorder tends to be defined in terms of a whole array of professional practices and ideas – only some of which belong to medical psychiatry. In that respect, to understand what psychiatric disorder is, one has to take into account the ideologies and practices of professional social workers, nurses and psychologists, as well as medical psychiatrists. That in itself is of sociological interest because it invites us to explain how a medical monopoly on the definition of certain types of mental 'diseases' and illnesses which existed at the opening of the century, fragmented into an array of competing professional claims.

The Nature of Paresis

Physical Signs – Amongst the earliest of [the] signs is loss or sluggishness of the pupillary reflex to light. . . . An important reflex, the pharyngeal, disappears early in General Paralysis – stimulating the back of the throat with a feather frequently produces no discomfort. . . . Tremors of the hands are also quite noticeable, and later, the manual and other actions are quite uncoordinate. . . . Muscular weakness and incoordination result in a shuffling gait, and finally the patient is bed-ridden, with muscular wasting and contractures. Congestive seizures occur sooner or later in the vast majority of cases [and these] . . . are of an epileptiform nature. Consciousness is usually completely lost [and] after each seizure the patient shows marked deterioration, both mentally and physically. The heart's action becomes gradually weaker . . . [whilst] at the onset of the disease there is always considerable loss of weight . . . . The bones become fragile, so that fractures may arise from slight injuries. The finger-nails may become grooved . . . herpetic eruptions are sometimes seen.

Mental Symptoms – There is a gradual blunting of all the special senses. . . . Memory is impaired . . . . The association of ideas slackens . . . . The patient loses all insight into his condition. . . . In expansive cases, patients boast of their superhuman strength and of their untold wealth. The exalted cases imagine themselves to be Kings, Princes, Millionaires, or even the Deity. Such delusions entail endless trouble in the early stages, before the patient is placed under care. The patient spends all his money on useless articles . . ., or he may accidentally commit suicide in some absurd attempt to fly without an aeroplane or to swim across the Atlantic . . . . There is an element of grotesqueness and exaggeration in General Paralysis which is unusual in other cases of insanity. . . . In the majority of cases, the disease runs its course to a fatal termination within three years. (Cole, 1913: 174–81 *passim*)

This abbreviated description of the symptoms of Paresis (more commonly referred to as general paralysis of the insane or GPI) was taken from Cole's *Mental Diseases* (1913: ch. 14). During the early part of this century, Paresis was far from being an uncommon disease, though it was a disease which was mainly restricted to males and one which was found particularly among ex-military men and sailors. The aetiology of the disease was not, however, at all clear during the early 1900s, and up to that time many kinds of fanciful theories were proposed to account for it. As with most mental diseases it was often assumed to have an hereditary basis. Though Bruce, in his *Studies in Clinical Psychiatry* (1906), claimed that it was a disease associated with the arduous and strenuous life of cities. Some commentators believed that it had a specifically physical aetiology and among the front runners for the role of the 'excitant' was syphilis. Thus, Stoddart in his *Mind and Its Disorders* (1908), and Stewart in *The Diagnosis of Nervous Diseases* (1908) specifically advanced the notion that syphilis was the cause of GPI. Unfortunately for the epidemiologists, however, not all men who manifested symptoms of tertiary syphilis went on to suffer from paralysis of the insane (in fact, only 4–5 per cent of those displaying signs of syphilis did so), and not all maniacs could be associated with venereal infection. Consequently, the exact nature of the causal mechanism remained mysterious.

In 1913, Noguchi and Moore (1913), keen students of the spirochete *Treponema pallidum*, demonstrated the presence of the living organism in the brains of 12 out of 70 (and later, 48 out of 200) Paresis victims. More interestingly, a link between this type of spirochete and syphilis had been pinpointed a few years earlier, in 1905, by the zoologist Schaudinn and his colleague Hoffman in Berlin. The latter had argued (incorrectly) that there was a constant association between the spirochete and the presence of syphilitic symptoms. And from there it seemed to be a relatively short step towards the serum diagnosis of syphilis in humans. It is usually Wasserman who is credited with inventing the blood test for syphilis (c. 1908), but the reasons as to why Wasserman sought evidence of syphilitic infection in the blood, and the processes by means of which the Wasserman reaction became recognized as a valid test for syphilis, are issues which raise central and interesting questions about the nature and structure of scientific discovery and validation. In this particular case, of course, Ludwig Fleck has already done the work for us, and in his *Genesis and Development of a Scientific Fact* (1979; first German edition 1935) he highlights the problems and ambiguities involved in regarding *Spirochaeta pallida* as the cause (or even a cause) of syphilis. Indeed, Fleck eventually argued that the spirochete ought to be defined by syphilis rather than the other way around. But this is to digress from his central point that scientific facts, and especially facts about disease, are never 'out there' ready and waiting to be discovered. Instead, they are constructed in accordance with the dominant beliefs and conceptual structures of the age – so it was with the causes of syphilis. From the standpoint of the newly emerging discipline of psychiatric medicine, however, the lesson of the Paresis research programme was clear, namely, that by searching for the germs which were present in the nervous systems of maniacs, melancholiacs and dementia sufferers one could only advance the cause of scientific psychiatry.

Whilst the organic origin of GPI was believed to be well determined by 1913, an effective treatment for the disorder eluded researchers for another five or so years. Naturally, there were numerous chemotherapies available for the treatment of syphilis during the first decade of the present century, and new preparations were continuously appearing (some early twentieth century treatments are mentioned by Mulzer, 1910). For GPI, however, no effective treatment was available until 1918 when Wagner-Jauregg instituted his malarial therapy. The new therapy seemed relatively straightforward. The GPI patient was either injected with a benign form of malaria, or alternatively two or three carefully selected malarial mosquitoes (of the same species) were allowed to feed on the patient. Soon after that, within a period of 48–72 hours, malarial fever appeared. The patient was monitored and managed through the fever, and once the febrile crisis was surmounted Wagner-Jauregg claimed to see a gradual but definite improvement in the behaviour of the previously maniacal individual. The paralysis abated, the manic delusions subsided and then disappeared, the handwriting became steadier, thought processes became clearer and mortality was averted. Wagner-Jauregg (1922) pronounced the cure effective and efficient. And convinced of its success, other therapists attempted to treat unrelated mental diseases by the same technique. Thus Rudolf, who was the assistant medical officer at Claybury Asylum (Essex), discussed in his *Therapeutic Malaria* (1927), the nature and use of the technique for GPI, syphilis and dementia praecox. (Dementia Praecox or adolescent psychosis was increasingly referred to as Schizophrenia after 1911.) The Board of Control – responsible for the welfare of lunatics in Britain – investigated the matter, and in its 1929 Report concluded that the treatment 'produces beneficial results'. Unlike other advocates, however, the Board's adviser also indicated that of the 1,597 patients treated by means of malarial therapy and investigated over a five year period, 75 per cent either died or remained in hospital. In other words the 'miracle cure' had positive effects on only 25 per cent of patients (Meagher, 1929).

Whatever the success rate, however, it was never clear to contemporaries why malarial therapy should have any effects in the first place. Rudolf (1927) suggested a number of possibilities: that the treatment worked because it encouraged leukocytosis (that is, an increase in the number of leukocytes in the blood); that the trauma of fever was of positive psychological benefit to the patient; that the high temperature of the patient's body destroyed the spirochete; that the new infection encouraged antibody formation; that the treatment generated some new metabolic process, or perhaps encouraged vasodilation. In effect, however, neither Wagner-Jauregg nor Rudolf, nor any other commentator could offer a plausible theoretical answer as to why such a therapy should lead to the remission of either the syphilitic or the Paresis symptoms. It was of little consequence however, because all that really mattered to the medics was their conviction that the therapy was deemed 'effective'.

This brief and sketchy history of Paresis and its therapy is abundantly instructive to those who wish to understand the treatment of psychiatric disorders during the twentieth century, and there are numerous points which can be usefully extrapolated from the story. First, it demonstrates how disparate and diverse symptoms of mental and bodily disorder were classified as belonging to a single condition and viewed as a unity. That unity was regarded as a disease process which had its own 'natural history'. Indeed, as far back as 1895, Kraepelin (1856–1926) had regarded GPI as the paradigm case of a psychiatric disorder, on the grounds that it had a distinct organic cause, a definite course, and a determinate outcome. (Though other researchers continued to refuse GPI the status of a disease entity right into the 1920s – see Meagher, 1929.) Secondly, we can see clearly from this example how what was considered to be a mental disease encompassing both organic ailments as well as purely psychological dysfunction was nevertheless diagnosed purely according to its clinical symptoms – that is to say, there was no independent pathological (laboratory) test for the disease. Thirdly, and relatedly, we can see how it was assumed that psychological impairment correlated with physical impairment – that the two were necessarily and not merely casually related (though in fact the psychological symptoms of GPI were not in any way specific to its assumed cause). Fourthly, the history of Paresis demonstrates faith in the belief that the causes of mental disease should be sought first and foremost in relation to the physical impairment, rather than the psychological dysfunction. In that sense, and by using Paresis as a paradigm case, many psychiatrists believed that they had good grounds for thinking that the causes of mental illness in general were likely to be found in the physical domain. Finally, we can see how a specific (malarial) therapy was readily used on patients on the basis of empirical judgements alone. There was no theoretical justification for such a therapy, and nor was any such justification thought to be necessary.

These several elements of the Paresis story also appear in other guises and other contexts of recent psychiatric history. For example, many of the major therapeutic developments during the twentieth century were as devoid of theoretical backing as was malarial therapy in the 1920s. And the belief in the organic base of many psychotic and some neurotic disorders is as sound today as it was in the 1910s (see, for example, Scharfetter, 1983). The history of schizophrenia, in particular, is replete with parallels to the history of GPI (Boyle, 1990). Despite such parallels, however, it would be quite wrong to suggest that physicalism has provided the only canopy under which psychiatric research has operated during the modern era. Nor would it be correct to imply that the study of Paresis provided a set of rigid precedents in terms of which all subsequent investigations were executed. The history of Paresis does, however, reflect a powerful tendency within twentieth century psychiatry to comprehend serious psychiatric dysfunction as having an essentially physical or organic base. Such a tendency is evident, for example, in the World Health Organization's *International Statistical Classification of the Causes of Diseases, Injuries and Causes of Death* (1977), where a distinction is made between the neuroses which have no 'demonstrable organic basis', and the functional psychoses (including schizophrenia), which are assumed to have such a basis, even though that basis is not always clearly evident. This faith in organicism is further evident in the 1987 Medical Research Council's report into the investigation of schizophrenia which recommends virtually nothing other than neurological and genetic research into that disorder. Indeed, this belief that mental illness is something which can be located in the body and which can be modified or treated by physical interventions is one which affects the lives of hundreds of thousands of psychiatric patients in the Western world. As we shall see, it certainly forms the basis on which the patients in the study group were treated. But before we examine further the nature of somatic visions of mental illness, let us first examine a psychodynamic interpretation of such illness.

The Nature of Hysteria

During various periods between 1880 and 1892 Josef Breuer and Sigmund Freud analysed the symptoms of hysteria in a number of female patients (Jones, 1964). The results of their examinations and their accounts of their therapeutic method were first published in 1895. The English (Breuer and Freud, 1955) translation was entitled *Studies on Hysteria* (*Standard Edition of the Complete Psychological Works of Sigmund Freud* – henceforth SE – Vol. 2). By their own admission this was a study of the members of an 'educated and literate social class' (SE.2: xxix), and Freud and Breuer's accounts and descriptions of such people 'often touches upon [the] patients' most intimate lives and histories' (SE.2: xxix). This was so because there was always an 'intimate' connection between the patients' suffering and their personal biography (SE.2: 161). Indeed the precipitating causes of hysterical symptoms were invariably located deep in the biographical histories of the subject. As Freud himself stated, the cause was quite frequently 'some event in childhood' (SE.2: 4). Each symptom, however, had its own cause and in the exploration for causes no detail of a biography was too small or too trivial for examination. In the case of Lucy R., for example, Freud 'decided to make the smell of burnt pudding [which Lucy R. frequently experienced] the starting point of the analysis' (SE.2: 107). And we know, after Freud adopted and developed his 'free association' methods between 1892 and 1895 (Jones, 1964: 214), no detail of a person's life could be dismissed as irrelevant or extraneous to the analysis. But it was the connection between the biographic detail and the detail of the symptoms which truly interested Freud. A connection which had necessarily to be drawn out in the dynamic process of what Breuer's patient, Anna O., had called the 'talking cure' (see Ellenberger, 1972).

This emphasis upon personal detail, especially private biography, and the inner development of self was, of course, closely tied in to Freud's theorization of mind as a psychological entity. And in developing that psychology he not only created a new geography of the mental, but extended it into an entirely new realm – namely the unconscious. In doing this, Freud and Breuer simultaneously created a new kind of mental patient. And this new patient – a patient with a mind of her own – was allocated a central role in the illness process. That role was an active one such that, together with the therapist, she was to work conjointly for the resolution of whatever psychological problem presented itself. And that resolution in turn was dependent upon the unveiling of the mind's secrets to the patient herself. In fact it was a process correctly called psychotherapeutics, directed as it was to that 'psyche' which Freud was to so deftly construct throughout his working life. Indeed, it is on the supposed existence of this psyche that Freudian therapeutic practice is based, but before we examine the sociological implications of such therapeutics any further we must first clarify some points concerning the relationship between psyche and soma in early Freudian psychology and the manner in which Freud and Breuer believed mental disorder to be 'in' the patient.

Freud was by early inclination and training a neurologist and his main biographer, Ernest Jones, indicates that he had achieved some distinction in that discipline long before his work as a psychoanalyst was either developed or acknowledged. Indeed, it is a feature of Freud's life which most Freud scholars (such as Gay, 1988; Stewart, 1969; and Sulloway, 1979) emphasize. In recounting his career in neurology, Jones (1964) at one point quotes a recollection of the master concerning his marked ability to predict post-mortem pathology of the brain from clinical diagnoses, and the later shame he (Freud) felt concerning a particular occasion when he diagnosed a case of neuroses as 'chronic localized meningitis'. This shame flowed from his having accepted, rather uncritically, the premisses of somatic medicine on which the diagnosis was built, but by way of excuse Freud states that at that time, 'greater authorities than myself in Vienna were in the habit of diagnosing neurasthenia as cerebral tumour' (Jones, 1964: 186). In questioning such (anatomically inclined) diagnoses Freud was to some extent following the ideas of one of his many mentors, Charcot (1825–93), who had demonstrated the presence of physical dysfunction in his patients despite the absence of organic disease. Indeed, Charcot, through the use of hypnosis, had even managed to artificially induce the existence of sensory and motor dysfunction in some of the Salpétrière inmates. So much so that, according to Freud, Charcot's work 'relegates physiological considerations to a second place' (Freud, 1966a: 135). The description and interpretation of hysteria as a pathology without organic base, however, flew in the face of some of the most serious scientific propositions of nineteenth century medicine, and it is, perhaps, in his apparent willingness to re-examine such propositions as valid starting points for the study of the neuroses that the kernel of the Freudian revolution is to be found.

There seems to be considerable debate among Freud scholars about the extent to which there was or was not a radical discontinuity between neurology and psychoanalysis in the Freudian corpus. It is a debate which need not concern us here (see, for example, Gay, 1988; Sulloway, 1979; Wollheim, 1971). But there are some broad and somatically inclined propositions about the nature of the human mind which Freud did have to contend with and we need to mention just two of these at this point. The first concerns the thesis that, as Gall and Spurzheim (1809: 6–7) put it, 'the brain is the organ of the mind [*de l'ame*], and the material base of the human spirit'; and the second concerns the thesis of cerebral localization (that is, the notion that different mental functions can be localized to specific areas of the brain).

Both theses found increasing theoretical and experimental support during the latter half of the nineteenth century, and there can be little doubt that Freud, as an eminent neurologist in his own right, would have been aware of all of the crucial developments. Yet, and as I have already indicated, it is not at all clear how he related these theses to his own mode of psychoanalysis. In fact, and as Gedo and Pollock (1976) indicate, the *Studies* exhibit all manner of ambiguities and contradictions concerning the relative significance of physiological and psychological explanations in the writings of both Breuer and Freud. What is clear, however, is that in the analysis of mind, Freud was concerned with much more than mere sensory-motor functions of the central nervous system and that he did not fully accept the mechanical image of cognition and consciousness within which such functions were usually examined and theorized. As far as the pathology of hysteria was concerned, for example, he was clear that, '[T]he lesion in hysterical paralysis must be completely independent of the anatomy of the nervous system since . . . *hysteria behaves as though anatomy did not exist or as though it had no knowledge of it*' (Freud, 1966a: 169; Freud's emphasis). Consequently, he argued that the neuroses were not caused by pathological features of the human brain, but by the dynamic processes of the human mind. In other words, he seemed to work on the assumption that there was a limited amount to be gained by correlating functional pathology with anatomical or physiological lesions. Psychology, not neurology opened up the pathway to understanding, and it is a point which can be well illustrated by reference to a tiny detail in one of the five case histories of hysteria; the case of Katharina. Thus, when Katharina says 'The truth is, sir, my nerves are bad' (SE.2: 125), Freud does not pick up and relate to the statement as a laywoman's description of her own anatomico-physiological system, but as an entrée into an entirely new level of analysis, namely, into the depths of Katharina's *unconscious*.

'Little mention will be made of the brain and none whatever of molecules', stated Breuer (SE.2: 185), as he opened the theoretical section of the *Studies*. Instead, the focus was to be placed on 'psychological' factors, and in order to sharpen this focus a new semantics of mind was called forth. The very first mention of the 'unconscious' (in its psychoanalytic sense) occurs in the *Studies* (SE.2: 45), 'repression' gets its first airing (SE.2: 10), 'conversion' (SE.2: 166), and 'symbolization' (SE.2: 180) also appear together with the newly minted concept of 'overdetermination' (SE.2: 212). The new conceptual framework is designed so as to redraft our image of the human mind and when this semantics is further developed in *The Interpretation of Dreams* (Freud, 1953; hereafter SE.5), numerous other key notions are added to the Freudian corpus, such as the preconscious (SE.5: 499), and the division of mental functioning into primary (wish-fulfilment) and secondary (inhibitory) processes (SE.5: 599). The Freudian mind, then, was beginning to emerge, and it did so as a dynamic psychological phenomenon rather than as an anatomico-physiological entity. Yet as powerful as it was, this theoretical revolution did not necessarily gain widespread acceptance. Thus Stewart, in his second (1908) edition of *The Diagnosis of Nervous Diseases*, stated very plainly that 'the old definition of a neurosis as a nervous disease devoid of anatomical changes is inadequate. Disease is inconceivable without some underlying physical basis' (1908: 338). And as far as public medicine was concerned, it was the like of Stewart, rather than Freud, who was to be the more influential.

Some Objects of Psychiatric Study

We have so far referred to a physicalist interpretation of mental illness and a psychodynamic one, and from that comparison alone we can see immediately that it would be misleading to suggest that psychiatry ever had a monolithic vision of its task and its domain. Scientists, even within the same recognizable disciplines rarely study common objects, or even different but related objects in a common framework. Kuhn's idea of a 'normal science' – a science defined by a single 'body of accepted theory' (1970: 10) – is in that sense a chimera. Thus, different schools within a single science or form of practice, tend very often to study and deal with entirely different objects of inquiry. And the objects differ precisely because the styles of theory and practice within which they are constructed differ. In this respect, the history of twentieth century psychiatry offers some excellent examples of diversity in theoretical schemes and their associated forms of practice. As with the history of the mental hospital, however, it is not possible to slot such diversity into a simple evolutionary framework in which earlier developments can be seen as precursors or elemental forms of later ones. So we would not, for example, be justified in describing changes in modern psychiatric practice in terms of a move from soma to psyche, or from psyche to family relationships. Instead we would more likely be forced to recognize that the numerous objects of psychiatric practice – body, mind, neurological system, behaviour, social relations – are forever overlaid one upon the other, and what is scored against the historical record is not so much their presence and absence, but the ways in which they are differentially evaluated and placed. In what follows, therefore, we shall seek to highlight some of the more common objects of study which have appeared in twentieth century psychiatry and to look at some of the frameworks in which they have been represented. In following through this exercise, however, we should forever recall the diverse and complex nature of psychiatric theory, and how a concentration on any one path of theoretical development must necessarily produce a fractured and fragmented insight into the nature of psychiatric practice in general.

The fragmentation of psychiatric theory is in many ways evident in the texts contained within the library of the Royal Society of Medicine. For there it is possible to approach the early twentieth century study of lunacy, neuroses, psychoses, mental illness and mental dysfunction (note the diversity of terms), from at least two directions. The first is through works on psychiatry, and the second is through works on neurology. In so far as one is interested in the nature of psychiatric thought between the turn of the century and, say, the 1940s it is both possible and viable to start with either route – simply because the objects and theories relevant to the one subdiscipline were likely to be cross-referenced against the other. Indeed, faith in the construction of a neurologically based psychiatry was evident throughout most of Western Europe and North America during the period in question. Somewhere around the 1940s, however, the subject matter, theories and directions of interest of these two subdisciplines diverge, at which point it seems that (in the UK at least), the vision of a neurologically based psychiatry was lost. Such a watershed is, for example, rather neatly represented in Brain's 1940 edition of his *Diseases of the Nervous System*, wherein (and in contrast to statements in the first (1933) edition), he admits that, 'Neither psychiatry nor psychotherapy, as such, fall within the province of neurology' (1940: 889). Yet until that point, it was firmly believed that neurology held the key to the mysteries of mind.

Given this broader context, Cole's *Mental Diseases* (1913) reveals a great deal about early twentieth century British psychiatry. Cole, as the title of his book suggests, believed in mental as well as physical diseases and also used the concept of mind. But for him, as with so many late nineteenth and twentieth century commentators, mind was not an independent entity or an entity without a material base. In fact, Cole was quite clear on this point and asserted that the substratum of the mind was the brain. 'That the brain is the organ of the mind now appears', stated Cole, 'as a truism scarcely worthy of mention' (1913: 16). Furthermore, Cole believed that it was possible to localize mind to the cortex of the cerebral convolutions. Given such beliefs it was inevitable that he and his readers would interpret mental disorder as nothing more than bodily disorder under another guise. Thus, 'the medical student will do well to follow out mental processes as far as possible on a neurological basis. . . . He will find that in insanity there is bodily disorder' (1913: 70). For Cole, then, as with so many other authors, mental diseases were primarily neurological in origin even though they manifested themselves through the medium of psychological processes. These ideas concerning the material base of mental processes and the notion that physical substrata underlay mental processes had been advanced primarily by Hughlings Jackson in the 1880s. The work of the latter, together with work on the localization of mental functions ensured that the old phrenological claims about the brain being the organ of the mind were, by the 1910s, regarded as being basically correct. And given such beliefs, it is hardly surprising that for Cole the pathology of insanity was to be located in the central nervous system and most likely in the brain.

In similar manner, Stoddart, who dedicated each edition of his *Mind and its Disorders* to Hughlings Jackson, also adopted the old phrenological claims. In the first (1908) edition, for example, Stoddart's stated goal was to 'induce the reader to think neurologically of mental processes' (1908: vii). And the psychiatric task was viewed as one which attempted to 'correlate mental processes with their physical substrata in the nervous system' (1908: vii). Such physicalist interpretations of mind, somewhat paradoxically meant that the primary object of psychiatric practice was not the mind at all, but the body. (In many ways it is only during the 1920s that hospital psychiatry begins to address itself to the mental.) Yet despite this, and whilst the nervous system, and especially the brain, figured as primary points of focus for early psychiatry, it would be wrong to think that madness (as it was then known) was something which could be localized solely in the nervous system. Indeed, madness was visible on the body as well as in it. Mental disease could be seen in the so called 'physical stigmata' of degeneration, that is in the atavistic features which were visible in the forehead, the jaw, or the ears of the patient, to say nothing of the cranial abnormalities which were 'dependent upon anomalies in the shape of the brain' (Stoddart, 1908: 166). Naturally, early psychiatric texts always reproduced photographs of the insane to verify the claims that mental disorder could be seen clearly in somatic gestures. These claims concerning the correlation of mental disorder with facial and bodily features were also underlined in texts dedicated to the development of this particular thesis. Thus, in his *Physique and Character* (1925; first German edition 1921), Kretschmer attempted to associate manic-depressive disorder and schizophrenia with specific body types – schizophrenia being said to manifest itself in the schizothymic body type. And this emphasis on body is further evident in the contents of the early twentieth century case notes of the asylum which serves as the reference point for this book. For, as the century progressed, the case notes incorporated photographs of the insane as visual aids to diagnosis.

Of all the early twentieth century texts, however, it is perhaps those of Stoddart which are (sociologically speaking) the most interesting. This is so because he, more than anyone, personifies a revolution in thinking which occurred during the early part of the twentieth century. In the third and fourth editions of his text (1919 and 1921 respectively), he proclaims his mistake in thinking that mental illness had its origins in bodily disorder. Indeed, by the 1920s he was claiming that the origins of madness were to be located in forms of 'intrapsychic conflict' rather than in neurology. In fact, following Freudian teaching, a new chapter on the ego was inserted into the second edition. Furthermore, and whereas he had previously discussed insanity in terms of disorders of action, judgement and sensation, by the third edition he discussed it in terms of neuroses and psychoses and proclaimed that psychical causes of insanity were primary and had to be taken account of in all mental disorders – even those which were recognized as being organic in origin. Thus stated Stoddart:

> When the [textbook] was first published, my endeavour was to induce the reader to think neurologically of mental processes, normal and morbid, and to study them from a neurological point of view. Since that time, however, owing to the psychological researches of Freud, and previously Janet and others, it has been found that we gain a clearer insight into mental processes when we approach them from a purely psychological standpoint. (1921: v–vi)

Stoddart's work, in this respect, serves to underline the ways in which, during the interwar period, psychoanalysis became a powerful force in mainstream psychiatry. Though whether we would ever be justified in claiming that psychoanalysis was 'the major influence on psychiatry' during the early twentieth century (Mora, 1959. I: 23), is doubtful. In any event, it is not surprising that the impact which Freud had on Stoddart's understanding of mental disorder was also evident in the work of other authorities. Diethelm's *Treatment in Psychiatry* (1936), for example (an American text designed for the medical psychiatrist), is written almost entirely within the psychoanalytic framework. Like Stoddart, Diethelm emphasized the role of the ego in the analysis of mental disorder and asserted that psychiatry was essentially the science of personality rather than body or mind. Thus, for Diethelm, 'The concept of personality as a unit replaces the psychophysical parallelism of Wundt [which] insists on a division of body and mind' (1936: 1). For Diethelm, then, methods of treatment included such things as dream analysis and the free association technique, word association methods and relaxation therapies. In siting personality at the heart of psychiatry Diethelm was further reflecting a quiet but steady change which had occurred in psychiatric practice in general and which was to become increasingly pronounced after the 1930s. That change concerned the popular perception of patients as having identifiable 'personalities' rather than just minds and bodies (personality is not a term which one finds in early twentieth century British psychiatric texts). So much so was this the case that the personality eventually came to be regarded as the core and essence of human being. This emphasis on personality reflected in part a growing interest of psychologists in such an object during the 1930s. Stagner's *Psychology of Personality* (1936), Allport's *Personality* (1938) and Murray's *Explorations in Personality* (1938), for example, all reflect the trend. This is to say nothing of the emergent series of personality tests – Rorschach, Thematic Apperception Tests, Word Association Tests and the like – which arose during this period.

From the fourth decade onwards, then, psychiatrists of all hues, be they physicalists or otherwise, recognized personality as a major object of psychiatric intervention. In some cases, of course, the psychiatric vision of personality was heavily influenced by biological understandings, and it would be incorrect to think in terms of biological or neurological objects of psychiatric attention having been replaced by psychological ones during the period under consideration. However, the emphasis on personality did tend to tilt psychiatric attention away from the vision of the purely biological 'instincts' which had so dominated earlier psychiatry, and towards a consideration of the complex modes of action and reaction which individuals adopted towards their own specific circumstances. For example, Stoddart (1908) had originally recognized instinctual behaviour as ubiquitous and talked readily of such things as an 'out-of-doors instinct' and a 'make believe instinct'. This emphasis on instincts, of course, was held in common with Freudian work. Instinct talk, however, laid a heavy burden on the biological determination of personality and even within the work of Freud's followers this biological emphasis increasingly came under attack during the 1930s and 1940s. Both Sullivan (1892–1949), and Horney (1885–1952), for example, to say nothing of Fromm (1900–80), in their different ways came to emphasize the role of social relationships in personality development. In fact, H.S. Sullivan had suggested that interpersonal relationships rather than instincts were the ultimate source of human anxiety. Thus, in a 1930 address to the American Psychiatric Association he stated that psychiatry 'is not an impossible study of an *individual* suffering mental disorder; it is a study of disordered interpersonal relations nucleating more or less clearly in a particular person' (Sullivan's emphasis) (1962: 258). Whilst Horney, in *The Neurotic Personality of Our Time* (1937), laid emphasis on the role of socially produced and variable human culture in the creation of psychic conflicts. Even outside of psychoanalysis – as in Kurt Lewin's theory of personality – there was a growing recognition that interpersonal factors could form the basis for the study of both normal and abnormal psychological characteristics. And this switch of focus on to the social pointed the way towards a consideration of objects which, though alien to the 1900–30 period, were to emerge in hospital psychiatry with increasing frequency during and after the Second World War, and which eventually were to form the foundation of community psychiatry.

So far I have suggested that body, brain and neurological system figured prominently during the first three decades of the present century, and that mind as a psychodynamic entity also emerged as an object of psychiatric attention. Naturally, the role and significance of any or all of these objects to psychiatric practice during the 1900–39 period can be easily attested to by consulting the key texts of the day. Were one to do that, however, one could not fail to notice that all of the objects so far discussed, were further studied against the backdrop of something called 'disease', and in many ways it was this latter which formed the true focal point of psychiatric attention. Bodies and minds were, in that sense, manipulated by psychiatrists only because they contained diseases – diseases which cried out for cure. Thus, dementia praecox (and from 1911 onward, schizophrenia), depression, mania, alcoholism and many other such diseases were believed to be the prime objects of psychiatric practice. Naturally these diseases manifested themselves in individuals, but during the earliest part of the century individuals were regarded as little more than carriers of pathology rather than as active creators of it. So in terms of the principles of Kraepelian psychiatry, for example, the discipline was concerned first and foremost with the description and classification of disease rather than with the relationship of disease to the life circumstances of specific human beings (Kraepelin, 1902, 1904).

This somewhat domineering role of disease did not, however, go entirely unchallenged, and Meyer (1866–1950) in particular (who in retrospect now appears to be one of the most far-sighted of modern psychiatrists), began to question the primacy of disease very early on in the century. The key concept of Meyer's psychiatry was psychobiology, and it was developed to emphasize how debates about body and mind were superfluous and irrelevant to psychiatry – on the grounds that any specific individual was always a unity of both body and mind (soma and psyche). Furthermore, each individual was unique and could not therefore be described accurately in terms of abstract and generalizing disease categories. On the contrary, as far as Meyer was concerned, it was essential for the psychiatrist to examine the patient in the context of his or her past and present empirical circumstances. At interview, for example, Meyer argued that a *life chart* should be constructed, and the essential elements of personal biography noted down. He believed that attention should be paid to the various external circumstances in which the patient existed and how that patient reacted to them. In fact, for Meyer, it was the *reactions* of the patient to these varied circumstances that held the key to any psychological symptoms of disorder. And herein lay the source of Meyer's notion of psychiatric illnesses as reaction types. It was a notion of illness which was to have a profound influence on modern psychiatry and was, for example, given the imprimatur of the American Psychological Association in the first publication of its Diagnostic and Statistical Manual (DSM-I) in 1952. In addition, Meyer's ideas were to be expounded in a whole series of influential psychiatric texts written by both his pupils and his followers. Diethelm (1936), for example, pays full homage to the work of Meyer, whilst Henderson and Gillespie's *Textbook of Psychiatry* (1927), is directly indebted to Meyer's work. Other texts which base their methods of diagnosis and treatment on Meyer's principles were Curran and Guttman's *Psychological Medicine* (1943), and Mayer-Gross *et al.*'s *Clinical Psychiatry* (1954) in which the principles of the psychiatric interview were most fully developed. (For a discussion of Meyer's influence on British psychiatry, see Gelder, 1991.) Indeed, by 1943, Curran and Guttman were noting how 'social medicine' was assuming 'increasing importance' in psychiatric affairs (1943: 3). The authors then proceeded to argue that mental illness did not always have a physical base, and that the psychiatrist should pay heed to personal biography and social conditions of the patient in both diagnosing and in treating illness. But perhaps this interest in the social expressed itself most forcefully in the work of the social psychiatrists of the Tavistock Clinic and especially those whose efforts centred on the development of therapeutic communities. Thus, Maxwell Jones, for example, underlined his concern with social factors by arguing that, 'As the psychiatrist widens his focus to include the matrix of relationships in which the patient is involved, he will begin to think much more in terms of "social assessment" and "social prescription"' (1968: 14), rather than just biological assessments and chemical prescriptions. In a similar fashion, during the late 1950s and early 1960s, R.D. Laing emphasized how his patients lived within networks of social interaction which could either foster their fulfilment as individuals, or lead to their destruction (Laing, 1961). Whilst in *The Divided Self* (Laing, 1959), he sought to produce an 'existentialist' account of 'madness', with the emphasis on self as a product of interaction with others and a vision of schizophrenic behaviour as expressive of what he called the concrete conditions of an individual's existence.

These latter developments are important for us on at least two grounds. First, because they represent an ontological understanding of disease which was quite different from that which dominated the psychiatry of Kraepelin, and the likes of Stewart, Stoddart and Cole. And secondly, because they represent the beginnings of a recognition of the role of the social interaction in the aetiology of mental illness. The ontological change was significant because it questioned the extent to which one could divide a population into the sane and the insane. The aetiological redirection was important because it threw into doubt the extent to which *hospital* medicine could adequately deal with psychiatric disorder. Taken together, these two developments represent fundamental changes in psychiatric theory which when fully expressed, would eventually undermine the foundations of traditional hospital centred psychiatric practice. We shall return to trace the impact of some of these theoretical considerations in Chapter 5; for now, however, we need only mark down the fact that post 1940s psychiatry had added a patient's social relationships and patterns of social interaction to the list of objects within its legitimate domain of study. So much so was this the case that by 1965 Merskey and Tonge in their *Psychiatric Illness* were able to ask 'Who is the real patient?', and to answer that, 'The family is the basic group in our society, and therefore when one of its members seeks advice about an emotional disturbance it can be taken as an axiom that the whole group is more or less disturbed' (1965: 54). The age of the isolated, asocial patient had come to an end.

It only remains at this stage to list the entry of one further significant object of professional interest into psychiatric practice. That object is 'behaviour'. As a category for study behaviour had existed in psychology for some decades. Even within the realms of psychiatry, a paradigm case of a learned 'neurotic reaction' had been in existence since 1919. The latter was an account of little Albert's phobia of white rats – a phobia which Watson and Reynor (1919) had induced in the infant by the use of classic Pavlovian conditioning techniques. Yet, despite that, behaviour as an object for therapy held only a marginal role in psychiatric practice until some decades later. In fact, the first mention of behaviour therapy in a psychiatric context, was probably that made by Eysenck (1959). In this latter paper, Eysenck chose to discuss neurotic disorders as nothing more than conditioned emotional responses – and further argued that what was conditioned could therefore be, so to speak, unconditioned. During the 1950s, therefore, numerous forms of aversion therapy were developed for dealing with 'abnormal behaviours'. And on a wider scale, techniques of behaviour modification were also used to induce behaviour changes in patients. The token economy system, whereby approved or positive patient behaviour was rewarded with tokens which could then be exchanged for goods or favours, was one such expression of this. (Token economy techniques were often discussed and sometimes used in the study hospital.) But more important, perhaps, than the use of any specific techniques was the fact that behaviourist theory and language emerged as a dominant postwar influence on both the education of nurses and of psychologists. One consequence of this was that many of the techniques which were and are used to assess and to describe psychiatric patients were designed in overtly behaviourist forms. So much so in fact, that by 1959 Ayllon and Michael (1959) were referring to the psychiatric nurse as a 'behavioral engineer'. And the language of behaviourism also came to shape broader psychiatric thinking. Thus, Merskey and Tonge in their *Psychiatric Illness* (1965) (despite their leanings towards social psychiatry), came to define psychiatry precisely as the study and treatment of 'abnormal behaviour' (1965: 3). An understandable reaction, perhaps, in a culture where (as Ryle (1949) put it in *The*

Concept of Mind), there was no need to assume a 'second theatre' of activity (i.e. mind). We could infer all that we wished to know about mental processes from personal bodily behaviour alone.

In a WHO paper on the teaching of psychiatry and mental health published in 1961 it was argued that the individual patient lived in a social environment. It was therefore important for the physician to be able to 'place' the patient in his or her social context before any physical examination took place. This theoretical exercise, however, could only be carried out on the basis of information acquired and disseminated by non-medical specialists, and in that sense psychiatric practice required a multidisciplinary response to the problems with which it was confronted. Indeed, this call for a multidisciplinary approach marked a recognition of the wide array of objects which had fallen under the domain of theoretical and clinical psychiatry during the postwar years, and a realization that much more than bodily illness was involved in psychiatric disturbance. These days, of course, the call for multidisciplinary involvement is common enough, and many psychiatric texts adopt an eclectic approach to the analysis of psychiatric health problems (see, for example, Wolff *et al.,* 1990). Yet despite its broadened vista, we should nevertheless remain alert to the fact that of all the objects to which psychiatric practice is addressed, it is still the body which holds centre stage. Minds and social relations may not be dismissed, but in the everyday concerns of psychiatrists it is ultimately bodies that are stabilized rather than social relationships. This is not just because bodies are usually easier to control than immaterial entities like minds and social networks, but also because psychiatry still holds to a belief that the real problems of psychiatry are material ones – upon which the other, superstructural problems, are constructed. This pre-eminence of the body was clearly present in the study hospital, and we shall eventually see how, in various ways, the physical body provided a well defined space within which clinical psychiatry could operate. Equally, we shall be able to see how the non-physical properties of individual patients – such as family, social and economic relationships – were the ones which were most readily allocated to supervision and analysis by non-medical specialists. In that sense, the distinction between the physical and the social properties of the individual patient provided the fundamental framework in terms of which the professional division of labour was organized.

Some Therapeutic Strategies

Objects of psychiatric practice are represented in numerous fields – in texts, therapies, everyday conversation, buildings, artefacts, as well as in the division of professional labour which surrounds the psychiatric patient (or, more recently, the psychiatric client). In this chapter we have so far restricted ourselves to textbook discussions of disorder, and we have seen how the diverse objects of theory intermingle and overlay one another – each one highlighted only within the terms of a specific theoretical matrix. Social relations highlighted in social psychiatry, dynamic psychological properties highlighted in psychoanalysis, objective properties of behaviour in behaviourism, the role of the central nervous system in neuro-psychiatry and so on. In this section we are going to take another fix on this array of objects – this time from the perspective of therapy rather than of theory. We will note how objects of therapy – as with the objects of theory – have taken numerous forms during the twentieth century. But more importantly we will see how those objects are in large part constituted through the application of therapeutic techniques themselves.

Therapies for Mind
We shall take as our starting point Freud and Breuer's analysis of hysteria in which the object of attention was psyche, and the essence of their therapy circulated around 'catharsis' and 'abreaction' – terms first introduced by Breuer (SE.2: 8) – rather than medication or surgery. Indeed, in the psychoanalytic context, and as we have already seen, the patient came to adopt a central role (probably *the* central role) in the therapeutic process. Thus, as far as Breuer was concerned, 'To cure [the] symptoms the psychical process must be brought back to its *status nascendi* and then given verbal utterance' (SE.2: 6). In other words, language serves as a substitute for action and only when the patient is incited to a confession can a cure take place. Thus, with Anna O., 'each symptom disappeared after she had described its first occurrence' (SE.2: 40).

> For we found to our great surprise at first, that each individual hysterical symptom immediately and permanently disappeared when we had succeeded in bringing clearly to light the memory of the event by which it was first provoked and in arousing its accompanying affect, and when the patient had described that event in the greatest possible detail and had put the affect into words. (SE.2: 255)

In this light, we can begin to see that the nature of the sick role and the organization of therapeutics were intimately related to the semantics of mind which the two psychologists introduced. It was a semantics which ushered into the world a knowledge of new levels of the (un)conscious, and which thereby generated new forms of investigation and therapy. Indeed, the therapy was quite properly referred to as 'psychotherapeutics' – a term first introduced by Bernheim (1891). Hence, we know intimate details of Katharina's sexual experiences, and of Fraulein Elisabeth's pains and desires because they are central to the theorization of the pathology to which they belong. So too with Frau Emmy's loss of appetite, her nervous tics and stammers, not to mention Anna O.'s linguistic convolutions and hallucinations. Each symptom was, of course, to be dealt with singly and in terms of its own unique history. The theory of the neuroses demanded intimate detail and intimate detail could only be gained through the structuring of intimate situations – the psychotherapeutic 'confession'. Indeed, in the contemporary reviews of the *Studies* it was the very nature of this psychoanalytic penetration into private life that most struck many of the reviewers, and it was the therapeutics rather than the psychology which appeared to be most in question to Freud's contemporaries (on the reception of Freud's early work, see Bry and Rifkin, 1962; Decker, 1971; Ellenberger, 1970). Thus, it was the wandering associations of his patients, the incidental and apparently meaningless details of everyday life, even their dreams, which mapped out for Freud the central terrain of his analysis. And deeper still were buried the secrets of their sexuality, a sexuality which dominated the aetiology of the neuroses (Andersson, 1962; Stewart, 1969; Sulloway, 1979). No wonder Ernest Jones came away from his reading of 'Dora' with 'a deep impression of there being a man in Vienna who actually listened with attention to every word his patients said to him'. Something which Jones 'had never heard of anyone else doing' (Jones, 1959: 159). It is a stark contrast to the dearth of knowledge which we have about the inmates of Europe's state asylums – inmates whose dreams were never recorded, whose sexuality was never spoken of and whose therapeutics extended only so far as the administration of potassii bromide, chloral hydrate, or a strait-jacket. But that starkness, was of course a product of a radically different vision of the relationship(s) which were assumed to hold between mind and body and upon which the imposing structure of the lunatic asylum was built.

Therapies for Bodies and Brains
It is perhaps naive to expect the world of text and the world of practice to be finely synchronized in any field of action. And it is certainly the case in psychiatry that what was and is done to patients

in empirical circumstances very often diverges from the grand theoretical principles expounded in psychiatric texts. In that respect, the study of empirical detail serves as an essential and necessary check on images and expectations derived from theoretical discussions. More positively, however, the study of empirical detail can also provide a new and more direct set of images concerning the practical nature of the psychiatric enterprise. In this context it is interesting, for example, to examine the old case books of the study hospital – for they reveal far more clearly than any text, what early twentieth century psychiatrists actually did for their patients.

Given the 'nervous' and hereditary dispositions of asylum inmates, it is perhaps not surprising to discover that the therapeutic effort of the asylum staff was directed mainly towards the insane body. And on the basis of case records of the study hospital there can be little doubt that asylum therapy was first and foremost about the control of the body – the category of 'mind' appears only dimly in the case-book accounts. Indeed, the details of medication which appear in the records seem, for the most part, to be directed towards the manufacture of docile bodies. So patients were regularly dosed, for example, with potassii bromide and foul tasting paraldehyde. Thus in 1904, inmate 6864 was dosed with what seems the excessive amount of 320 grains of bromide. Inmate 6227 was unfortunate in that his acute melancholia and suicidal impulses were treated with both bromide and chloral hydrate (ether also figures in his therapy). For an episode of acute mania 6658 was dosed with potassii bromide (30 grains) and spirits of ammonia. The suicidal 5970 (who had slit his throat to such an extent that when he drank water it gushed out through the oesophagus) was dosed with morphine. Inmate 7375 was dosed with sulphonal (25 grains) and paraldehyde (3 drachms). The luckier 7648 seemed to be unaffected by any of the substantial doses of paraldehyde or bromide which were administered to him and was therefore treated with cannabis.

In addition to sedatives and hypnotics for the quelling of loud behaviour, great attention was also paid to bowel movements and endless doses of calomel, potassii sodium and dilute hydrochloric acid were dispensed to the intestines. Enemas were also frequently used. The comatose and dying 6371, for example, was nevertheless given an enema of oil of ricin and turpentine, whilst 6387 was fed beef tea and whiskey through a nasal tube in the mornings and given an enema each evening. (For a wider discussion of asylum posology see, Cullum, 1905.) When chemical control failed, mechanical restraint was used in its stead. Inmate 6658 was placed 'in seclusion' (that is, in the cells) for a number of hours. Though the use of seclusion is little recorded. More frequent is reference to the 'refractory division'. Thus, the hyperactive 5914 was dosed with potassii bromide and spirits of ammonia for three months to no effect. Subsequently, her medication was changed to bromide and tincture of cannabis. Two weeks later the medication was again changed – to chloral hydrate and bromide. When that failed she was taken off all medication and subjected to the mechanical restraint of the refractory division alone.

It is clear, then, that the therapeutics of the asylum were primarily directed towards restraint and confinement. There is no hint here that anyone confronted the delusions and imaginings of the insane on anything other than a physical basis. In fact, it was the body which was observed and treated and dosed with bromides. The mind was left to its own devices. In that sense the asylum was an instrument of chemical and mechanical restraint and the social relations which were associated with these means of restraint were, in the nature of things, repressive. Unlike the intimacy of the Freudian confession, the therapies of the asylum were public in all sense of that word and were solely directed towards the physical frame.

This emphasis on body – and especially the nervous system – was, as we have seen, characteristic of early twentieth century psychiatry. And although, as the century progressed, numerous other objects of psychiatric work came into play, the body as a theatre of practice never truly lost its primary role. Mind and social relations may well have figured prominently in psychoanalytic or milieu therapy, but even there physical and somatic therapies were frequently utilized – at least for the short term control of the grosser symptoms of psychiatric disorder. And we must add to this observation numerous other relevant considerations: firstly, the fact that in large public institutions the use of individual modes of psychoanalytic therapy was hardly feasible, and consequently tended to be restricted to patients in the private sector – as we saw in Chapter 2; secondly, that it was and is, usually, far easier to manipulate bodies than it is to manipulate social relationships, and far easier to exercise influence on physical symptoms than social deprivation; whilst thirdly, people with psychiatric disorders more often than not report their problems in bodily rather than in mental terms, and for numerous other material, ideological and contingent reasons soma usually takes precedence over psyche. During the twentieth century, this primacy of soma was further underlined and emphasized by a series of significant therapeutic developments which appeared in relatively quick succession during the 1930s. (And the treatments which emerged were to dominate psychiatry through to the 1960s and beyond.) In fact, most of the older patients in the study group had been subjected to at least one of these therapies, and for that reason alone it is essential that we understand something about their nature, origin and rationale.

In 1944 Sargent and Slater published their *An Introduction to Physical Methods of Treatment in Psychiatry*. The book celebrated the 'big advances' which had been made in psychiatric therapy during the 1930s. Sakel (in Vienna in 1933), for example, had induced his patients into an insulin coma with favourable results. Also in 1933, Meduna induced epileptic convulsions into his patients in the mistaken belief that schizophrenia was contraindicated by epilepsy. In 1936 Moniz instituted his surgical treatment for the psychoses by using the technique of lobotomy. And in 1937 Cerletti and Bini had, by means of a simple device, chosen to subject their patients to a series of electric shocks. These were not, of course, the only somatic treatments to be used on psychiatric patients during the twentieth century, nor were they the first. Kalinowsky and Hoch (1946), for example, in their review of shock and other somatic treatments in psychiatry mention Lundvall's use of sodium nucleinate to induce a 'blood fever' in his patients (*c*. 1907), Wagner-Jauregg's malarial therapy (*c*. 1917), Klasi's use of barbiturates to induce prolonged narcosis in his patients (*c*. 1922) (sometimes lasting up to three or four weeks), and Talbott and Tillotson's refrigeration therapy (*c*. 1941).

What is interesting about these various treatments is that despite the fact that they operated directly on the body, their focus was non-specific. That is to say, they were simply directed at the body in general rather than to any specific organ system or specific physical lesion. Even the technique of lobotomy – which was directed at the frontal lobes – was simply a crude and general strategy aimed at the 'emotional nucleus' of psychosis. This lack of direction in therapy was matched by an ambiguity concerning their theoretical bases. So there was in short, no apparent reason or collection of reasons as to why such things as shock therapy, convulsive therapy or surgery should actually make any difference to the mental functioning of what were referred to as psychotic patients. It is, therefore, not surprising perhaps that in one of the key psychiatric texts of the 1940s – Kalinowsky and Hoch's *Shock Treatments and Other Somatic Treatments in Psychiatry* (1946) – no attempt was made to offer any theoretical justification for the therapies which it discussed. Instead, the various editions merely offered the reader the technical details as to how to execute shock, convulsive and other therapies, and then added some selective data on favourable outcomes.

This dearth of theoretical insight is evident, for example, in discussions concerning insulin coma therapy, for in none of the early (or even the later) discussions was any plausible explanation given as to why it should prove effective in the treatment of psychiatric disorder. The insulin induced coma was merely described as being able to neutralize or muffle the 'excitant' which caused psychosis. Or, in the words of its inventor, Sakel: 'restore the balance of certain vegetative centres' (1938: 1). Equally, electric shock therapy (EST), was assumed (not unsurprisingly), to induce fear into the patients and this in itself was believed to be therapeutic. Surgical intervention was similarly devoid of theoretical support. Thus Freeman and Watts's *Psychosurgery* (1942) – a surgical text which is littered with pictures of the smiling patients who had undergone psychosurgery – entirely lacks any coherent statement concerning the rationale for the surgical procedures. Instead they merely assert that under lobotomy, 'The emotional nucleus of the psychosis is removed, the "sting" of the disorder is drawn. Even though the fixed ideas persist and the compulsions continue for a while, the fear that disabled the patient is banished' (1942: xiii). In fact, this reference to fixed ideas lies at the heart of the therapy in the sense that Moniz, its inventor, had argued that in the frontal lobes there were groups of cellular connections which sometimes became 'more or less "fixed" leading to fixed ideas and emotions' (Moniz, 1936: 13). Lobotomy destroyed the fixed connections and thereby loosened the previously fixed ideas of the patient. Furthermore, the observation that lobotomy resulted in apathy and lowered rates of activity was seen as being of specific benefit to what were otherwise excitable patients.

Sargant and Slater (1944), of course, were keen to point out that judgements concerning the efficacy of these physical treatments rested on purely empirical grounds, and that when it came to evaluating the results of psychiatric therapies, theory would just have to bow before empirical fact (as Charcot had argued some 60 years previously). Somewhat interestingly, however, these same authors threw aside empiricism in favour of intuition and privileged professional judgements when rigorous evaluation of the surgical and other techniques began to throw doubt on their therapeutic effects. Thus, when researchers (using randomized clinical trials) began to question the efficacy of insulin shock therapy and even of psychosurgery, Sargant and Slater retained their faith in such treatments because, 'The attentive and discriminating observer has the possibility of insights which can be gained in no other way and are certainly beyond the reach of experimental design' (1963: viii). In other words, these therapies had become nestled within a self-supporting *weltanschaung*, which assumed mental disorders to be dependent on physiological changes. Therefore the only therapies which could possibly be effective were those which addressed themselves to the physiology of the human frame.

By the mid-1950s of course it was chemical rather than physical methods which had come to dominate psychiatric therapy. Chlorpromazine and reserpine were, for example, introduced into psychiatric treatments increasingly after 1953. Yet once again the theoretical basis of their introduction was sorely lacking. Thus Delay *et al.*, (who were responsible for introducing chlorpromazine into clinical psychiatric practice), linked the use of largactil to a notion of artificial hibernation. The drug apparently rested the 'neuro-vegetative' system and preserved patients from stress and shock (Delay *et al.*, 1953). What is more, during the early years at least, chlorpromazine seems to have played a role similar to that played by the bromides during the 1910s and 1920s. Thus in a letter to *The Lancet*, Davies (1954) outlines the use of chlorpromazine for controlling the behaviour of patients in an understaffed hospital for the mentally handicapped – and made no pretence that the tranquillizer was in any way directed to a cure for psychiatric malaise. The early use of lithium salts also lacked theoretical justification. Thus, Rice, who was an early advocate of the use of Lithium for the treatment of manic depression claimed that, 'As so often in medicine the original decision . . . to use Lithium in the treatment of psychiatric conditions of excitement, seems to have followed a chance and almost accidental observation' (1955: 608). And that observation concerned the apparent benefits to 'maniacs' of drinking certain kinds of well water. Perhaps it is not surprising then, that when Sargant and Slater (1963) approved the use of such drugs they did so, once again, solely on the basis of 'empirically established facts' – though as we have already noted, such facts, 'were founded on clinical experience and not on the basis of planned experiment' (1963: 305). Over the decades, of course, increasingly sophisticated technical explanations referring to such entities as neurotransmitters and brain cell receptors have been developed to explain how the drugs actually 'work' – and these in turn have led to the emergence of new images of schizophrenia and depression (see, for example, Healy, 1990). Naturally, these *post hoc* technical assessments, explanations and descriptions of psychiatric disorders and their treatments fall far beyond the scope of this book. And all that we can note here is that despite their radically altered physiological and chemical images, body and brain as fields of action and objects of study are as central to the psychiatry of the late twentieth century as they were to the psychiatry of the first two decades of this century. So although patients in the study hospital had (at various times) been engaged in forms of occupational therapy, behaviour therapy, family therapy and (occasionally) even psychotherapy, the only genre of therapeutic response that was consistently administered was chemical therapy.

Ideas and Organization

The hidden agenda of this chapter has been ultimately concerned with the hospital to community transition. In fact, by concentrating on vade mecum knowledge, it has sought to demonstrate how the big organizational changes which have occurred in the field of psychiatry during the twentieth century have been intimately related to theoretical developments within psychiatry itself. So, for example, it has been shown how, during the earlier part of the century, psychiatry addressed itself to objects of practice which were especially well suited to medical treatment in hospital settings, and how brain, nervous system, degenerate or infected bodies were phenomena which readily lent themselves to management in terms of medical expertise and medical understanding. It has also been demonstrated how mainstream (textbook) theorizations of mind and the mental were essentially founded on neurological images of brain, rather than on any psychodynamic understanding of psyche. Indeed, it seems that 'mind' as an independent entity did not really figure in hospital psychiatry before the 1920s. (And even today, 'mind' is not something which figures in any way prominently in psychiatry texts – see, for example, Gelder *et al.*, 1988.) When, of course, the crass physicalism of the earlier part of the century subsided, other objects of study did enter into the field of focus – personality was perhaps the most prominent of these. And from the 1940s onwards we see a range of other non-physical objects falling within the domain of professional psychiatrists. Of the latter, the study of social and, especially, family relationships had perhaps the most profound effect on ideas about how psychiatric services ought to be organized. In addition, of course, we have noted how aspects of social and physical behaviour also came under psychiatric scrutiny, and how they proved conducive to new forms of intervention. Naturally, many of these later objects of psychiatric theory and practice (abnormal behaviour, stressful social relationships, family dynamics, and so on), were not objects which were especially well suited to hospital care or treatment, and in that sense their emergence served in part to highlight the limitations of asylum care. But having said that, we should not underestimate the extent to which – during all of these transitions and alterations of focus –

the body retained its place as the primary object of psychiatric focus. (Though its primacy is something which is, perhaps, better highlighted through the study of psychiatric therapy rather than of theory.)

Somewhat interestingly, most of the aforementioned trends and developments were accurately reflected in the nosologies of twentieth century medicine. Thus both Bertillon's *Nomenclature des Maladies* (1903), and the International Commission's *Nomenclature of Disease* (Commonwealth of Australia, Bureau of Census and Statistics, 1907) originally placed 'insanity' (together with hysteria and GPI), under 'Diseases of the Nervous System'. And that style of classification persisted in every revision of the nosology up to and including the fifth revision (1938). It is not until 1948 that the International Statistical Classification of Disease includes a separate category of disease referred to as 'Mental, psychoneurotic and personality disorders', and this is also the first time that the psychoses are distinguished from the psychoneuroses. The category of nervous diseases still existed of course, but it now included only identifiable somatic disorders of the cerebral functions and vascular or central nervous system. By 1952 the American Psychiatric Association in the first edition of its *Diagnostic and Statistical Manual* (DSM-I), had in any case abandoned the division between the neuroses and psychoses and built its nosology on Meyer's concept of reaction types. Disorders were still arranged in an informal hierarchy ranging from the organic through to the behavioural, but by that stage it was possible to see psychiatric illness as a reaction to a wide spectrum of conditions – only some of which were organic and many of which were psychodynamic, interpersonal or even 'social'. And although the concept of reaction was later abandoned by the Association (in DSM-II), later editions of the Manual continued to lay emphasis on the manifestations of mental disorder rather than on their causes. Thus, in the third (1987) revision (DSM-III), psychiatric disorder was conceptualized in terms of 'clinically significant behavioral or psychological syndrome[s]' (1987: xxii). The nosology was 'atheoretical with regard to etiology' and avoided any assumption that each mental disorder was a 'discrete entity with sharp boundaries'. In short, the old notion of neurologically determined and sharply defined psychiatric disease entities had vanished.

4
Networks of Professional Practice

Discourse is both the bearer of a message and the instrument of
action.

Emile Benveniste (1971: 67)

The Division of Labour and its Consequences

In Volume One of *Capital* Marx discusses the significance of the
division of labour for capitalist production. In particular, he draws
our attention to what he regards as two fundamental characteristics
of the process. First, he notes that it necessitates and entails a
decomposition of the product (that is, a breakdown of the product
into separate components), and secondly he notes that this in turn
involves a decomposition of the producer. Marx, of course, was
overwhelmingly interested in the nature and consequences of the
division of labour for manufacture, but his analysis carries interesting implications for many other forms of activity. Indeed his twin
themes have been picked up and developed in a variety of contexts
by a number of authors. In this book, however, we need to
concentrate mainly on the first of Marx's two claims and in
particular to examine the ways in which changes in the division of
professional labour have encouraged what we might call a decomposition of the objects of psychiatry, and hence changes in the ways
in which psychiatric disorder has been represented through diverse
forms of professional practice.

In Chapter 1 it was argued that mental illness is essentially
defined through the sum total of practices which surround it. And
given that, it follows that the organization of the division of labour
necessarily reflects a great deal about what such illness is considered
to be at any one time. Thus, as each profession marks out different
and unique areas of activity, it tends to underline novel aspects of
what psychiatric work is all about. Indeed, the ways in which
different professional groups section off, or partition their chosen
aspects of patient life and existence tells us a great deal about how
objects of study and practice are organized and perceived. Thus we
are, for example, most likely to perceive the significance of family
interactions to mental illness in so far as they are highlighted

through the activities of social workers and community nurses. Equally, we are most likely to perceive the significance of physio-chemical objects mainly in so far as they are highlighted through the work of psychiatrists – and the significance of behavioural characteristics mainly in relation to the ways in which they are emphasized, described and classified through the work of hospital nurses, psychologists or occupational therapists. And it is not just that various kinds of professional activity highlight different aspects of the human condition, but that these same activities also serve to constitute the nature of psychiatric disorder in itself. This is so in the sense that specific and identifiable psychiatric conditions only broaden in scope and nature under the gaze of the different professions. Thus, the schizophrenia of Bleuler, for example, is not the same disorder as is discussed and analysed in psychiatry texts of the 1990s, if only because the modern form now incorporates a social and behavioural assessment of that disorder in a way that would have been unimaginable within Bleuler's original conception of it (see, for example, Boyle, 1990). In fact, not only schizophrenia, but most objects of psychiatric study and practice have, during the twentieth century, become dispersed and diffused over a much wider range of professions than Bleuler would have recognized. And as practice has been diffused, so knowledge about psychiatric illness has followed in its wake. For as Berger and Luckman so forcefully argued in their 1967 work, the division of labour always entails a division of knowledge – that is to say, a division of practical and theoretical expertise which fundamentally alters the ways in which objects are classified, analysed, organized and integrated into the social order.

As well as resulting in the decomposition of objects of study and therapy, the division of labour has also brought other consequences. In particular, it has led to the decomposition of both the professional and his or her patient/client into numerous self-contained fragments. For example, and as we shall read later on, patients in the study hospital tended to be fragmented into different behavioural components, and their capacities and problems were frequently split into numerous subdivisions, before being parcelled out to the various professions. In fact, different client needs were usually addressed by the members of specialist professional groupings, so that the numerous components of an individual life were subdivided in terms of a broad array of professional psychiatric practices. Furthermore, as a corollary of the decomposition of the client, work roles were also decomposed in such a way that professionals rarely encountered the *homo totus* directly, and more likely dealt with clearly partitioned segments of their client's existence. Indeed, in many psychiatric settings members of professional groupings can often be found seeking lines of demarcation, and a division of professional expertise which ensures that their differing professional interests do not overlap. In terms of the professionals who dealt with the members of the study group, for example, the lines of demarcation seemed to be especially problematic for social workers and community nurses – mainly because members of both groups sought to base their work in 'family dynamics'. But not only do professionals come face to face with problems of demarcation – they are also confronted with the problems of strategic positioning. That is to say with marking themselves out as members of an autonomous profession *vis-à-vis* the medical profession. This is so because it is psychiatrists who represent the 'dominant profession' (Freidson, 1970), and the other professions are subordinate to it. In fact, for Freidson, medicine (or in our case, psychiatry) is dominant in the sense that much of the technical knowledge on which the work of other professionals is based is either discovered, enlarged upon or, at the very least, approved of by physicians. And the tasks of paramedical and non-medical professionals are normally ordered by physicians, so that the members of these latter groups tend to assist rather than replace the focal tasks of diagnosis and treatment. Naturally enough, one way in which the non-medical professions can carve out for themselves a domain of professional autonomy is by developing their own body of theoretical knowledge and expertise. And it is in the development of this realm of knowledge and expertise that the subordinate professions are most likely to emphasize specialized aspects of mental illness. The capacity to create a new knowledge base, however, has a tendency to go hand in hand with the emergence of new terrains of practice – terrains free from medical governance. This is yet another reason why the transition from hospital dominated, to community psychiatry is so important to questions of social organization. For it was only when the paramedical and associated professions stepped beyond the shadows of hospital psychiatry that they could discover, and then colonize, new spaces in which to operate (here child guidance clinics, there the family and later the community itself). Naturally, the creation of new knowledge and new strategies for coping with psychiatric disorder did not close either the professional debate or the rivalry between professions. Thus, psychiatrists, for example, may still try to assert that it is the 'illness' which constitutes the base problem in psychiatry, and that the social, family and material conditions of a patient are secondary to the central psychiatric problem. Other professionals, however, often prove keen to argue that such a base/superstructure view of psychiatric disorder belittles the significance of non-somatic factors (such as interpersonal relationships) in generating and sustaining psychiatric illness – and thereby diminishes the centrality of paramedical and non-medical professional work in the management of psychiatric maladies.

In the light of these remarks, we shall seek to examine some of the more common representations of psychiatric disorder which have appeared in the texts of various professional groupings – such as nurses, social workers, occupational therapists and psychologists. Our focus will be on how the development of specialist forms of knowledge and practice have given rise to new images of mental illness and how in that process of change, professionals have tended to reorganize and re-present their own particular roles.

Nursing Mental Illness

In 1923 the Medico-Psychological Association published the seventh edition of its handbook entitled *Handbook for Mental Nurses*. The previous six editions of this work had been entitled *Handbook for Attendants of the Insane*, but as the authors of the seventh edition pointed out, there had been (during the first two decades of the present century) a change of perspective on the asylum, and that change had rendered the concept of an overseeing attendant somewhat redundant. Nursing, claimed the authors, was now directed towards remedying mental illness and not merely supervising the insane, and that was also why the term asylum was beginning to give way to the notion of a mental hospital.

We have already noted these movements from asylum to hospital, from insanity to mental illness, and from attendant to nurse, in relation to at least two other contexts – namely, changes in legal practice and psychiatric theory. This third appearance underlines still further how fundamental these changes of concept and vision actually were. Naturally, the existence of a custodial role did not diminish or disappear simply because of a change of title in a handbook, and custodial practices were to persist in mental hospitals for some decades (the studies cited in Chapter 2 provide proof enough of their extent), yet the new terminology is nevertheless important because it marks a threshold over which a paramedical profession was crossing. The 1923 text was not, of course, the first text for 'nurses' as opposed to attendants, but the handbook was among the very first to mention the broad based nature of the changes which had affected care and treatment of the insane during the earlier part of the century. In that respect it contrasts markedly with, say, Mills's *Nursing and Care of the*

Nervous and the Insane, published in 1915 (note the title), a text very firmly lodged in the culture of insanity.

The new profession of mental nursing did not, however, bring in its train any new or unique objects of therapy. The *Handbook* for example, offered nurses little more than a diluted form of the knowledge which was present in the more specialized texts on neurology and psychiatry. Thus, nurses were clearly informed how, 'it is now generally recognized that the brain is the organ of the mind' (Medico-Psychological Association, 1923: 5), and following this they were introduced to anatomy and physiology – especially in relation to the nervous system – and then to first aid and hygiene. In other words, nursing knowledge was little more than a pale reflection of medical knowledge and there was no real attempt to develop any specialized forms of nursing theory or forms of practice. Thus, there was no mention of family relations for example, or group relations in general, and the prime object of nursing attention remained the physical body – that is, the body as defined in terms of medical anatomy and physiology. The primacy of neurology to nursing is, for example, evident in the frontispiece of Sands's *Nervous and Mental Diseases for Nurses* (1928) which contained a lateral image of a human brain, whilst the first chapter concerned itself with a description of nerve cells and other neuro-anatomical features. Chase's *Mental Medicine and Nursing* (1914) likewise begins with a discussion of the central nervous system and even has a separate chapter on neurons. Unlike psychiatry texts, however, both the *Handbook* and the other texts took time to elaborate on the relations which they thought should be fostered between nurse and patient. So nurses were told, for example, that they should ensure the occupation, amusement and comfort of patients, and generally play a nurturing role in the life of their charges. (It is this image of the nurse as a nurturer of human qualities which has, of course, been notably emphasized in modern feminist analyses and critiques of the profession's history.) This emphasis on the creation and development of affective relationships with the patient, then, served to mark out what was considered to be one of the most fundamental and distinguishing features of nursing work, though it was not a theme developed in a sophisticated theoretical sense. Indeed, it was not until the 1930s that nursing texts began, as a matter of routine, to include discussions of psychodynamics in their accounts of mental illness – though when they did appear, these discussions usually contained little more than a faint echo of the more specialized terms and theories which were available in the texts of professional psychiatrists. Thus, Sadler's *Psychiatric Nursing* (1937), for example, included discussions on the subconscious, the neuroses and psychoses, and psychotherapeutics (in addition to the inevitable treatise on the anatomy of the nervous system), but no attempt was made to use the psychotherapeutic framework to develop a measure of professional autonomy – as for example happened in child centred social work. Instead, the patient was still viewed as an isolated, and to a large extent, asocial individual whose fate was under the direct and absolute control of the professional psychiatrist. And without the development of its own specialized sphere of knowledge and practice, psychiatric nursing in the interwar years remained prey to easy domination by a medical profession which ordered and regulated its activities. In fact, more often than not, nursing followed quietly and subserviently in the wake of divisions and distinctions which were generated within psychiatry. Thus, as psychiatry distinguished more and more clearly between mental deficiency and mental illness, the nursing profession subdivided itself so as to accommodate the division. A separate training certificate for mental deficiency nurses was introduced in England in 1919. And gradually, nursing texts were developed for the respective parts of the profession – a separate edition of the *Handbook*, for example, was published for nurses of the mentally deficient in 1931 (see Day and Jancar, 1991), and texts dedicated to the instruction of the latter became common after this date.

In terms of objects of therapy, then, the primacy of the mental patient's body in nursing discourse is clearly evident in most texts and this fact is underlined, first and foremost, in terms of the amount of space given to discussions of nervous anatomy and physiology. But as with objects of therapy in general, this pre-eminence of soma was represented many times over and in many different ways. For example, it was further represented by means of various pictorial representations of nurses standing next to baths, items of electrical equipment, strait-jackets, chairs and numerous other mechanical devices – all of which were to be used to control and modify the patient's body. Sands (1928), for example, discusses such things as electrotherapy, hydrotherapy and mechanotherapy, and includes along with each of these a description of their application and the occasional photograph of nurse and equipment *in situ*. Similar photographs are visible in Buckley's *Nursing Mental and Nervous Diseases* (1927) and other texts. In fact, this juxtaposition of the nurse and various bits and pieces of technical apparatus also served to reflect back on the role of the mental nurse itself. For the pictures offered a representation of the nurse primarily and foremost as a therapeutic technician – and as someone who merely administered the prescription which was ordered by the psychiatrist. Unlike the work of the medics, the work of the nurse was in that sense seen essentially in terms of the physical and the practical, and this tended to further emphasize the division of labour which existed between the (intellectual) work of psychiatrists and the (manual) work of nurses – a state of affairs which Gamarnikow (1978) would argue to be common to both general and psychiatric nursing. Nowhere in the nursing texts of the first half of the century, then, do we find an attempt to develop a specialist form of knowledge and practice. And nowhere in these texts do the authors question whether nurses should ever instigate therapy, or develop a therapeutic role in any other than the purely technical and subordinate sense. It is a strange contrast with the 1950s where questions about what constituted therapy, and who was to administer therapy, were pushed very much to the fore in the wake of the therapeutic community movement (see, for example, Greenblatt *et al.*, 1957).

The 1950s contains a watershed as far as nursing is concerned. It is a watershed which was linked in the long term to that all embracing hospital–community transition which affected so many features of psychiatric practice. In fact, the latter transition enabled (and possibly encouraged) nurses to develop and colonize areas of .theory and practice which were far less tightly controlled by medics than were those found in psychiatric hospitals. In the short term, however, the revolution in nursing stemmed not so much from the overall demise of the psychiatric hospital, as from the creation of the therapeutic community in the hospital grounds. The latter with its emphasis on the democratization of therapy – in which patients and nurses as well as psychiatrists were allocated a therapeutic role – formed the occasion for a radical reassessment of the tasks of the psychiatric nurse. For in the therapeutic community proper, such tasks were no longer to be confined to the technical duties specified by psychiatrists, but rather to encompass diagnosis (even if only at a level of common sense rather than professional knowledge) and active participation in the design and execution of the treatment process. Naturally, many of these changes took a long time to filter through nursing theory and practice. Thus, at the opening of the 1950s many of the (textbook) visions of mental nursing which had existed during the 1930s and 1940s were still present. A 1955 report on *The Work of the Mental Nurse* (Mackenzie, 1955), for example, claimed that overseeing patients, the execution of technical nursing tasks and the general comfort of the patient were the prime goals of psychiatric nursing. Not surprisingly, the members of the committee who drew up the document also emphasized the nature of patient–nurse 'rapport' and the intangible set of affectual relationships which supposedly lay at the core of nursing, but they still saw all these tasks as being executed solely in the intramural world of the mental hospital, and they still failed to argue for the development of a body of specialized knowledge which would serve to mark out nursing as a profession autonomous from medicine. The first of these failings was, however, to be put to the test quite rapidly. For, by 1959, the *Report of the Ministry of Health* (1959, Part II), whilst recognizing that the mental hospital would 'remain a place for diagnosis, treatment and nursing skill', was discussing the need for the creation of a comprehensive mental health service in which hospital nursing would play only a limited role. And by 1961 the Chief Male Nurse at Warlingham Park Hospital (Croydon), was reporting the establishment of a community oriented out-patient programme (Moore, 1961) – a programme which was developed into the first fully fledged community psychiatric nursing service in the UK a few years later (May and Gregory, 1963). Meanwhile on a much broader front, a WHO document on 'the nurse in mental health practice' (John *et al.*, 1963) was arguing for the establishment of a multidisciplinary, integrated and community centred team approach to the nature of mental health and illness – albeit an approach which was quite clearly under the direction of psychiatrists.

The ninth edition of the *Handbook* had, by 1963, caught up with many of these developments. It discussed the 'increasing emphasis on the therapeutic value of the hospital environment', as well as social therapy and the care of the patient in the community (though community care was discussed in less than two pages). The authors pointed out that psychiatric patients were not afflicted with diseases but suffered disorders of the 'whole person', and that the first aim of the psychiatric nurse was to form an affectual bond with that person. Indeed, the fact that the early chapters of the *Handbook* were now based in psychology rather than neuro-anatomy reflected many of the changes which we have reviewed in previous chapters. Despite this, however, the role of the nurse in the psychiatric system was one which was still discussed almost entirely in terms of an institutional environment. And this vision of nursing as essentially a hospital and ward based activity was further reflected during the 1960s in two quite separate official UK reports on nursing. Thus, the report on *The Post-Certificate Training and Education of Nurses* (Ministry of Health 1966) – on general nursing – and, more significantly, the Ministry of Health Report *Psychiatric Nursing: Today and Tomorrow* (1968), both located the nature of modern nursing in hospital contexts. In fact, the latter Report was in many ways exceptionally narrow in focus, concentrating as it did on the ward rather than the hospital as the hub of nursing practice. Moreover, and despite the futuristic flavour of the Report's title, absolutely nothing was said about community care or community based nursing – indeed, the latter did not even 'fall within [the committee's] terms of reference' (1968: 46). Instead, the authors predicted a rise in psychiatric hospital populations until 2001 accompanied by a possible increase in the number of psychiatric units in general hospitals. And given these 'expert' deliberations, it is not surprising, perhaps, that psychiatric nursing texts (such as that of Maddison *et al.*, 1963), continued to anchor all discussion concerning the role of the mental nurse firmly in hospital practice. Thus, only in the third (1970) edition of their text did the latter include a chapter on community psychiatry and discuss the possibilities of community nursing. And this same switch of focus is exceptionally well represented in the Preface to the ninth edition of Mereness and Taylor's *Essentials of Psychiatric Nursing* (1974), wherein they stated that, 'One of the primary reasons for [the new edition], was the recognition that emotionally ill people are often treated outside hospital. A decade ago this was not true.' And in line with this observation one sees, from the 1970s onwards, a proliferation of texts on community mental health nursing, in which the emphasis tends to be on health rather than illness, on the group rather than the individual and on community rather than hospital.

It was, perhaps, the creation of a therapeutic space outside of hospitals which essentially provided the material base in terms of which new theoretical developments in the field of nursing could grow and new objects of practice emerge. The development of such a space was partly reflected in, and partly encouraged and accelerated by, the emergence of such things as therapeutic communities, halfway houses and specialized psychiatric units (for children, alcoholics and old people). Ultimately the new therapeutic territory was truly opened up by professional psychiatrists themselves – especially in their recognition that family and other social relationships could be seen as central components of psychiatric disorder. Naturally, the foundations of the new terrain needed to be underpinned by legislative and political policy initiatives, and in both the UK and the US, there was extensive political support for the move from hospital to community centred psychiatry from the 1950s onwards (Ramon, 1985). Thus we see in the Joint Commission on Mental Illness and Health report, *Action for Mental Health* (1961), a demand for the provision of community mental health centres (CMHC) throughout the US (one CMHC for every 50,000 of population). And it was in spaces such as these that the nursing profession proved ready to develop its theoretical and practical autonomy. Family therapy, which in the 1950s had been virtually restricted to work with 'schizophrenic families', for example, was expanded so as to cope with a wide range of psychiatric disorders, and during the 1970s specialist nurse training programmes were designed to encourage the use of the technique. In fact nursing texts now spoke of the unique 'fit' of the nurse for family therapy (Fagin, 1970). Similarly, various forms of psychotherapy, group therapy and milieu therapy which had, during the late 1950s been restricted to use in therapeutic communities, were also developed for extramural use. And the same can be said of the various types of behavioural therapy, aversion and operant conditioning techniques – all of which now appear in modern nursing texts as a matter of routine (see, for example, Janosik and Davies, 1989). In the UK these changes were further reflected in the development and approval of new nursing syllabuses by the professional bodies involved: a section on community care included in the Registered Mental Nurse syllabus in 1974, a syllabus for community psychiatric nurses proposed in the same year and a course in behavioural psychotherapy approved in 1977. And by 1986, the Cumberlege Report (DHSS, 1986), was calling for 'a switch of resources within the health service' so that neighbourhood rather than hospital would form the focal point for schemes of nursing practice and nurse training.

These developments did not merely impinge on the changed and changing role of the psychiatric nurse, but further reflected on the diverse objects of therapy which now fell under the scrutiny of a key paramedical profession. Observable behaviour, behavioural deficits, learning deficits, social skills, social relationships and various aspects of the human psyche were now queued up with the older notions of (organic) disease entities as subjects for study and objects of therapy. In tandem with this, nurses also attempted to generate a body of specialized theoretical knowledge to underpin the new developments. Models of nursing were constructed and presented in diverse and inventive ways, though they always held at least one thing in common – namely an opposition to the 'medical model' of theory and practice. For the patient, or more properly, the client, was now seen as something far more than a mere assemblage of anatomical and physiochemical functions; something far more than a mere 'case' of disorder (Burr and Budge, 1976). Indeed, the patient/client now had a social persona and a social location which had to be accounted for and dealt with appropriately. As Reynolds and Cormack (1990) stated in their review of the theory and practice of modern psychiatric nursing, 'There is an increasing effort among nurses to dissociate themselves from the medical paradigm, and to define the boundaries and goals of their discipline as being essentially different from those of medicine. This has been particularly true of psychiatric nursing with its distinct psychosocial emphasis' (1990: 9).

The Role of the Social Worker

In 1962 Jones and Sidebottom published a review of a different kind. It was a review of three English mental hospitals at work. In the first of these hospitals (referred to as Crown Lodge), the authors noted that there was no social worker available. (In fact, according to Titmuss (1963) there were only 24 full time Psychiatric Social Workers in England in 1959.) On investigating the shortfall further, the authors were told that 'very few social work problems' existed in Crown Lodge and that the few which did were dealt with by the medical staff (Jones and Sidebottom, 1962: 48). This notion of a social work problem as something sporadic and peripheral to the everyday routine of hospital life is one of the key notions which characterized the hospital age. It was a notion based in large part on the rough and ready principle that what went on within the bounds of the hospital was a medical problem and something that should be properly under the control of the medical profession, and that what went on outside of the hospital was peripheral to the various forms of psychiatric illness contained within, and could therefore be placed in the hands of non-medics. So, as happened with the nursing profession, psychiatric social work (PSW) only developed as an autonomous form of professional practice in the therapeutic spaces which existed beyond the boundaries of the asylum walls. In that respect, it was if anything the child guidance clinic which provided the 'conditions for a new beginning in social work' (Timms, 1964: 4), and it was there that social workers proved able to foster the various forms of specialized theory and practice which helped to guarantee their professional development.

Child guidance clinics (which, in the long run, were also responsible for bringing a whole new range of disorders into the orbit of psychiatry) were developed in the UK mostly during the 1920s and 1930s (the first London clinic was opened in 1926). The Child Guidance Council recognized 18 such clinics in 1935, 46 in 1937, and during the 1940s and 1950s their numbers expanded rapidly (Timms, 1964). Somewhat paradoxically it was psychiatrists and psychologists who were to benefit most from the employment opportunities which were created by these openings, but social workers also gained in so far as they were eventually to find something of a therapeutic role at these sites. Theirs was therefore a position which differed markedly from the one which they were allotted within the hospital system. For, during the early years of the century, hospital social work was primarily seen in terms of the preparations of pathways out of hospital and as securing the material conditions in the home before the patient returned to the family. In other words psychiatric social work was dominated by the concept of aftercare. Thus, Meyer (who advocated the use of social workers from the very earliest years of the century), can be heard arguing in 1911 that social work was necessary only for securing a healthy domestic environment for his patients (Winters, IV, 1952). Though, as he develops his notions of reaction types – including the notion that psychiatric disorders are, in essence, reactions to environmental circumstances and not merely organic disorders – he begins to argue that social workers are also essential for dealing with 'life problems' in general. A relatively radical image of the social worker's role was also evident in one of the earliest of the American treatises on psychiatric social work, *The Kingdom of Evils* (Southard and Jarrett, 1922). The primary aim of this text had been to illustrate how doctor and social worker could, 'co-operate in the care of the mentally deranged', but in doing that, it also provided a new image of the psychiatric patient. For the latter was now seen as someone involved in a network of social relations and also as someone with a 'social history'. Since many of the patient's difficulties were hypothesized as originating in this history, it was consequently regarded as essential that each patient underwent a 'social examination' as well as a medical examination on entry into hospital. The examination was, however, just the last part of an innovative package which had been introduced into US hospitals from the earliest years of the century. Thus, the Neurological Clinic of the Massachusetts General Hospital had engaged its first social worker in 1905, whilst the 'Psychopathic' wards of the Bellevue Hospital (New York), had done likewise in 1906. In contrast, these same styles of practice were relatively slow in reaching the UK – the first psychiatric social worker in London being employed under that title only in 1936. (The (British) Association of Psychiatric Social Workers was inaugurated only in 1930.) And even then, social work in the UK was viewed, in general, almost entirely in terms of philanthropic and aftercare work rather than in terms of therapeutic interventions. Even as late as 1926, for example, The Royal Commission on Lunacy and Mental Disorder spoke only of the need for aftercare of the recovered mental patient and made no mention of any further tasks which could be carried out by a social worker. In fact, the role of the latter was ignored to the extent that the title was not even mentioned in the final report.

The principles of casework which had been well illustrated in *The Kingdom of Evils*, and which were to serve as a cornerstone of much twentieth century psychiatric social work practice, were further extended by the likes of Meyer, Southard and Jarrett into community psychiatric work in general. Meyer was, of course, a founder of the American mental hygiene movement which sought a preventive as well as curative role for psychiatry. And this interest in preventive work encouraged many East Coast hospitals to open out-patients' departments and social services departments in the hospital complex. It was in such departments that the psychiatric social worker's role grew. Southard, for example, who was based at the Boston Psychopathic Hospital, must have been among the very first psychiatrists to have spoken of 'social psychiatry' (1917: 567; Southard and Jarrett, 1922: 523) – a psychiatry which focused on the patient's social as well as his or her medical problems – and also among the first to mention explicitly the family conference, in which the social worker was to play a major part. This twin track approach directed at both case work and prevention was seen as characteristic of US psychiatric social work in the interwar period. It is, for example, clearly represented in Odencrantz (1929), as well as in French's *Psychiatric Social Work* (1940). Though it is equally clear from the latter that by the 1940s hospital social workers were also seeking a well defined therapeutic role in the management of psychiatric disorders. Thus, French argued that the social worker should be seen as an essential part of the hospital based clinical team and not 'just an errand girl', and this notion of the social worker as a key member of the clinical team was in part premised on a changing vision of what psychiatric difficulties were all about. Indeed, there were at least three separate developments which occurred during the 1930–50 period and which encouraged social workers to try and establish themselves as an integral part of the psychiatric system. The first of these saw social factors as being intimately involved in the causation of mental disorder. This was a notion introduced to psychiatry through the work of Meyer, Southard and Sullivan, among others, and which was to be empirically supported by numerous sociological studies of mental illness. The second produced a vision of psychiatric disorder as being widespread in the community, and not simply restricted to a limited number of organically degenerate individuals – and this is something which we will discuss in the next chapter. Whilst the third encouraged an expansion in the kinds and number of symptoms regarded as 'psychiatric'. This latter state of affairs was, as we have seen, something which was well reflected in the sixth (WHO, 1948) revision of the *International Statistical Classification of Diseases* wherein were included for the first time a range of psychoneurotic and personality disorders, anxiety reactions, neurotic-depressive reactions, disorders of character and behaviour, together with such things as occupational neuroses and homosexuality. And it was this expansion of psychiatric vision into the realm of what others considered to be nothing more than forms of social deviance which inspired later writers such as Szasz (1960) to talk of the 'myth' of mental illness, and others (Castel *et al.*, 1982) to talk of the psychiatrization of society.

This expansion of the psychiatric arena was in part reflected through the work of the child guidance clinics in which relatively minor emotional difficulties were often psychiatrized. Indeed, the very concept of child guidance invited multiple professional involvement in 'case management', and it provided social workers in particular with an opportunity to engage in various kinds of therapeutic practices. In many ways it was only through the child that social work could enter directly into a treatment relationship with the patient and his or her family, since hospital based therapy was, as we have seen, virtually monopolized by psychiatrists. Thus, in contrast to hospital based social work, we find in the history of child guidance practice a discussion of therapeutic intervention from a very early stage. Thus, Robinson (*A Changing Psychology in Social Case Work*) can be heard arguing from as early as 1930 that the social worker in the child guidance clinic should enter into a full blooded therapeutic relationship with her patients as soon as possible, (especially with an eye to practising 'attitude therapy'). And this desire to intervene in personal case work acted so as to stimulate an interest in the wider theme of social therapy. As Robinson pointed out, 'Clinical experience has revealed the significant fact that while the starting point of treatment is the patient, there may be other members of the family who are also seriously maladjusted' (1930: 238). In a similar manner French (also speaking in terms of child guidance) argued some ten years later that, 'The treatment of parents must be carried along with the treatment of the child' (1940: 156). The PSW, consequently had to recognize tensions which arose in the family and learn how best to release the attendant strain. Yet the social worker's journey into therapy and therapeutic relationships was not to be based on any unique theoretical insights, or specialized skills. On the contrary, social casework principles were essentially to be derived from studies in psychology and psychoanalysis – so much so, that by 1949 Garrett (1949) was asking whether there was any real difference between casework and psychotherapy. And not surprisingly, social work texts in general came to adopt the language of psychoanalysis for both their titles and their content. Social work was thus interpreted in terms of the concepts of 'diagnosis', 'treatment', 'therapy', 'relationships' and even 'transference'. Wootton (1959) traced in great detail the impact of this kind of language on social work texts of the 1950s, and argued that by that stage social work practice had become so deeply engaged in 'hidden psychological issues' that it was in danger of 'deliberate disregard of practical problems' (1959: 278). This influence of psychoanalytic thinking on social work was further evident in the nature of professional training programmes. Thus, trainees in the UK during the 1950s and 1960s, were routinely introduced to studies on the nature of human personality and the psychology of family relations (rather than, say, aspects of community life), as a precursor to their fieldwork activities (Timms, 1964). In fact, the new training programmes merely underlined the extent to which social work had moved away from a simple concern with material need and towards a concern with 'psychological maladjustment'. Thus, even when clients sought assistance with straightforward material problems, the social worker had to be trained to see that these were mere 'presenting problems' (Miles, 1954), and that a deeper malaise probably existed elsewhere. Indeed, as Armstrong (1947) had stated a few years earlier, social work practice (in the mental hospital) should never be restricted to the 'commodities of welfare' alone.

The dominance of psychoanalytic language and thinking in social work practice was eventually to generate demands for the 'social' to be brought back into the profession (Wootton, 1959). The centrality of personal casework to the social work task was not, however, to be easily challenged – this despite the fact that what casework consisted of was never really very clear. Timms (1960), for example, devoted two papers to the problem without providing anything approaching enlightenment. So not surprisingly, the question of how casework was to be carried out was always a matter of considerable debate – a debate which even re-emerges in recent writings such as those in the Barclay Report (1982: App. B). Naturally, during the post Second World War era, the precise methods of professional intervention changed as much in social work as they did in, say, nursing, and so practical techniques came to include behavioural therapy, social skills training, cognitive therapy and various forms of personal counselling. But in almost every respect, social work failed to develop its own distinct body of theory and turned instead to the claim that its professional autonomy rested on the nature of its specialized practice and perhaps even the unique 'skills' which the social worker was called upon to use in casework practice (Butler and Pritchard, 1983;

Hudson, 1982). In the UK this notion was possibly given its fullest expression in the Inter-Departmental Report (1968) on the organization of social services in England and Wales – more commonly known as the Seebohm Report. For Seebohm, the PSW, in particular, was to be placed under the authority of social services rather than medical personnel and was to be trained in common with social workers covering other kinds of need (so called generic training). This was assumed to be possible because the skills required of social workers were believed to be common to all casework settings, and thus there was no call to train the PSW any differently from the social worker who specialized in work with, say, children or with old people. But of more relevance was the belief that the focus of social work was now supposed to be placed on the family rather than the isolated individual and so practitioners had to be prepared to deal with all kinds of presenting problems. Indeed, Seebohm sought to anchor social work in general in 'community based and family oriented' services (1968: 11), and in so doing she foreshadowed an emphasis which was to reappear with some force in the 1980s. Despite these attempts to reorganize and redefine their tasks, however, social workers experienced considerable difficulty in specifying just what was unique about their particular skill base. This, together with the lack of a distinct theoretical territory, was often reflected in a dispute about what social work really was (see, Timms and Timms, 1977). Perhaps because of these ambiguities, many social workers in both hospital and community settings continued to be dominated, and to feel dominated, by medics. Thus a 1970s DHSS Report on social service teams indicated how social workers often felt undervalued by medics and also subordinate to them *in practice* – 'They [medics] don't think much of us', being one published response from the study, (Hill, 1978). (In the study hospital, the subordinate position of social workers was in part reflected in the tendency of many of the psychiatrists to refer consistently to the team social worker as 'my' social worker.) In so far as that was so, social work had not really moved any further than when Goldberg (a psychiatrist) had discussed the role of the PSW in the community in 1947. His views, reprinted in the *British Journal of Psychiatric Social Work* in the late 1950s (Goldberg, 1957), were that the PSW had an essentially subordinate role – limited to 'paving the way toward treatment', aftercare and educational work. Therapy and treatment were not, therefore, issues which figured in the remit of the social worker. In a similar vein, Rushing (1964) pointed out how the role of the hospital based PSW often remained undefined and, at best, contentious. So whilst the social workers in his study defined their role in terms of casework treatment, the psychiatrists tended to see it in terms of 'welfare'. And interestingly, this vision of social work – as an essentially extramural welfare activity – was also one supported by nurses and projected from nursing texts. Thus, the *Handbook for Psychiatric Nurses* (Ackner, 1963) asserted that the Psychiatric Social Worker dealt with relatives and the patient in his or her environment – that is to say, the non-hospital environment – whilst the nurse was concerned with problems of the patient as a disordered individual. Even during the 1970s, authors of nursing texts continued to see the social worker as facilitator, dealing with the patient as a member of a family, or other social group, whilst the nurse confronted the patient as an individual person with an illness. Thus Maddison *et al.*, in the third (1970) edition of their *Psychiatric Nursing*, claimed that it was the social worker who provided the 'social diagnosis', and the social worker who acted as a bridge between the two worlds of hospital and community. The nurse on the other hand restricted him- or herself to getting the patient well. It was only in the fourth (1975) edition that the chapter on the PSW was rewritten to emphasize the shared aims and goals of the nurse and social worker, and the consequent overlap of practice.

Despite these somewhat dated visions of nurses and psychiatrists, we can nevertheless see in social work practice, from the 1960s onwards, the same moves towards community based objects of focus as we have already encountered in nursing. First, in a recognition – presaged by Seebohm – that the community as well as the individual should constitute a field of social work practice (though the exact nature of the relationship between social work and community work was not clarified). Secondly, in the official encouragement given to social workers in the UK to devote attention to the development of informal social networks as a means of care. So the Barclay Report (1982), for example, argued that social workers should be more concerned with mobilizing systems of social support which are latent in their client's social networks than had traditionally been the case. In that sense, argued Barclay, the social worker should aim to become a *community* – even, perhaps, a neighbourhood – social worker, rather than a personal caseworker.

It is evident, then, that coincident with the rise of care in the community policies, there was a growing demand that social work should move away from client-centred social casework to something else. Though exactly what that something else might be, remained unclear. Consequently, given the overall context, it is not perhaps surprising that the relationship of social work to serious mental illness remained unclear. Thus, social workers might claim that mental illness is, 'a multidimensional concept requiring a multidisciplinary response' (Huxley, 1985: 82), but in practice, and as far as mental illness is concerned, social work contributions are rarely to be found in such key areas as diagnosis and therapy (and in so far as social workers do engage in therapy, it is likely to be in terms of providing counselling sessions for people with neurotic disorders). This, despite the fact that since 1983 the social worker's involvement in serious mental disorder had been enshrined in law. Hence social work often remains on the sidelines of the therapeutic system and engages itself mainly with what we might call the client's wider, material conditions of everyday life – the commodities of welfare as it were. These latter are, of course, every bit as fundamental to understanding what constitutes mental illness as are the biological conditions of existence, but they also lie in a domain which is easily marginalized by medical psychiatry (and even by General Practitioners). More significantly perhaps, they inscribe a field of activity from which social workers themselves constantly try to escape.

The Inactive Patient

In 1933 the Board of Control for England and Wales published a *Memorandum* on occupational therapy for mental patients. After discussing the numerous advantages of occupational therapy for the mentally ill it mentioned the necessity to employ specialized occupational therapists (henceforth OTs). 'The latter', it said, was 'a new class of officer who has to be fitted into an organization designed in the first place without any thought of the intrusion' (Board of Control, 1933: 16). This recognition that occupational therapy (OT) was very much an afterthought in the design of mental health programmes, more or less sums up the position of such therapy throughout most of the twentieth century. Indeed, even today, the status of OT as an add-on feature of psychiatric treatment is very often reflected in the kinds of buildings in which the OT finds him- or herself – namely, temporary buildings which have been roughly converted to accommodate OT, and very often separated and placed on the margins of the hospital grounds.

The introduction of OT into psychiatric practice was originally achieved through the work of the self same psychiatrists who were involved in the introduction of social workers into mental hospitals. Among such innovators, however, the name of Adolf Meyer stands foremost. In fact Meyer is often regarded as a founding father of OT – probably because the concept of occupational and life therapies fitted in so well with the implications of his psychobiology, and especially his notion that an individual's relation with his or her environment was crucial to abnormal psychological processes. We can, for example, find him talking about OT in a 1921 paper on the philosophy of that subject – a paper in which he elaborated upon his conception of mental illness as being composed of 'problems of living' (Winters, 1952: 88), and in which he indicated that one such problem was often the absence of an organized work pattern. For Meyer, work provided discipline, and as such it enabled patients to adapt more readily to the outside world and to the pressures of modern life. 'Work in itself is of value' stated Meyer. He did not, however, provide any empirical or detailed theoretical justification for this claim (in the same way that there was to be little or no justification for the introduction of various forms of shock and surgical therapies into the psychiatry of the 1930s and 1940s). Unlike the *post hoc* rationalizations which were produced to support medical therapies, however, justifications for the use of OT usually took on a distinctly moral tone.

It is, perhaps, the emphasis given in the early writing on the subject to the need for 'personal discipline' which justifies this last remark. The Board of Control's *Memorandum*, for example, had advocated the use of OT partly on the grounds that 'good [personal] habits are induced and maintained'. And in an article in the *Lancet* in the same year, Haworth made the claim that the induction of the habits of personal discipline into the mental patient was among the most significant benefits of OT. This was why OT had 'its greatest use in the mental hospital' (1933, I: 171), and why the establishment of 'habit training' centres was called for. (The notion of habit training had in fact been a key notion of one of the founders of the American OT movement: Eleanor Slagle.) Indeed, in the following decade, Haworth and Macdonald's text on OT, *The Theory of Occupational Therapy* (1940), was to underline and further emphasize this message. Hence, in their discussion on the uses of OT for chronic mental patients, Haworth and Macdonald listed among their justifications for its use the observation that 'the devil makes mischief for idle hands', and further, that it was in some sense a duty to society to provide occupation for mental hospital inmates. In a similar fashion Dunton and Licht (1950) emphasized the negative effects of idleness and the positive effects of activity. For 'the idle patient either expends his energy in destructive violence or in preoccupation' (1950: 7). And Willard and Spackman (1947) also advocated habit training and its benefits. Thus, there was undoubtedly an element of Protestant moralizing involved in the theory of OT. Work was its own reward: valuable in itself, and always preferable to idleness and inactivity. Even Maxwell Jones's Social Rehabilitation Unit – opened in 1947 – was originally designed for patients 'who were primarily seen in terms of their poor employment record' (Rapoport, 1960: 2). And this emphasis on the intrinsic value of productive activity is still evident in many modern OT publications, in which such things as the use and allocation of time, the planning of leisure pursuits and the cultivation of good work habits still figure prominently. Indeed, and in many respects, the very concept of an occupation is itself the linguistic expression of a culturally based preference for an organized and disciplined use of time and skill to achieve specified goals. And it is, in fact, to this 'rational' approach to the organization of time, work and leisure that OT adheres. Consequently, for those authors who have argued that the institutionalization of the insane represented a means by which unproductive labour could be regulated and controlled (such as Rothman, 1971; Warner, 1985), the twentieth century 'theory' of OT provides much supportive material.

By 1940 the place of OT in English mental hospitals was more or less guaranteed by the publication of the Board of Control's *Suggestions and Instructions* for the building of hospitals (Board of Control, 1940), wherein the OT centre figured as an integral component of treatment. And this was not simply because OT inculcated the habits of industrial discipline into inmates but also because other benefits were believed to result from such therapy. Henderson and Gillespie's *Textbook*, for example, had included a chapter on OT since its very first edition in 1927. Therein OT was viewed as providing a means for bringing patients into social contact with each other and developing the social life of patients. Similarly, Haworth and Macdonald (1940) had argued that OT had a 'normalizing effect' on patients by encouraging group activity, responsibility and cooperation. 'A normal life includes work, play and exercise', and patients had to be educated for all three. And these arguments, of course, link in with those wider changes in psychiatric theory by means of which mental illness was partly redefined in terms of its social dimensions. In other words, for Henderson and Gillespie and the other followers of Meyerian principles, mental illness always had a social component which was expressed either in the patient's human relationships with others, or in their relationship to the economy and the wider environment in general. Therefore, therapy had to be directed as much towards these wider relationships as it was towards mind or physiology.

As with the other professions, however, OT found itself unable to assert a truly autonomous identity in the absence of theoretical specialization. As the 1933 *Memorandum* put it, OT was always to be provided 'under medical direction'. And as with nursing and social work, occupational therapy could not escape from medical dominance unless it developed its own specialized forms of knowledge and practice. It is not surprising, therefore, that from the 1950s onwards we find numerous attempts to theorize OT in increasingly complex ways. The Fidlers, for example, in their *Introduction to Psychiatric Occupational Therapy* (Fidler and Fidler, 1954), tried to represent OT as a collaborative therapeutic relationship in which the patient, the psychiatrist and the OTs were all equally involved. The OT room was in this view a 'laboratory' for treatment. And almost a decade later (in the 1963 edition of their text) these same authors represented OT as an important 'communicative process' for both patient and therapist. Indeed, these texts presage the production and publication of endless 'models' of OT, most of which were forced to borrow their theoretical principles from psychology – for example, behavioural models, models based on the notion of social skills and social skills training, and sometimes neurobiological models (for a selection of these see, Briggs and Agrin, 1981). And the dominance of psychology in OT is plainly demonstrated in introductory texts on the subject (Willson, 1983, 1984). In fact, OT often ends up evaluating the self same objects of psychiatric practice as does nursing and clinical psychology – namely behavioural and physical deficits in the individual (see, for example, Hemingway, 1988). And the history of psychiatric nursing and that of OT, often overlap for this very reason. But whilst OT often highlighted the ways in which mental illness in the modern world was composed of more than just 'mental' dysfunction, it proved singularly unable to move beyond a vision of the isolated individual as the origin and location of all that was significant about psychiatric disorder. In the final analysis, therefore, psychiatric OT, rather like OT in general, was ultimately concerned with deficits of personal and economic 'functioning' and the rectification of poorly organized 'skills' in the patient. The social relationships which lay around the patient, and the wider social and economic circumstances in which the patient found him- or herself, were never to become objects of OT practice.

The Psychometric Technician

In Rushing's (1964) study of a (US) psychiatric hospital staff, he pointed out how psychologists often felt undervalued – especially in their relationships with psychiatrists. This was so, in large part, because the latter demanded that the former only be capable of executing routine testing functions.

This image of the psychologist as psychometric technician reflects at least two significant features of the clinical psychologist's place in the network of professional practice. Firstly, the importance of tests and testing in the psychologist's workload and secondly, the subordination of clinical psychology to medical psychiatry, (a relationship which was re-emphasized in the deliberations of the (UK) Trethowan Committee (DHSS, 1977a)). Naturally, the importance of psychometrics in the broad history of psychology is not something to be overestimated, but there can be little doubt that as far as the history of hospital work is concerned, it is central. In fact, the very presence of the psychologist in mental hospital settings is related to the valuation which practising psychiatrists placed on data derived from psychometric tests. And the primacy of psychometrics was emphasized over and above the fact that it was psychology which rested at the base of many of the major theoretical developments which appeared in academic and clinical psychiatry during the twentieth century. We can list among the latter such things as the construction of psychological (as opposed to physicalist) concepts of mind, the invention of the neuroses and the emergence of the modern concept of personality. These, taken in conjunction with that other conceptual pillar of twentieth century psychiatry – behaviour – sum up to a formidable contribution. In addition, and as has already been stated, nearly all of the major theoretical developments in nursing, social work and occupational therapy also arose out of the speculations of psychologists. Yet, for the most part, these higher level (conceptual and theoretical) advances were ultimately absorbed into psychiatric practice through routine and well worn academic routes rather than through practical work at ward or hospital level. Indeed, at ward level, psychology remained forever overshadowed by medical psychiatry. Consequently (and as with each one of the other psychiatric related professions), the emergence of clinical psychology as an autonomous and independent activity ultimately depended on the creation of a professional space outside of that which was controlled by medical psychiatry – and, as with social work, it was the invention of the 'clinic', and especially the child guidance clinic, which served to underpin the professional development of clinical psychology (Watson, 1977).

Naturally, the technology of 'mental tests' (the term was first used by Cattell in 1890), was a technology intimately tied up with the history of measurement and statistical inference (Gould, 1984). And the impetus to test and measure mental functions was executed in the belief that the measurements reflected what were otherwise considered to be hidden, and unknown, but nevertheless real properties of the individual. When tests were applied to human groups it was further assumed to be possible to make accurate assessments concerning the range of mental capacities in entire populations. Thus the Binet test, for example, was assumed to tell us something about mental age and its normal distribution. As with all such schemes of measurement, however (and we shall encounter some others in the following chapter), scores of mental age or general intelligence did not offer any truly independent measures of objective properties 'in the world', but rather offered some practical reflections of the complex and intricate theories which had generated the tests in the first place. In that sense, test scores merely helped to realize theoretical properties. (The intricate connections between the early theories, the tests and measurements of intelligence are, for example, thoroughly reviewed by Gould (1984).)

The history of general intelligence and its measurement is not, of course, of primary concern here. But what we can note with advantage is that the development of intelligence tests opened up the opportunity of assessing such things as degrees of mental defect among the inmates of early twentieth century asylums. So in the US, for example, Goddard (whom we shall meet once more in Chapter 6) adapted Binet's tests for use with mental defectives in the Vineland Training School. Whilst the UK Commissioners for the Care and Control of the Feeble Minded (1908), having noted US developments, advocated the use of such tests for the classification of all institutionalized mental defectives. The perceived virtues of scores for such things as mental age were, however, relatively short lived in the UK because it was quickly recognized that the category of 'mental defective' involved social as much as intellectual judgements. So by 1929, the Board of Control had decided on a social definition of mental defect rather than a psychological one stating that it was the capacity or incapacity for 'independent social adaptation' which marked out the true defective. And even Penrose (1938) who was committed to accurate scientific description of mental conditions, and who disliked the social definition proposed by the Board of Control, noted that mental age scores alone were far from being sufficient to characterize mental defect. Yet despite this, IQ test scores were used for diagnostic purposes throughout the century (and they were certainly used in the study hospital).

As well as assessing what eventually became known as IQ, clinical psychology also embroiled itself in the discovery and assessment of attitudes and personality traits. The concept of personality is not, of course, one which looms large either in psychology or in psychiatry before the second decade of the current century when Freudian concepts began to take root in intellectual life. (And we have already noted the impact which Freudian teaching had on textbook psychiatry during the 1918–39 period.) In terms of clinical psychology, for example, Whipple's *Manual of Mental and Physical Tests* (1910), contained no mention of personality whatsoever. Yet by 1917 Woodworth had developed his *Personal Data Sheet* (later to be called the *Psychoneurotic Inventory*) and by 1921 Rorschach had developed his eponymous test for psychodiagnosis – which involved the use of projective techniques derived in large part from Jungian psychology (Rorschach, 1942). In the 1930s (which was in many ways a central decade for the development of personality theory) the Thematic Apperception Test was devised. The latter apparently aimed at demonstrating how the 'underlying dynamics of personality' could be revealed by getting subjects to 'project' their experiences or fantasies on to pictures (Morgan and Murray, 1935). And these projective techniques fitted in well with many of the Freudian and neo-Freudian precepts which had saturated mid-century clinical psychology (see, Schafer, 1948). Personality tests were, of course, assumed to be capable of revealing hidden facets of 'character', and some psychologists (such as Schafer) moved on to suggest that one could even use such tests to profile disease states – that is, to diagnose hysteric, neurotic, addictive or schizophrenic personalities. Yet, in so far as the personality tests of the 1920s and 1930s – and even later ones such as the Minnesota Multiphasic Personality Inventory (devised 1940) – were built on a concept of inner consciousness and hidden psychodynamic entities they came to be regarded with considerable suspicion by many psychologists. This was especially so in the post 1945 era. Thus Eysenck (1953), for example, charged that psychoanalysis was 'unscientific' and lacking in rigorous propositions and consequently that the personality tests based on psychodynamic theory were equally unscientific. These arguments predated by some years the vehement claims of Cattell (1965), who spoke of the Rorschach and the TAT tests as nothing more than mere 'gadgets'. And this attack on projective techniques was usually combined with a call for the accurate measurement of specific personality traits. Cattell, for example, had observed that 'There is not a single measurement in the work of Janet . . . Freud . . . Adler . . . Jung' (1965: 15), and Kraepelin, and that their work should therefore be dismissed as belonging to some prescientific stage of his discipline's history. More important than calls for measurement, however, was the increasing tendency to focus in on a distinctly twentieth century object of psychological theory – behaviour.

In 1925 J.B. Watson had asked, 'Why don't we make what we can *observe* the real field of psychology?' (1925: 6), and had gone on to argue that what really mattered about individual persons was not consciousness but the *'behaviour or activities of the human being'* (1925: 3, Watson's emphasis). It was not until after the Second World War, however, that behaviour as a major object of psychiatric attention came to the fore. In the UK, for example, Eysenck (1959) suggested that there might be 'new ways of curing neuroses' – based on behavioural principles, and that psychologists should be used as diagnosticians of behaviour abnormalities and designers of behaviour therapy programmes. They were claims taken up with some force among clinical psychologists, and the latter became heavily engaged both in the design of behavioural measures and, to a lesser extent, in the execution of behaviour therapy techniques. (Even in the study hospital, one of the major concerns of the clinical psychologists was the design of a new behavioural instrument which could be used to describe and then to classify the patients in some objective fashion.) In addition to operant procedures, of course, clinical psychologists also utilized aversion techniques, cognitive methods, token economy techniques (used in the study wards), thought stopping methods, social skills training and numerous other methods. (For a list of such methods together with an indication of their approximate points of introduction, see Slade (1990).) The claim that psychologists should have a therapeutic role was not, however, one to be easily conceded. So the Trethowan Committee (DHSS, 1977a) on the position of psychologists in the health care system, for example, argued that in the National Health Service there was 'a continuing medical responsibility which [could not] be handed over to any other profession' (1977a: 25), and that whilst psychologists might express an interest in developing therapeutic programmes, their work could only be carried out under the direction of psychiatrists.

With the advent of community psychiatry, of course, we see in clinical psychology the emergence of a new range of instruments – often directed towards such things as the measurement of 'independence' and 'social support'. More recently and in line with the times, psychologists have also been concerned to develop measures of 'quality of life' (see, for example, Bowling, 1991). In general, however, and as Pilgrim argues (1990: 223), clinical psychologists have more often sought 'to make a bid for legitimacy to manage the "neurotic" population, leaving madness to the medical profession'. But it is not our concern to trace the detailed history of psychological practice and its impact on hospital and community populations. All that is of importance is for us to note, albeit briefly, how psychology was responsible for bringing new objects of attention into the domain of psychiatry, and how psychologists sought to realize those objects through the construction of numerous measuring instruments. In fact, in more recent years clinical psychology has even attempted to 'operationalize diseases' (Thompson, 1988: 4) – that is to say, provide precise indicators of disease states. (A task which seems to have become ever more prominent since the publication of DSM-III in 1980, when calls for the operationalization of specific psychiatric disorders were explicitly made.) This latter task, however, has been based on the belief that diseases are names of things rather than names for theories, yet as Wing *et al.* (1981) pointed out, such a belief is an erroneous one. Indeed, it is clear that the objects of psychology – whether they be personality, mental age, behaviour, or quality of life – are not in any sense timeless, immutable and objective properties of the real world, but cultural constructions which are forged in theory, honed through practice and made visible only through the use of the self same instruments which are supposedly designed to measure them. And somewhat inevitably, as the instruments change so do the objects of analysis.

Occupations and Illnesses

> You cannot gain a fundamental understanding of mathematics
> by waiting for the result of a theory.
>
> (Wittgenstein, 1979: 129)

For Berger and Luckman (1967: 92), 'roles *represent* the institutional order'. Consequently, the simple appearance (or disappearance) of specific roles tells us a great deal about the changing nature of social organizaton in general. More directly, the appearance of the roles of occupational therapist, social worker, community psychiatric nurse and clinical psychologist, reflect both changes in the occupational structure and changes in our understanding of what mental illness is and how it ought to be organized. Indeed, the very existence of such roles underlines the fact that, in the closing years of the twentieth century, mental illnesses are far from being perceived as purely medical and organic problems.

In that respect, the appearance of different occupational roles also implies a great deal about fundamental changes in the division of knowledge. And it is really in terms of this latter division that different representations of mental illness arise. In this chapter, of course, we have not really attempted to focus in on particular kinds of illnesses – such as schizophrenia, or depression, or senile dementia – and have contented ourselves instead with documenting the ways in which new theoretical objects have entered into various forms of professional practice. Thus, we have noted how psychology has been responsible for drawing psychological and behavioural objects into the orbit of professional psychiatry, and how the activities of social workers and community nurses have brought an interest in family and other forms of social relations into consideration. It might be tempting, of course, to regard such things as poor employment records, discordant family relations and deficits in social skills as being merely peripheral to mental illness – as mere symptoms of deeper organic pathologies. And this viewpoint is sometimes expressed in modern psychiatry texts – especially in relation to the more serious disorders (see, Gelder *et al.*, 1988). The sociological task, however, is not to evaluate the significance of different signs and symptoms of disease, and still less to place any such signs in positions of relative importance, but rather to note the points at which new signs are recognized, and how they have been integrated into various forms of professional activity. Indeed, the real nature of any given mental illness, for all practical purposes, always lies in the sum total of signs and symptoms in terms of which it is described, analysed and organized. So in that sense, the nature of, say, schizophrenia is to be found as much in the existence of disordered family, interpersonal and work patterns as in any assumed organic or genetic pathology. In fact, some clinical psychologists – Bentall (1990) – have recently suggested that instead of investigating disease entities such as schizophrenia, it would be more productive to concentrate on individual symptoms. By implication, and as with Wittgenstein's arguments about mathematics, we can argue that one is unlikely to gain any fundamental understanding of schizophrenia by waiting for a theory. Its nature lies in the very activities which confront it.

5

Representations of Psychiatric Disorder in the Community

The meaning of a word is its use in the language.

Wittgenstein (1967: 20e)

The Centrality of Community

In the late twentieth century, the community is regarded as a 'cornerstone' of psychiatric and many other forms of medical practice (Goldberg and Huxley, 1980), and modern services are deliberately organized around the concept as a matter of routine. The nature of a community, however, takes many forms and what is often overlooked is that in the history of modern psychiatric practice, communities have been just as readily found within hospitals as they have in the extramural world at large. In this respect we have already encountered, for example, references to the hospital as a therapeutic community, and we have also heard about the ways in which colonies were constructed as self-contained and self-supporting communities. In fact, these older notions of organized care developed in an age which saw no contrast and no antagonism between the nature of community and the nature of asylum. As a consequence, during the first half of this century, the concept of care in the community could just as readily have been applied to asylum care as to care in the world beyond the asylum walls. But given this, how are we to explain why a professional interest in the extramural community of people with psychiatric disorders came to eclipse an interest in the intramural community of the insane? And how can we explain the centrality of community to contemporary psychiatric practice?

In many respects, the material contained in earlier chapters has gone some considerable way towards answering both questions. Thus, we have seen how the objects of professional psychiatric practice altered during the decades, and how modern objects of treatment failed to readily lend themselves to the earlier notions of asylum care. One cannot, after all, treat social relations or normalize behavioural deficits in an artificial and isolated medical setting in the way that one might, perhaps, treat a physical disease or a malfunctioning brain. But in addition to this technical change of focus it also became clear, as the twentieth century moved forward, that psychiatric disorder was far more widely distributed in modern populations than had previously been allowed. This was partly because the range of things which counted as psychiatric disturbance expanded considerably during the century, and partly because the once sharp line which existed to divide sanity from insanity was gradually blunted. Thus, the emotional disturbances found in the child guidance clinic, the nervous reactions found in the General Practitioner's surgery and the behavioural abnormalities found in the out-patients' clinics came to be regarded as just as central to the psychiatric enterprise as did the 'lunacy' contained in the old asylum. Indeed, as lunacy waned, the neuroses and the behavioural disorders waxed. And with that came the recognition that mental disorders were not things set apart from the everyday, but merely the more extreme forms of what were otherwise normal thought and behavioural processes. So as Penrose (1938) put it in his study of mental deficiency, there were degrees of defect and all that distinguished the normal from the abnormal was an arbitrary line. Add to that one further ingredient, namely a recognition that psychiatric disorder always developed in some kind of a social context, and that it tended to have a distinct social distribution, and we begin to see a suitable mix of reasons as to why the psychiatric and related professions turned their attention outward – beyond the asylum walls and into non-institutional settings. This switch of focus was neither a hastily conceived change, nor a hastily executed one; it was, however, distinctly noticeable. Thus in the introduction to his mental health survey of a rural area in Southern Scotland, Mayer-Gross (1948) was able to assert that:

> During the last thirty years the interest of psychiatrists has shifted from the major psychoses, statistically relatively rare occurrences, to the milder and borderline cases, the minor deviations from the normal average. Their dependence on social conditions and their influence on the social life of the patient himself, or his family and of the community [have formed the subjects of psychiatric study]. (1948: 140)

And it is primarily to the study of the distribution of psychiatric disorder in the (non-hospital) community that this chapter is devoted. It seeks to trace the route by means of which psychiatric disorder was discovered in the community, and thence to examine how community life was seen to contribute to the causation of such disorder. It ends by considering changed visions of community in psychiatric discourse.

Disorder in the Community

In the third edition of *Clinical Psychiatry*, Slater and Roth (1969) opened their preface by stating that during the 1960s the developments in psychiatry had been extensive and profound. The most important of those changes, stated Slater and Roth, emanated from epidemiological findings, and in particular from the recognition that mental illness had social as well as physiological and psychological causes. Perhaps it was in deference to the latter findings that they incorporated a whole new chapter on social psychiatry into their book. In any event, they were certainly moved to argue for the adoption of what they called a multidisciplinary study of psychiatric disorder rather than one based merely on neurology or psychopathology. Nowadays, of course, it is a commonplace call and one which is echoed in numerous modern texts (see Wolff *et al.*, 1990). Our interest in that call, however, originates in the fact that the first steps towards a recognition of social factors as causal agents of psychiatric disorder depended not so much on tightly designed epidemiological studies of mental illness, as on a recognition that such illness had an identifiable social distribution – and that discovery, in turn, depended on surveys and censuses of community life.

It was not until the late 1920s and 1930s that studies of the distribution of mental illness in the community were widely undertaken. Though the first (and most frequently cited) study of the prevalence of community wide mental disorder was that of Rosanoff (1917) carried out in Nassau County, New York. On the basis of his research, Rosanoff suggested a prevalence rate for mental disorder of 16 per 1,000 of population, but much more interesting than his suggested prevalence rate was the fact that his study involved not merely medical assessments of what constituted mental disorder, but also social assessments concerning questions of 'adjustment' and 'maladjustment'. For it was essentially by means of such socio-psychological assessments that the range of recognizable psychiatric disorders broadened out during the twentieth century so as to encompass what Mayer-Gross was to refer to as the 'minor deviations from the normal average', and what others referred to as minor psychiatric disorder.

Mapping the extent to which psychiatric disorder was nestled in the community was, of course, just one specific manifestation of a much broader 'clinical gaze' which has characterized twentieth century medicine in general (Armstrong, 1983). In the UK the earliest census of mental disorder in the population at large was that carried out by Lewis (1929). The latter study was commissioned by the Mental Deficiency Committee which reported in 1929, and Lewis concluded that the prevalence of such deficiency – 8 per 1,000 – was much higher than had been previously assessed, and also that it tended to be greater in rural as against urban areas. Using both survey and census techniques other European researchers also sought assessments of the prevalence of mental disorder in non-hospitalized communities. Schwab and Schwab (1978), for example, list 10 European prevalence studies carried out between 1929 and 1949 – not including Lewis's. Thus Brugger (1931) had made an attempt at a census in two counties of Thuringia (eastern Germany) during 1929 – discovering, among other things, that more than one half of psychotics were living outside of hospitals. Whilst in Denmark (1933–6) Strömgren (1950) had made an assessment of the prevalence of disorder in an island community in which he discovered quite high rates of lifetime prevalence for mental disorder and again a relatively high percentage (35 per cent) of people with psychotic symptoms living in the community. In like manner, a number of North American studies came to similar conclusions *vis-à-vis* community disorder and non-hospitalized cases of serious mental illness. Thus, Lemkau *et al.* (1941) assessed prevalence in the Eastern Health District of Baltimore on the basis of hospital data. Once again they pointed towards the existence of relatively large proportions of psychotics living in the community and, more importantly, to quite high rates of psychoneurotic symptoms in the general population. And a similar tale was produced as a result of Roth and Luton's (1943) studies in rural Tennessee.

Following the Second World War, epidemiologists sharpened up both their concepts and their technology. Distinctions were drawn between incidence rates (rates at which new cases of mental illness appeared) and prevalence rates (rates of existing mental disorder). Different kinds of prevalence were specified and new technologies of sampling applied in an attempt to assess ever more accurately what the 'real' rates of mental disorder in the community might be. Probably the most important of the methodologically sophisticated survey studies of the post 1940 era were those of Stirling County in Nova Scotia (Leighton, 1959), and the Midtown Manhattan Study of the 1950s (Srole *et al.* 1962, 1977). The former suggested that 57 per cent of their 1,150 respondents were 'genuine psychiatric cases', and the latter estimated that of their 1,660 subjects 23 per cent were mentally ill and only 18 per cent were 'well'. This reconfirmation of extensive rates of psychiatric disorder in the community was matched and duplicated in yet other studies in Europe and North America. In the UK, for example, Shepherd (1966) in his

Psychiatric Illness in General Practice, argued that up to one fifth of the adult population was in need of psychiatric treatment and that there was a 'reservoir' of cases far greater than the rate of referral to psychiatrists indicated. A potential prevalence rate of 70 per 1,000 was suggested. The majority of psychiatric patients, however, were found to be suffering from relatively minor disorders and only 4 per cent of their sample were assessed as displaying psychotic symptoms. And numerous studies centring on Camberwell in South London during the 1970s also showed reasonably high prevalence rates of depression and anxiety states in the general population, though only minimal presence of schizophrenic, paranoid and manic disorders (see, for example, Wing *et al.*, 1981). In terms of both sociology and psychiatry, however, these various community surveys and censuses eventually raised fundamental questions about the nature of psychiatric disorder and its distribution in general. For in seeking to count the extent to which mental illness was present in any population the researchers had first to confront the question of what mental illness actually was, and how a real case of psychiatric disorder could be identified.

At the commencement of the century, problems concerning the identification of mental illness had been, for the most part, posed in terms of Kraepelian psychiatry. The latter, as we have seen in Chapter 3, was constructed on the premiss that mental illnesses (or forms of insanity) were the product of pathological physical processes in the patient's body. These processes followed a 'natural' course which could be specified in terms of recognizable symptoms. The sum total of symptoms added up to a recognizable disease. In other words, it was assumed that physical reality manifested itself in natural divisions (for Kraepelin, dementia praecox and manic depression were two such divisions). In that sense diseases were regarded as ontologically real entities. And in so far as the Kraepelian vision of psychiatric disease processes was adhered to, the problem of enumerating cases of psychiatric disorder in a population ultimately resolved itself into the problem of recognizing a small number of symptoms in specific individuals (for given some symptoms, others were bound to follow). Unfortunately for psychiatry, however, human beings proved to be far less tractable than Kraepelian classificatory principles would allow, and the problem of matching dynamic human symptoms with lifeless categories created endless anomalies. Since no commonly agreed somatic pathology was ever satisfactorily established for any specific form of insanity (not even for GPI), psychiatry had nothing left to interpret but variable clinical symptoms. And it was dissatisfaction with the rules and principles by means of which clinical diagnoses were executed that led various authors to question the reality of disease categories in themselves. Thus Meyer, for example, declared himself to be unhappy with classificatory categories as early as 1907 (see Winters, 1952) and, later, preferred to speak of individual reactions to life experiences rather than of diseases. Whilst Menninger (1948) advocated the abandonment of diagnostic categories altogether – preferring instead to focus in on specific symptoms. These conflicting viewpoints (of the ontologists and the nominalists) were never to be resolved during the twentieth century, and the question as to how psychiatric diagnoses can be standardized or operationalized continues to cause dissension. Kendell (1975) and Wing *et al.* (1981) have argued (in different ways) that there is some kind of technological fix to the problem – that the use of well constructed instruments allied to modern statistical techniques can reduce significantly the amount of error involved in diagnosing, say, a case of depression, or of schizophrenia or of paranoia. Nominalists (such as Szasz (1960), and Sedgwick (1982)), however, have protested that the problem of defining mental illness is not a problem of achieving concordance among psychiatrists, but about the nature of human reality itself.

Leaving aside these intractable problems of ontology, however, it is at once obvious that a number of questions can be legitimately posed about what it was that the various studies cited above actually identified. Did they, for example, reveal a real (independent) rate of disorder in the community or did they in some sense construct their own rate of disorder according to variable definitions of what was and what was not a 'case'? For whereas most of the investigators who worked between 1916 and 1970 took it for granted that their surveys were netting real rates of prevalence, a number of later investigators began to seriously question the instrumentation involved in such surveys and, more problematically, the issue of how cases of psychiatric illness were to be identified in the first place. Thus, Copeland (1981) argued that what was and was not a 'case' depended on the purposes of the survey being undertaken, and Wing *et al.* (1981) argued that no single definition of case could be given for all surveys. In short then, the suggestion began to take root that community surveys did not mirror some real and true state of affairs in an independent world, but rather discovered only what the researcher's instruments (or principles of identification) set out to identify. During the 1970s and 1980s the number of such instruments (and the popularity of their use) increased markedly. Instruments were designed and used to measure functional ability, psychological well being, life satisfaction, depression, general health, anxiety and many other features of human existence (for a review of such instruments see, Bowling, 1991). But once the certainties of the ontologists were dispensed with, it became increasingly easy to argue (in various ways) that such instruments could in effect only produce what Bachelard (1984: 133) once called 'instrumental products'. That is to say, they could only produce the phenomena which they were supposedly designed to discover and measure. And in that respect there was a sense in which the problems of community prevalence rates lent themselves to sociological considerations. For example, by arguing that a case was not so much to be defined in terms of isolated and decontextualized instruments alone, but in terms of professional practice in all of its complexity. In this view, what made a 'case' was treatment of a disorder by a psychiatrist (which is akin to the position adopted in this book *vis-à-vis* diagnoses of schizophrenia, manic depressive illness and so on). Such a distinctly sociological approach to the problem was hinted at by Goldberg and Huxley (1980) when they argued that 'psychiatric illness proper' is marked out by admission to a psychiatric out-patient or in-patient department. (And in this context it may be worth noting that the rates of referral to psychiatric out-patient services in the study hospital catchment area were 11 per 1,000 and rates of first admission to hospital were 2 per 1,000 of the population.) Naturally, such an emphasis on the role of professional practice undercuts at once the claims to the existence of hidden disorder. For in the absence of professional recognition, there can be no psychiatric disorder *per se* to hide – though that, of course, is far from claiming that only professionally recognized forms of disorder are real or problematic for the individual.

Whatever the philosophical problems involved in the study of morbidity rates, there is no doubt that community surveys had a very real impact on psychiatric practice in at least two respects. First, the discovery of the 'reservoir' of mental illness in the community suggested that the presence of the asylum wall no longer acted as a natural physical boundary between the sane and the insane. So the segregative function of the asylum lost its rationale once it was demonstrated that mental illness could be found almost anywhere and everywhere. Secondly, the discovery of a high proportion of people with psychotic symptoms who were not hospitalized suggested that there might be valid alternatives to institutionalized life for people with serious mental disorder. Taken on their own, of course, such conclusions would have carried little weight with those who planned psychiatric services, but taken in conjunction with a changing vision of what constituted psychiatric disorder and how it was caused, the evidence provided by community surveys eventually served so as to undermine the rationale for isolated and self-contained psychiatric hospitals, and to lay the basis for a new rationale for community based forms of psychiatric work.

Communities as the Source of Disorder

In both lay and professional thinking, mental illness has usually been viewed as a property of isolated individuals – it is people who are 'mad', not families or community groupings, still less whole societies. The origin of such illness, however, is not necessarily to be located in such individuals – though that is by far and away the most popular assumption. In fact the supposition that psychiatric disorder might have an extra-personal as well as a personal psychological dimension emerged in twentieth century psychiatry through a slow and piecemeal process. Indeed, we have already encountered reference to some currents of psychiatric theory and practice which turned towards interpersonal relationships for an understanding of the nature and origins of mental illness. The flow of those currents was, however, interlinked with numerous other forms of activity, and among the latter one would have to include the extensive mapping of prevalence rates which was generated as a result of the community surveys cited above. But more to the point perhaps, one would also have to recognize the fact that in the process of mapping prevalence rates and distributions, epidemiologists (under various guises) began to document how mental illness could be perceived as having social correlates and distinctly social origins, and it is really the changing understanding of those correlates and points of origin which is of interest to us here.

The breakdown of the institutionalized insane into subcategories of age, sex, occupational grouping, marital status and even religion and nationality is far from being a twentieth century concern. Indeed, the cross-tabulation of disease categories by such factors had been executed throughout the latter half of the nineteenth and right into the early twentieth century. Thus, the UK Census Reports, for example, regularly analysed institutional populations along all of those dimensions, and the reports of the Lunacy Commissioners analysed inmates according to most of them. By the opening of the current century, therefore, the enumeration of madness in terms of what we now refer to as social categories was well established. In that sense the government reports to which I have just referred might appear to the contemporary reader as unusually modern. There are, however, at least three considerations which must be immediately taken into account when considering the representations of mental disorder to which the aforementioned reports contributed. First, and most importantly, their data referred only to institutionalized cases of insanity, and no attempt was made to assess the extent of disorder 'in the community'. Secondly, most if not all of the categories which were used to enumerate the distribution of mental disorder (such as age, sex and nationality), were invariably viewed in distinctly biological terms, rather than as social categories. So, the observation that certain diseases (such as hysteria, for example) had a well defined distribution among women, would not (and could not) have been used by alienists as a starting point for an enquiry into female lifestyles or roles, but only as evidence of different biological propensities of males and females. And thirdly, we have to remember that the cross-tabulations of such categories as marital status, occupational grouping, sex and age, against disease categories was not executed so as to reveal the strength of causal associations between social conditions and disease, but merely as an accounting exercise in political economy. Indeed, at the opening of the century, the causes of insanity were still located in a strange array of factors – reprehensible personal habits, exposure to adverse or unusual weather conditions, hereditary influences, personal setbacks and misfortunes – all of which were seen to operate on a weak biological constitution. The *Census of Ireland (1901): General Report* (1901) provides interesting examples of causal logic which prevailed.

In short, then, what the early twentieth-century cross-tabulations showed were the contexts in which biological (and particularly hereditary) processes operated, rather than any data on the social distribution of mental illness. In part we might assume that this was because the entities which we now refer to as sex-roles, age-roles, or race, class and disorganized communities were not conceptualized in their modern sociological senses until very much later on in the century. (The modern sociological conception of role analysis, for example, is normally traced to Linton (1936).) But that, in many senses, would be to put the cart before the horse, because what the emergence of the sociological concepts of age-role, sex-role, race and community themselves depended on was a radical change of world view which saw the realm of the social as an autonomous realm – free from determination by biological forces. Indeed, nowhere was this willingness to elevate the social from a mere subcategory of the biological more evident than in the work of Durkheim, and especially in his 1897 work on suicide – perhaps the earliest example of a sociological analysis of what was perceived to be a specific form of insanity (see Durkheim, 1952). Durkheim's work, however, was just one part of a much broader strand of thought which struggled to argue that human beings could and should be seen as other than biologically determined organisms – or instinctually driven creatures – whose sociality was merely subservient to independent biological needs. And during most of the twentieth century that struggle formed the essence of a subplot which ran throughout almost every sociological text which was concerned with the causes and origins of mental illness. It certainly formed an integral part of the research work which was first responsible for establishing an empirical basis for belief in the social causation of psychiatric illness – Faris and Dunham's *Mental Disorder in Urban Areas* (1939) – and it is to their work that we must now turn.

The work of Faris and Dunham (1939) was essentially concerned with the distribution of mental illness in the Chicago metropolitan area. Their study was executed in a theoretical frame which paid extensive attention to the distribution of social phenomena in urban 'zones'. This notion of zoning had emerged partly out of the work of R.E. Park, who had established the broad programme of urban research in Chicago as early as 1916, and partly out of the work of E.W. Burgess, who had discussed the zoning of cities in 1925. By 1929 when Zorbaugh (another member of the Sociology Faculty at Chicago) published his *The Goldcoast and the Slum*, the vision of Chicago as a city composed of various socio-economic and cultural zones was well established, and in a sense it was only necessary for Faris and Dunham to fit their own empirical data (mostly derived from hospital admission statistics) into the general framework. Their thesis and conclusion was that personal disorganization (mental illness) was directly related to the prevalence of social (urban) disorganization. And they believed that studies of the social distribution of mental illness acted not simply as descriptive aids as to where such disorder may be found, but also told us something about the nature of causation. Given the prevailing ethos of biological determinism, however, they assumed that social causes could only ever be secondary to the primary biological causes. And this was exactly the position which Burgess adopted in his introduction to the Chicago study in which he cited the work of Abraham Myerson on the inheritance of mental disease. In fact, he used Myerson's claims to suggest that since the primary causes of insanity were biological, social factors played only an indirect (though important) role in the aetiology of mental illness. And it was in that rather circumscribed context that Faris and Dunham argued that insanity rates for the different psychoses varied by geographical district (the 'Negro' areas as against the white areas; the rooming house zone *vis-à-vis* the suburbs; the poverty-stricken areas as compared with the affluent ones, and so on). On this basis they observed, for example, that the schizophrenias were prevalent in the lower half of the social scale, whilst manic depressive psychoses seemed to be more readily found in the more advantaged sectors of the city, and in the private as opposed to state mental hospitals. This thesis that social disorganization was closely associated with personal disorganization was of course, a much favoured theme of the Chicago school of sociology in the interwar period. Naturally, it was only suggestive of a link between social conditions and personal misfortune and as with all ecological studies it fell victim to that famous fallacy. Nevertheless, the Chicago study was among the very first to trace in detailed form the links which existed between multiple social factors and insanity. In a similar vein, of course, during the second, third and fourth decades of the century, epidemiologists of physical ailments were also beginning to examine the relationships between somatic diseases and social processes.

In addition to collecting and re-presenting empirical data on the distribution of hospitalized psychiatric patients, Faris and Dunham also sought to advance explanations for their observations. In fact, their study generated, directly and indirectly, a number of important hypotheses concerning the relationships between mental illness and social life which were to be much discussed in later decades. Two in particular stand out. The first was a social isolation or social breakdown hypothesis which argued that loss of social contact(s) was in some way causally related to the onset of illness. Whilst the second was highlighted by Myerson (1940) in his review of Faris and Dunham's work and which later became known as the downward drift hypothesis. This latter posed the question as to whether the inverse association between higher rates of mental illness and social status which Faris and Dunham had discovered was a product of mentally ill people drifting down the social scale (as a result of their inability to function in a modern urban economy), or whether it was a reflection of the fact that people in lower socio-economic groups really were more prone to mental illness on account of their social conditions. The first of these two alternatives supported the viewpoint of the biological determinists (of whom Myerson was one), whilst the second supported a distinctly social aetiology. In later years numerous empirical studies were designed either in whole or in part so as to 'test' the reliability of the attendant claims. In the short term, however, the Chicago study tended to do little other than encourage a search for insanity areas in large cities. In fact, the distinctly ecological style of the original research was eventually to spread across the Atlantic, and it was still being executed during the 1950s and 1960s. Hare's (1956) study of Bristol,

Clausen and Kohn's (1959) study of Hagerstown (Maryland), and Rowitz and Levy's (1968) 1960s study of Chicago being just three examples of the genre.

The methodology of the original Chicago study was, perhaps, crude by modern standards, and not so far removed from that which had been adopted by Durkheim in his study of suicide. It essentially consisted of plotting instances of the phenomena under study onto maps and charts and attempting to describe areas with high rates of schizophrenia, suicide or whatever, in terms of other known characteristics. (In terms, for example, of the number of rooming houses, or rates of criminal activity in a given zone.) The fallacy involved in these studies emanated from the fact that one could never be certain that the people who were classified as schizophrenic or as suicides, were the same people who actually lived in the rooming houses or who were in low status or marginal economic positions. And the shortcomings of using such aggregated data were only to be overcome when epidemiologists began to design sophisticated random surveys of individuals – it was only after the Second World War that the technology for constructing such surveys became widely used. Among the first of the postwar studies to address itself to questions of psychiatric epidemiology, however, was that of Hollingshead and Redlich who investigated the distribution of mental illness in New Haven, Connecticut, in 1950 (their results being published in 1958). In the 1958 publication the authors traced the precedents for an examination of the social causes of insanity. The sum total of their references was six – two of which referred to Faris's and Dunham's work, and a further two of which had looked solely at the geographical distribution of insanity – one in Scotland and one in the US. Naturally, the methodological details of the New Haven work need not overconcern us here, except to note that the researchers had by this stage translated an interest in urban zones into an interest in social class – or what they called class status. The study was designed to focus on the ways in which social location was related to prevalence of mental illness and forms of therapy, and the authors concluded that '[S]ignificant interrelations exist between class status and the ways patients reach psychiatrists, how their difficulties are diagnosed, how they are treated, and expenditures on treatment' (Hollingshead and Redlich, 1958: 335).

For example, they discovered that apart from a much higher rate of prevalence of treated psychiatric disorder in the lower social classes, there was also a much higher rate of psychotic disorder than would be expected. Furthermore, patients from different social classes gave expression to different kinds of symptoms, and patients from the lower social classes were much more likely to be subjected to organic or custodial treatment in state mental hospitals than were the middle classes, who were more likely to receive some form of psychotherapy in a private medical setting. A further (and much larger) study of prevalence rates and patterns of causation was also inaugurated a few years after the New Haven study, in 1953. This time, however, the new technology of survey research was applied to a discrete area within New York City (Srole *et al.*, reported on the findings in 1962 and 1977). The results of the study were almost as extensive as the research programme itself, but the authors once again made reference to the inverse relationship which seemed to hold between socio-economic status and psychological 'impairment', as well as to a positive correlation between impairment rates and age, and a significant relationship between marital status and impairment. More important than the specific results obtained, however, was the conceptual framework into which the findings were slotted, for this made extensive reference to a relatively new intervening variable between the mental functioning of individuals and the social circumstances in which they found themselves. The new object of interest was 'stress', and it was a term which the researchers had borrowed directly from engineering parlance. Its use symbolized the fact that human beings could now be viewed in a way akin to steel rods or wooden beams – namely as objects which became deformed when placed under stress from an external environment. In the mechanistic world view of the authors, the most efficient index for predicting mental health risk was assumed to be that derived from the cumulative total of stress factors (such as economic deprivation, poor physical health, broken homes in childhood and so on) to which any given individual was subject. In fact an entirely new calculus of risk and outcome was computed in which psychiatric well being was viewed as a function of what were essentially social and economic stress factors. The claims of the Midtown Manhattan researchers were far from being the first to cite stress as a causal factor in the illness process (Dohrenwend and Dohrenwend (1969) traced the origins of stress hypotheses to 1940s wartime research on combatants and civilians). But in emphasizing the significance of social and economic stress factors for an understanding of mental illness, the Manhattan study epitomized the late twentieth century concern with the power of extra-personal circumstances to impinge on the mental lives of isolated individuals. In that respect the study underlined the theoretical distance which had been travelled since the likes of Kraepelin and Bleuler had surmised that the causes of mental illness were to be found entirely 'in the brain' (Bleuler, 1950: 463).

Perhaps it is characteristic of all scientific activity that its practitioners attempt to resolve what are essentially fundamental differences of world view by appeal to empirical detail – and the history of physical sciences is certainly replete with appropriate examples of such attempts. Yet, as Feyerabend (1975), Kuhn (1970) and others have argued, within any given field, what counts as evidence, explanation and even as relevant instances of the phenomena under study are themselves constantly open to question and vigorous debate. And in the present context it is instructive to analyse responses to the so called downward drift hypothesis as a very real instance of the kinds of incommensurable issues involved in such arguments, for they provide worthy examples of how a theoretical difference can be repeatedly subjected to empirical test without any definitive conclusions being reached.

Almost all of the researchers whose work touched upon the downward drift hypothesis noted the existence of an inverse relationship between social class and prevalence of psychiatric disorder. In fact, some 30 years after the publication of the Chicago study and following a review of 44 studies on social factors and psychiatric disorder, Dohrenwend and Dohrenwend (1969) emphasized that the most consistent result of epidemiological studies showed an 'inverse relationship between social class and psychological symptoms' (1969: 174). The scope of their review had extended across Europe, Asia and North America, and had naturally enough included the 1939 work of Faris and Dunham themselves. Indeed, they paid homage to the aforementioned authors for having posed the 'central issue' relating to social class and psychiatric illness (namely the issue of causation). But they argued that the nature of the association remained 'unexplained'. The problem according to the Dohrenwends was (as almost any elementary text on descriptive statistics might itself have put it) that correlation did not imply causation – so one might be able to demonstrate the existence of a statistical relationship between class and, say, prevalence of schizophrenia easily enough, but one could not thereby claim evidence of a causal link. Thus, whilst the authors of the New Haven and Midtown Manhattan studies felt able to evaluate the drift hypothesis negatively, Goldberg and Morrison (1963), on the basis of a study of hospitalized patients in England and Wales, felt able to evaluate it positively. Indeed, the latter claimed that 'gross socio-economic deprivation' was unlikely to be a factor of major aetiological significance to schizophrenia (1963: 802). The resolution of the broader debate was not, however, simply dependent on the accumulation of empirical evidence alone, but rather upon how one was to define mental illness, and where one was to place the phenomenon of 'socio-economic factors' in causal models. Indeed, whilst some researchers remained content merely to document the stark relationships between social class and prevalence of mental disorder, others maintained that reference to social class in itself explained little or nothing. So in a 10 year follow up study in the New Haven area, for example, Myers and Bean (1968), were happy to demonstrate the presence of 'social components in mental illness' (1968: 4), and to argue that 'social class is related to the outcome of psychiatric treatment and adjustment in the community no matter how they are defined or measured' (1968: 202). In their view, higher class patients were less likely to have had a hospital readmission within the follow up period, more likely to have received a hospital discharge, less likely to receive only drug therapy or custodial care, more likely to receive psychotherapy, and more likely to be able to reintegrate themselves into social networks and economic roles on their release from hospital. Whilst for the Dohrenwends (1969), on the other hand, references to class without mention of stress or social selection made little epidemiological sense. The latter, who had structured their study of social stressors and environmental effects in terms of social causation versus social selection hypotheses, had even devised what they referred to as a 'crucial test' of the social causation hypothesis, only to find that their empirical results were equivocal and could not in themselves provide a definitive conclusion to the debate.

During the late 1960s and early 1970s, this interest in stress factors was recombined with an interest in life events (as, for example, in the work of Brown and Birley, 1968). The significance of life events had of course been highlighted by Adolf Meyer many decades earlier, and had been linked to his recommendation that psychiatrists should construct 'life charts' of their patients. The latter were intended to record significant events in patient histories in the expectation that such histories would cast light on the unique, personal causes of psychiatric disorder. And in the UK, these ideas were quite readily adopted in the work of Mayer-Gross and his colleagues who, in their *Clinical Psychiatry* (1954), proved to be among the first to lay emphasis on the importance of life charts and systematically organized psychiatric interviews for subsequent diagnosis and treatment. The problem with recording life events, however, echoed the problems of recording relationships between class and mental illness in so far that, by themselves, such events revealed nothing about causal sequences. So what was taken to be a predisposing life event by one psychiatrist might simply appear as an effect of an illness to another. Nevertheless, the reinterpretation of the big structural factors (such as class and status), in terms of what were often viewed as randomly distributed, negative life events, generated something of an ideological shift in epidemiological theory. For the task now became one of understanding structural disadvantage in terms of the myriad detail of everyday personal life. One influential study of such processes was to focus on depressive disorders among women in South East London (Brown and Harris, 1978). As well as providing a wealth of information about the onset of illness episodes, the study also underlined the ways in which systems of social support and intimate interpersonal (family) relations could foster or retard the appearance of depression. Somewhat ironically, however, it achieved this during an era in which 'home' and family life were being promoted as havens from illness. In fact, policy makers continued to push ahead with their demands for a redirection of health service resources in favour of community – and especially family – based care and treatment irrespective of any such research findings. Thus many years after Brown and Harris (1978) and others had discussed the complex nature of the relationships which held between family interactions and serious psychiatric disorder, we could still find the healing powers of 'home' life being extolled in a DHSS Report on Neighbourhood Nursing, wherein it was argued that; 'There is an inherent feeling among the public that they recover [from illness] quicker, or at least feel happier at home, and that their quality of life is often better. Research justifies this view and we can see no reason to frustrate people's wishes' (DHSS, 1986: Foreword).

Community As Haven

Community is a word with many meanings.

(Barclay, 1982: xii)

According to Nisbet (1966: 47) community is one of the most 'fundamental and far-reaching' of sociology's central ideas because it points towards the very heart of what are supposed to be 'natural' human relationships. Indeed, in its original nineteenth century formulations, it was a concept which embraced a vision of such relationships as ones founded in cooperation and personal commitment, rather than in competition and impersonal contract. And there can be no doubt that for the likes of Toennies (1971), whose distinction between *Gemeinschaft* and *Gesellschaft* often provides the basis of discussions on the meaning of the community, the archetypical forms of this kind of social organization were to be discovered, above all, in kinship, neighbourhood and friendship. This was so because these latter were all rooted in the furtherance of what Toennies called intimate and internal social relationships (1971: 68).

Naturally, we need not concern ourselves here with the history of sociological thought, but we can note that whilst the concept of community left nineteenth century sociology as an abstract and generalizing notion, it entered twentieth century sociology as a descriptive, empirical term. In fact, empirical sociology quickly established that relationships in communities were not always as cooperative, intimate and supportive as the founders of sociology might have either argued or wished. So (as we have seen), the early research programme of the Chicago sociologists (1916–39) revealed that very different types of communities existed within different zones of the same city, and some of those communities were regarded by such sociologists as being 'disorganized' – and as fostering various kinds of deviant social behaviour. Thus, as Zorbaugh (1929) was to demonstrate; life on the 'Gold Coast' (of Chicago) was very different from life in the slum. Despite the Chicago work, however, the concept of community managed to preserve much of its rosy glow, so that even in the works of European based anthropologists and sociologists it was, broadly speaking, the cooperative, intimate side of human existence that was emphasized in empirical studies of rural and urban communities. In the British Isles, for example, a whole series of such studies published between the late 1930s and the early 1960s (many of which were reviewed by Frankenberg, 1966) emphasized the interdependent, communal and collaborative efforts of people living in small scale localities. And whilst one eye, at least, was always kept on the changing nature of social life, the discordant, disruptive or antagonistic features of community existence were rarely highlighted. In that respect, communities were viewed as a resource on which individuals could call in times of need, crisis, or simply during the occasion of the common *rites de passage*.

More pertinently, of course, it was (more than anything) this supportive and cathartic side of community life which was emphasized in the field of psychiatry. In some respects we can even see how the nineteenth century English asylum had been designed (if not actually organized) as a supportive community, and it is certainly the case that the early twentieth century colony system had been advocated partly on the grounds of its caring, supportive qualities. So as Scull (1989: 302) put it, 'any discussion of "community care" for the mentally ill must begin by paying serious attention to the mental hospital' – for the latter, if nothing else, was built on the intention of providing care in a community setting. Indeed, the possibility for improving the community features of hospital life was still being actively pursued right up until the 1960s, and nowhere more so was this the case than in the work of those who supported the therapeutic community movement.

The detailed history and evolving nature of therapeutic communities has been reviewed in numerous publications – see, for example, Bloor *et al.* (1988), Clark (1965, 1977), and Jones (1968) – and there is no need to recap that detail here. We can note, however, that two of the central figures in the development of such communities – Main and Maxwell Jones (at the Northfield and Belmont hospitals respectively) – only began to formulate their ideas on therapeutic communities during the late 1940s and to implement them during the 1950s. Jones, in his own account, recalls how his psychiatry began to 'focus far beyond the patient as a sick individual' (1968: 200) so as to look at 'problems in living' and systems of social support in general. The redirected vision then encouraged him to consider specific features of routine hospital organization as a potential psychiatric resource. And in particular he began to argue for the involvement of patients and junior nursing staff, as well as more established figures (psychiatrists, social workers, senior nurses), in the provision of therapy. In fact, he intended his therapeutic communities to be run democratically and constructively, and in this regard the daily 'community meeting' was to play a pivotal role in the development of both group life and in the life of the individual. Above all, however, in Jones's therapeutic community, treatment was regarded as a product of 'normal interactions of healthy community life' (Watson, 1953: vii), rather than as a product of drugs, shocks or psychotherapy. In that respect his therapeutic strategy was quite revolutionary, and during the 1950s the ideas of the therapeutic community movement had a noticeable impact on various forms of mental hospital organization. (Though according to Clark (1977) most organizational innovations were usually restricted to just one or two wards in the larger hospital environment.) Most important of all, however, was the fact that, as far as Jones, Main and even Clark himself, were concerned, the notion of 'healthy community life' was not in any sense inconsistent with life in an institutional setting.

Hospital based therapeutic communities were not, of course, the only kinds of communities to emerge and develop during the period under question. In fact, in psychiatric as in other fields, the therapeutic community movement began to appear in the world beyond the old asylum walls. The founding of the Richmond Fellowship in 1959, for example, led to a growth of therapeutic communities in ordinary urban settings, and during the 1960s Laing and his associates – in line with the times – moved out of 'Villa 21' in

Shenley Hospital to relocate at Kingsley Hall in East London. (The latter, in contrast to most types of therapeutic community, was specifically aimed at the needs of schizophrenic patients.) In discussing this move a few years later, Cooper (1967) was to argue that the move out of hospital was in itself a 'step forward' (1967: 104). Yet what was paradoxical about these moves from hospital to community was the fact that they were being carried out at the same time as the epidemiological studies were beginning to suggest that it was the accumulation of stressful events in everyday (community) living that was related to the onset of illness episodes. This apparent contradiction was, however, an inevitable result of psychiatry's focus on the social, wherein human relationships were increasingly viewed as holding the key to both the genesis of abnormal personality developments, and to their correction.

The community into which patients of the late 1950s and early 1960s were about to be moved was undoubtedly a poorly understood entity. This, perhaps, was not so surprising when we recognize that even in the academic world there was considerable ambiguity in the meaning of the term. (The American social scientist Hillery (1955), for example, felt able to cite some 94 different definitions of the word and to conclude that their only common factor was that they all referred, in some way or another, to people.) More interestingly, however, and during that same period, many anthropologists such as Barnes (1954), Bott (1957), and Mitchell (1969), had begun to analyse communities in terms of a new conceptual system. In fact, they proposed that individuals should be seen as the foci of social networks rather than as members of ill-defined communities, and further, that variations in an individual's social behaviour could be interpreted as a product of network links. This new and somewhat radical conceptualization of personal behaviour and group relationships in effect spelt out the demise of the old community concept, and so replaced an ambiguous and hazy term with one which could be operationalized through a series of measures and mathematical operations (Scott, 1988). It was a focus of analysis which was readily adopted by researchers in the field of psychiatry, and the popularity of the new terminology in studies of mental health is probably best attested to by the fact that during the mid-1980s Biegel *et al.* (1985) felt able to list more than 1,430 items in their bibliography on social networks and mental health. By implication, it was evident that, in the field of epidemiology at least, 'stress' was coming to be seen more and more as the property of network interrelationships rather than as the property of the poorly theorized entity called community.

Perhaps it is in the nature of social policy that it is slow moving in its adoption of technical ideas. In any event, it is certainly clear that the understanding of 'community' in British social policy hardly shifted between 1926 (which is marked by the publication of the Macmillan Commission on Lunacy and Mental Deficiency), and 1988 (the publication year of *Community Care: Agenda for Action* (DSS, 1988)). In fact, throughout that period community was equated simply and clearly with the non-hospital world. The Macmillan Commission had restricted its comments on community to features of what it called 'after care', whilst the more recent document placed the community at the heart of policy making, but in both cases there was an absence of any assessment about what a community might be, or of what it might consist. Only in the field of social work did any new assessment of 'community' appear. That assessment occurred in the Barclay Report, wherein community was defined 'as a network of informal relationships between people' (1982: 199). And as we have seen, the Report argued for a fundamental reorientation of the social worker's task so as to take account of such networks. Naturally, such a claim slotted in rather neatly with the contemporaneous discovery of 'informal care' and the centrality of family and kin to the social worlds of dependent individuals. Studies of how such networks might operate in practice, however, and what care in the community might mean for mentally ill people, remained rather thin on the ground.

As Kirk and Therrien (1975) argued (in relation to American experience), the policy of integrating hospitalized psychiatric patients into the community was 'devoid of any systematic analysis of what constitutes a relevant community' (1975: 213). And so in actual practice ex-patients were not so much reintegrated into community life but 'ghettoized' in the poorer and least desirable areas of US cities. This absence of research, and failure to analyse the community into which ex-patients were to live was also characteristic of the study region. In a similar fashion researchers like Scull (1984, 1989) argued that the process of 'decarceration' resulted not so much in 'deinstitutionalization', but in the transfer of patients from large hospitals organized mainly along medical lines, to smaller institutions which usually lacked any form of therapeutic facility. Such a process of what some researchers have referred to as 'transinstitutionalization' has also been accompanied by a 'transfer of care' (P. Brown, 1985) from medical to social welfare organizations, with all its attendant organizational consequences. And we shall shortly see how this process of transinstitutionalization was reflected in the fates of the study group patients (very few of whom were transferred to individual homes). For now, however, we need to note that the empirical evidence on the fates of patients who were transferred to community settings was, to say the least, equivocal. So whilst the conclusions of Korman and Glennerster (1990) and the Personal Social Services Research Unit (PSSRU, 1989) suggested favourable outcomes (at least for mentally handicapped patients), a great deal of US evidence and some UK evidence pointed to a tawdry tale of the neglect and isolation of ex-patients. (Scull, 1989 reviews a lot of the US evidence, and some of the UK evidence is reviewed by Prior, 1991a; Tomlinson, 1991.)

Yet, perhaps the most interesting of all the detailed findings on the fates of psychiatric patients in the community were those of Jodelet (1991), who examined the social worlds of community based psychiatric patients in the context of studying lay representations of mental illness. In that context she demonstrated how the 'otherness' of the psychiatric patient is forever underlined in interactions with those with whom they live and work. For madness, suggests Jodelet, is often regarded as a polluting substance which must be controlled and kept at bay – even to the extent of segregating people who live in the same house, or by the allocation of different eating utensils among the sane and the afflicted. In that respect her work replicates the findings of one of the very few studies into community attitudes to the mentally ill which was ever carried out in the hospital age. The study was that of Cumming and Cumming (1957), and one of its most telling conclusions was that, 'on the whole the people of [the study community] do not wish to have very much contact with mental illness either on the personal or social level' (1957: 109).

Mental Illness in the Community

When concepts change, stated Winch, 'that means that our concept of the world has changed too' (1958: 15). In this respect, an examination of the shifting discourse on community is more than just a clumsy exercise in etymology. For we can see how the distinct alterations in our notions of what mental illness might be, is in part dependent on our changed comprehension of what community is. Thus, a new understanding of community as social network, or a new understanding of community disorganization as class disadvantage, throws light on previously unexplored problems of aetiology. In fact, we can broaden this argument considerably to show how social science in general has altered professional representations of psychiatric disorder. For by borrowing, and then using the emergent sociological language of role, class, status and family, epidemiologists of psychiatric disorder proved able to construct radically new models of causation. So in place of a vision of mental illnesses as biological diseases, it became increasingly possible to understand them as a reaction to social isolation, or social disadvantage, or even to social and economic 'stressors'. In a similar way, new social scientific understandings of femaleness (from the 1970s onwards), provided the basis for new insights into the relationship between women and such disorders as depression and hysteria (Miles, 1988). Whilst the reinterpretation of biological 'race' as socially constructed ethnicity, provided a radical insight into the relationships which held between skin colour and the diagnosis of mental illness.

But in addition to the various theoretical and conceptual revolutions which occurred within psychiatric epidemiology, we can also see how surveys of community life, in themselves, produced alterations in professional understandings of mental illnesses. For such surveys opened up a vision of psychiatric disorders as being merely the more extreme forms of what could otherwise be considered as commonplace and ordinary forms of thought and behaviour. Consequently, survey data were often used to crush the old ontological notions of insanity (which had reified diagnostic categories), and to replace them with an image of psychiatric illnesses as things which were only quantitatively (rather than qualitatively) different from the normal. In other words, they helped to shift psychiatry away from notions of disease and towards an understanding of psychiatric disorders as syndromes. It was unfortunate only that these new images failed to have an impact on lay representations of illness, which – if the work of Cumming and Cumming (1957) and Jodelet (1991) is to be relied upon – continued to regard such illnesses as shameful and stigmatizing diseases. But perhaps the greatest change of all was truly to be found in the language of social policy rather than in the field of epidemiology; and in particular in a redefinition of the term community so as to exclude its older, religious connotations and to emphasize its geographical and locational ones. Hence, in the new lexicon of the late twentieth century, it became impossible to equate community with asylum, or havens with hospitals. Instead it was taken for granted that the worst home was always superior to the best institution.

6

Representations of Psychiatric Disorder in the Family

> Far from being the basis of the good society, the family, with its narrow privacy and tawdry secrets, is the source of all our discontents.
>
> Edmund Leach (1967: 44)

Deborah Kallikak and Dora

In his 1912 account of the travails of the Kallikak family, Goddard included a photograph of teenage Deborah – well dressed, comfortably seated and well occupied with a sewing task. The photograph was included so as to demonstrate to readers what could be achieved for people from Deborah's background. In Deborah's case that background included the all important fact that she was the great-great granddaughter of the feebleminded Martin Kallikak. This latter had some 480 descendants, of whom 143 had supposedly been 'defective' (feebleminded), whilst only 47 had been normal (the remainder were 'tainted'). Deborah, of course, was included among the former. As Goddard was keen to indicate, 'All this degeneracy has come as the result of the defective mentality and bad blood having been brought into the normal family of good blood' (1912: 69). And in making this reference to 'bad blood' Goddard was expressing a fundamental truism of early twentieth century psychiatry – namely that mental defect was an inherited characteristic transmitted from generation to generation through bodily fluids. It was a belief which was to persist at least until 1938 when Penrose concluded – on the basis of his studies in Colchester – that 'the aetiology of mental defect is multiple' (1938: 70). It was, therefore, neither a product of simple genetic, nor of environmental, nor of pathological causes alone, but rather a product of multiple causes interacting.

Our interest in genetics stems from the fact that, throughout the century, the family often entered into studies of mental illness by virtue of its function as a reservoir of hereditary influences. And it was certainly the case that during earlier decades most forms of mental defect and of mental illness were assumed to have hereditary origins. Thus, of the two major forms of mental illness which had been identified by Kraepelin – dementia praecox and manic depression – both were regarded as having a genetic cause. And this mistaken belief in the hereditary origins of mental defect and illness, combined with a very crude understanding of how Mendelian processes expressed themselves in human beings, encouraged the members of some interest groups (such as the eugenicists) to argue for the isolation of the mentally ill on the simple grounds that it served as a necessary, though far from sufficient, check on the reproduction of the biologically unfit (see Kevles, 1985).

It would of course be quite wrong to suggest that the theory of hereditary degeneration provided the only context in terms of which the family entered into deliberations about mental illness. For there was quite clearly a second context in terms of which illness and the family were intermingled, and its origins are to be found in a case history of another teenage girl – namely, one called Dora. Dora was a patient of Freud's during the very earliest years of the century; her case study was first published in 1905. Dora had presented Freud with both physical and psychological symptoms – mainly nervous coughing, migraine, and depression – which Freud grouped together as symptoms of *petite hystérie*. In analysing the cause of the girl's disorder Freud was keen to point out that he did not wish to 'give an impression of underestimating the importance of heredity in the aetiology of hysteria' (1977: 50), but he nevertheless felt that its true origins were to be located elsewhere – namely in, 'a psychical trauma, a conflict of affects, and a disturbance in the sphere of sexuality' (1977: 54). These trauma's and affects revealed themselves both in Dora's dreams and the psychotherapeutic process to which she became subject, and in her revelations Freud began to see the family in a different light from that of his contemporaries. In fact, for Freud, the family no longer appeared as a simple reservoir of hereditary influences, but as a dynamic social and sexual unit – the machinations of which lay at the origin of powerful psychological forces. And in offering us this vision, Freud opened up the possibility for new routes into the study of family life which were later to be adopted by members of paramedical and associated psychiatric professions. Indeed, it was Freudian theory, combined with growing sociological insights into the interactive structure of the family, which laid the basis for modern forms of family therapy. In spite of Freud's influence, however, psychiatric, nursing and social work interest in the dynamic properties of family life never entirely managed to eclipse the interests of the geneticists. So the assertion that mental illnesses – and especially serious illnesses such as schizophrenia – have a genetic base, has been persistent throughout the century (Boyle, 1990). These days, of course, there is what Lewontin (1992) has called the 'new eugenics', which is based essentially on the chemistry of the nucleotides (DNA). It is a eugenics which claims to explain most of what we need to know about human ailments (including psychiatric ailments), and in that respect it echoes many of the grand and fallacious claims of its forerunners.

An Illness Inherited

In his *Genesis and Development of a Scientific Fact*, Fleck (1979) points out that the test for syphilitic antibodies *had* to be a blood test – simply because late nineteenth and early twentieth century medical authorities regarded syphilitic infection, rather like madness, as being 'in the blood'. In other words, the (socially based) belief about infection being in the blood predated the scientific discovery. And in much the same way, it is clear that the origins of mental defect and mental illness were sought in the genes not because there was any scientific basis for the belief, but rather because belief in the hereditary transmission of mental disease was central to the ethos of nineteenth century (and even twentieth century) psychiatry. In other words, madness was believed to result from hereditary causes long before any systematic scientific theory of hereditary transmission was available, and well before any empirical evidence for such a belief was collected. Indeed, for much of the current century, still less the nineteenth century, it was not even clear what the unit of hereditary transmission in humans might be. Furthermore, until 1955 it was not even possible for biologists to state with any accuracy the number of basic units – such as chromosomes – which existed in human cell tissue. Yet despite this amazing dearth of fundamental information we can read in textbook after textbook how mental defects and mental illnesses were in essence, forms of inherited genetic disorder.

    R.H. Cole in the first edition of his *Mental Diseases* (1913), for example, appeared quite definite about the origins of dementia praecox when he stated that, 'Dementia Praecox invariably originates from a neuropathic stock' (1913: 157). And this exact same reference to the insane stock of dementia praecox patients can also be found in Stoddart's *Mind and its Disorders* (1908). In fact, in Stoddart's work, the genetic claims are combined with information concerning the ways in which the legacy of insane stock manifested itself in the physical stigmata of degeneration – which were supposedly visible in such things as the shape of the face, the jaws, the ears and the skull. Naturally, what was claimed about the origins of mental illness was also claimed of mental deficiency (though the distinctions between the two categories of disorder were not so clearly made during the earlier part of the century as they were during the latter part). Thus Tredgold (1922) in his *Mental Deficiency* distinguished between dementia (or decay), and amentia (the failure to achieve normal mental development). Amentia was subdivided into primary and secondary, and the former was defined a priori as being hereditary. (The term amentia was retained in the subtitle of Tredgold's texts until the tenth, 1963, edition when it was changed to subnormality.) Yet what an hereditary cause might be and how hereditary influences were transmitted through the generations was quite uncertain. So Maudsley, for example, in his *Heredity, Variation and Genius* (1908), could waffle on that, 'Everybody is typically what he is because his progenitors were what they were, like having begotten like; he inherits the form, traits and qualities of the stock from which he proceeds' (1908: 1). But more learned minds were well aware of the complexities involved in genetics. Thus Bateson, in his 1906 address to the neurological society on 'Mendelian heredity and its application to Man', openly stated that, 'The detection of systems of heredity is not a simple matter', even in the stock of sweet peas (1906: 178). Indeed, Mendel's papers on heredity, which concerned the transmission of characteristics of peas rather than maniacs, were published in English for the first time (in the Royal Horticultural Society's Journal) only in 1901. And Bateson's own *Mendel's Principles of Heredity* was not to follow until 1909, by which time he too began to talk of the 'sociological applications' of Mendelian principles.

At the biological level, therefore, things were far from clear. Hansemann, for example, had counted chromosomes in human tissue in 1891, but it was not until 1903 that the chromosome was established as the seat of the hypothesized hereditary units, the genes. And this latter discovery was achieved through work on the fruit fly rather than humankind (Hirschhorn and Cooper, 1961). In fact, the counting of chromosomes in human tissue remained an awkward and difficult business for most of the century – mainly because of the technical difficulties involved in preserving human cellular tissue. Between 1891 and 1923, for example, there had been at least 26 studies carried out on this very problem – producing various counts ranging from 16 to 48. But in 1923 Painter reported on his observation of tissue removed from the testes of three mental patients in the Texas State Asylum – each one of whom had been guilty of 'excessive self abuse coupled with certain phases of insanity' (Painter, 1923: 293). He concluded that both the Negro and the White tissue showed evidence of 48 chromosomes. And this count was persistently confirmed until 1955 when Tijo and Levan established that there were only 46 chromosomes in human tissue. (In fact, the correction does not actually appear in texts on medical genetics until the late 1950s and early 1960s – see, for example, Roberts's *Medical Genetics* of 1959.) Equally difficult was the problem of identifying a difference in the morphology of cell nuclei according to the sex of the individual providing the tissue. As with chromosome counts, numerous suggestions were made during the century as to how the identification could be achieved. Though the capacity to distinguish between males and females according to the chromatin body in the cells was only finalized in 1950. In short, therefore, during the first half of the century it was impossible to either correctly identify the number of chromosomes in human tissue or to identify the sex of the tissue donor on the basis of microscopic data. Yet such lacunas failed to impede eugenicists from claiming that recognizable mental disorders had a genetic base. In 1958 however, it was announced that Down's syndrome (Mongolism) might be attributable to the presence of an extra chromosome in the carrier – that is, someone whose cells contained 47 instead of the normal 46 chromosomes. (It was this latter discovery which further led some medical geneticists to claim the chromosome as their specialist 'organ' (Kevles, 1985: 249).) Following this, experts in the field of mental deficiency suggested that the term Mongolism (a term originally adopted with intentional racial connotations), be replaced by the more technical 'trisomy-21', or more neutral Down's syndrome.

Fortunately for the eugenicists, the attempt to explain mental illness as the consequence of inherited defect did not depend on developments at the cellular level. Indeed, from the turn of the century until the 1950s, the main claims concerning the inheritance of such defect hinged on the principles of mathematics rather than on the principles of biology. Thus, as Pearson had stated to Galton (in 1897), the problems of genetics were 'in the first place statistical, in the second place statistical, and only in the third place biological' (Pearson 1930, 3: 128). And it was primarily as a source of data for the statisticians that family histories collected by psychiatrists were really to come into their own. In this respect Goddard's work on the Kallikaks, and Dugdale's (1910) work on the degenerate Jukes (first published 1877), were precursors of a genre. And it was on the basis of family data that Henderson and Gillespie, in the first edition of their *Textbook of Psychiatry* (1927), expressed themselves as convinced of the inherited genetic basis of schizophrenia (the new name for dementia praecox) as were Cole and Stoddart before them. In fact, basing their conclusion on an assessment of family incidence – they claimed that 50 to 60 per cent of schizophrenics were known to have a genetic tendency to such a disorder. Indeed, psychiatrists in general believed that by combining genealogical studies with the principles of probability theory it would prove possible to draw valid inferences about the extent to which mental illnesses were or were not inherited. Though in actual fact, systematic studies of inheritance patterns of psychotics remained uncommon.

One of the earliest and most influential studies of the problem was that of Kallman (1938). Kallman had studied the clinical notes of some 1,087 schizophrenic patients who had been housed in the Herzberg Hospital (Berlin) between 1893 and 1903. His aim was to detect the hereditary basis of schizophrenia (not, one may note, to question the heredity thesis). Naturally enough this necessitated his gathering information on the ancestors of his selected study group. And rather like Goddard before him, Kallman had to allocate ancestors to some notional diagnostic category. In Kallman's case he wished to determine whether or not a patient's ancestors were 'tainted'. Given that most of the ancestors were dead by the time the study was carried out, it was to be no easy task, and consequently Kallman was forced to guess whether or not proband ancestors had any schizophrenic taints. The guessing was of course carried out on the basis of certain rules. Thus, 'taints' were said to be evidenced by the presence of death from suicide, tuberculosis and alcoholism in the family; or, failing that, the presence of cranks, eccentrics, or psychopathic types among earlier generations. In addition, the stubborn, perverse, recalcitrant and malicious were also included among the tainted. Thus, one of Kallman's so called case histories indicated that the patient's mother had been: 'Slovenly and very pious and had curious hobbies. [She] took offence easily, dressed conspicuously but without taste. Often behaved like a queer old bird' (1938: 202). Kallman diagnosed this woman as 'schizoid psychopathic'. And his position was no safer when he considered his sample of patients – for by the time that he came to carry out his study, members of the sample population (as with the ancestors) had either died or had left hospital and were therefore unavailable for direct study. Kallman, however, had deliberately designed his study as a retrospective one and he thus diagnosed the members of his sample group on the basis of hospital notes alone. Yet in spite of the somewhat dubious procedures on which his research was built, Kallman displayed few uncertainties when he came to draw his conclusions. Thus, said Kallman, 'The genotype of schizophrenia is a single recessive trait, penetrating only with a probable manifestation of approximately 70 per cent'

(1938: 163). In defiance of its manifest shortcomings, however, Kallman's work was cited in psychiatric texts as evidence for the existence of inherited schizophrenic traits right up to the early 1960s – and the 0.7 probability of inheriting the disease is still quoted as a plausible upper limit in numerous reviews (Brooker, 1990). Kallman's was far from being the only twentieth century study which focused on the inheritance of schizophrenia. More interestingly still, it was not the only such study to be shot through with serious methodological flaws – indeed, Boyle (1990) has recently reviewed much of the evidence concerning the inheritance of schizophrenic traits and found most of it wanting. Whilst a recent Medical Research Council Report has suggested that schizophrenia is far from being 'a simple genetic condition' (Medical Research Council, 1987: 20). But as was pointed out earlier, the broad plot and the conclusion of the story relating to the hereditary transmission of serious mental illness had already been worked out well in advance of any evidence and it was not therefore a belief which was likely to be upset by the mere absence of facts.

This concentration on inheritance stemmed in part from a confusion about what was genetic and what was inherited – textbook writers, in particular, tending to conflate the two. In human genetics, this particular confusion was laid to rest in 1930, but it took many decades for the distinction to percolate through to textbook level. In fact, the problem of non-inherited genetic disease had first arisen in the context of the study of haemophilia, where observations had shown that in spite of the fact that many haemophiliacs died before fathering any children, the incidence of haemophilia in the general population did not tend to diminish. Suggestions that contemporary haemophiliacs were the residue of a much larger ancestral group encouraged someone to calculate that if that were so, then the entire British population must have been haemophiliac in the tenth century AD. But in 1930 Haldane – one of the most influential of British geneticists during the interwar period – suggested, somewhat more reasonably, that the population of haemophiliacs must in fact be sustained by people becoming fresh carriers of the disease on account of mutation (see Kevles, 1985). And this was a suggestion which Penrose took up in his analysis of his Colchester data. Penrose was interested in epiloia – a disorder associated with idiocy, epilepsy and tumour formation in human organs. Since his patients did not reproduce in any number at all, he concluded that the appearance of the disorder must be attributable in part to mutation – the latter accounting for up to one-third of cases. Indeed, it was on the basis of his studies in Colchester that Penrose came to doubt the value of inheritance as a source of disease in the first place – estimating that no more than one-quarter of Colchester cases were attributable to heredity. Thus in his *The Biology of Mental Defect* (1949) Penrose argued that three conditions needed to be fulfilled for a disease to be called inherited. There should, he said, be a specific condition to identify; every affected person should have one parent affected, and about one half of sibs should be affected when there is an affected parent. Yet, he concluded, 'very few inherited diseases agree precisely with these specifications' (1949: 69).

Genetics during the interwar period, then, clearly drew its theoretical force from mathematics rather than biology, and it was only during the post Second World War era that the latter gained the ascendancy. The double helix structure of DNA, for example, was untangled in the early 1950s – though it makes its first appearance in many medical texts, such as Roberts's *Medical Genetics* (5th edition) only in 1970 – and by means of both that and many other discoveries concerning the ways in which genes produced enzymes, it became clear that single genes could only ever account for a small fraction of human disorders – most of the latter being, at best, polygenic and therefore not fully understood even at the end of the twentieth century. This has not, of course, prevented some authors from reasserting that schizophrenia and other serious disorders are genetically determined. In fact, and according to McGuffin and Murray (1991), the search is still on for the genetic markers of mental illness in families. Yet as Lewontin (1992) points out, such claims constitute part of a new ideological package which is as riddled with inconsistencies as was the old eugenics. In consequence it is clear that, in terms of hypotheses at least, we end the century more or less as it began. Modern biology has, however, introduced at least one new social role into the world – that of the genetic counsellor. It is not a role which impinges, as yet, on the field of mental health and illness, but its appearance serves to underline the ways in which throughout the century the family has been linked to illness in terms of its providing a genetic or chemical pool of disease, rather than as a generator of socially constituted illness.

In the light of these remarks, then, it is at least evident that although genetics was believed by the members of certain interest groups to be at the heart of 'mental' conditions, practising geneticists were never in a position to provide any diagnostic criteria by means of which specific psychotic (or neurotic) conditions could be distinguished. Even the differences between Tredgold's amentia and the dementias were never clearly sorted out on a genetic basis. Perhaps that is why the *Report of the Mental Deficiency Committee*

(1929) proposed that, 'The only really satisfactory criterion of mental deficiency is the social one.' That is, a mentally deficient person could only be distinguished from a normal person on the grounds that he or she was 'incapable of independent social adaptation' (1929: 13). And perhaps that is why Penrose had argued that the nature of mental deficiency was partly biological, partly mental (as might be evidenced by such things as abnormally low IQ scores), partly behavioural and mostly social. In any event, we know that for most of the current century a large number of the 'mental' disorders which necessitated institutionalization could only be recognized in terms of impaired social and cognitive functioning rather than as clearly distinguishable genetic diseases. And it is precisely because mental illness is seen as a product of complex interrelationships between social, organic and behavioural factors that the attribution of the term has been rendered so problematic in the modern world. Indeed, and as we shall discover shortly, it was only in and through a mixture of social, psychological, organic and behavioural assessments that the peculiarities of the patients in the study group were understood.

An Illness Nurtured

Freud published his first case of child analysis – that of 'Little Hans' – in 1909. From the outset Freud doubted whether Hans was a 'degenerate child condemned by his heredity to be a neurotic' (1977: 298), but the very mention of the possibility reflected one of the central cultural precepts in terms of which psychiatric work was being carried out in central Europe during this period. As with Dora, however, Freud ultimately located the origins of Hans's anxieties and phobias in sexual impulses – and especially those which arose in a family context – and in so doing he opened up the possibility of seeing the symptoms of neurosis in terms of effects which were present in social groupings rather than just individual patients. (Many years later Eysenck (1965) was to suggest that it was J.B. Watson's behaviourist analysis of Little Albert rather than Freud's analysis of Little Hans that should provide the paradigm case for a psychiatric understanding of neurotic reactions in childhood.) Whilst Freud pointed the way towards the exploration of family dynamics as a factor in the generation and sustaining of the neuroses, however, he nevertheless shied away from arguing that social, rather than internal psychological relations, should form the primary objects of study and practice. And this, of course, is why the case histories are written in terms of Dora and Hans rather than in terms of their families. In fact, the first psychoanalytic treatise to be concerned with the influence of family life on the psychology of individuals was not to appear until 1921 when Flugel's *Psycho-Analytic Study of the Family* was published.

In many ways, and as Freud's own deliberations suggest, the psychiatric analysis of the family was in large part dependent upon the emergence of the child as a distinct object of medical and psychiatric practice. In this respect the publication of his 'Analysis of a Phobia in a Five Year Old Boy', was itself a significant marker. Indeed, Freud's focus on childhood was but one expression of a much broader interest in children which was evident in and through various aspects of late nineteenth and early twentieth century medical practice (see Prior, 1992). In terms of psychiatry, for example, we have already noted how the Maudsley Hospital opened up a department for children in 1920, how the Tavistock Clinic followed in 1926, and how the very first London clinic for child guidance was opened in 1927. During roughly the same period, and on the theoretical front, psychiatry texts began to include chapters on the disorders of children and childhood. Thus, Henderson and Gillespie included a chapter on Child Psychiatry in the third (1932) edition of their *Textbook*. Though for most psychiatrists, the child's family continued to appear almost solely in the context of 'history taking' (that is, in terms of the search for insane ancestors of the patient), rather than in the context of social interrelations. This belief in the so called inborn causes of mental disorder (together with a recommendation for the adoption of a eugenic programme) was reflected, for example, in every Henderson and Gillespie text from the time of the first edition in 1927 right through to the time of the eighth edition in 1956. Even in Curran and Guttman's *Psychological Medicine* (1943), which was heavily indebted to the ideas of social psychiatry, the family only appeared to the extent that it might be considered as the source and origin of hereditary taints. And it was not really until well after the Second World War that mainstream texts in psychiatry began to address themselves to the family as something other than a biological source of disease.

As Ackerman suggested, the war had served to focus attention 'on the fundamental interdependence of the individual and the group' (1966, 3: 202), and thereby had given a tremendous boost to the claims of the social psychiatrists, and thence to those of the family therapists. But war in itself was far from sufficient to structure the distinct ways in which family life was to enter into psychiatric discourse in the post 1945 era. In fact that entry was primarily dependent upon modes of theorizing and conceptualization which had been developed in academic social science rather than in military medicine. And it was not really until sociologists began to analyse the family as a system of social relationships – instead of as a static legal and domestic unit – that family life was able to be properly theorized as an important and significant influence on personal psychological processes. Among the earliest steps taken in this regard were those of E.W. Burgess (of the Chicago School), in a paper published in 1926 in which he suggested that the family could be seen as a 'unity of interacting personalities' (1926: 3), rather than as a mechanism for controlling fixed and static human instincts. In so doing, he opened up the possibilities for studying the family as a dynamic socio-psychological entity, though somewhat unfortunately, he failed to provide any insight into the exact mechanism by means of which personalities could be formed or developed within the family setting. Indeed, it was not until the posthumous publication of G.H. Mead's work in the 1930s (Mead, 1934) that any real socio-psychological answers to problems of personality development appeared. When they did appear, it was the concepts of reflexive conduct and role taking which took centre stage. And it was, above all, the claim that human beings could in a sense 'internalize' social relationships which opened up the possibility for considering personal psychological properties as mirror images of social relations. These Meadian notions concerning the internalization of external social relations were, of course, to be further followed through by a wide range of sociological investigators during the early 1950s. Thus Parsons *et al.* (1953), for example, married socio-psychological notions of personality and self to the concept of a 'social system'. And by interpreting the family as such a system, they were then able to suggest how it could induct and then sustain its members in 'deviant' forms of cognition, perception and behaviour.

When these various ideas eventually infiltrated into the work of psychiatrists during the mid 1950s, it was perhaps inevitable that some would be tempted to see the family as capable of nurturing diverse forms of psychological disorder. Lidz *et al.* (1957), for example, argued that certain families absorbed into themselves divisions and distortions of reality which then resurfaced in the personalities of their (schizophrenic) members. So the fact of a marital 'schism', for example, might manifest itself in a personality schism. Whilst Wynne *et al.* (1958) argued that, in general, the 'overall family role structure', together with patterns of human interrelations within the family were, 'taken over into the child's personality structure' (1958: 642–3), and that where those structures and relations were perverse, schizophrenic personality types arose. Similarly, Vogel and Bell (1968), working on data gathered from a late 1950s research programme, analysed the 'emotionally disturbed child' and described such disturbance as a direct product of scapegoating mechanisms in the family. And most influential of all were the arguments of Bateson *et al.* (1956), concerning the 'double-bind' manoeuvre in families.

The paper written by Bateson and his colleagues was entitled 'Toward a theory of schizophrenia', and in it they sought to suggest that circumstances sometimes arose in families whereby one member in particular (called a victim), was repeatedly subjected to contradictory demands from another. The persistent and illogical nature of the process meant that victims eventually proved unable to respond to the demands placed upon them, and they consequently suffered a 'breakdown' in their ability to communicate with all others. The focus of Bateson *et al.* was essentially on child–parent relationships, and the authors saw in the double-binding process the genesis of schizophrenic reactions. During the 1950s and 1960s the theory proved attractive to a number of psychiatrists, not least because it broadened the focus of attention onto the group and away from the isolated individual. More specifically, it threw attention onto maladjusted parents as well as maladjusted children, for, as Cooper was to put it many years later, '[t]he real illogic, or illness of logic, is [now] seen to be in the parents' (1967: 45). (Interestingly, a number of parents of people in the study group had some knowledge of this and related theories concerning the genesis of schizophrenia, and invariably resented its implications – preferring instead to think of schizophrenia as a physical, even genetic, disease.) Naturally, many of the 1950s claims about schizophrenia and its relationship to family life were later to resurface in the work of R.D. Laing and his associates. And when they did, they became entangled in a broad *mélange* of ideas about labelling processes, the socio-genesis of mental illness, the essential rationality of madness and the intrinsic evil of institutionalizing the insane. More significantly, it was this (sometimes inconsistent) mixture of beliefs and suggestions which came to form the ideological core of what was eventually to be called the 'anti-psychiatry movement' (Tantam, 1991).

R.D. Laing's views on the nature of mental illness are by no means easy to decipher. This is in large part because he changed and revised his views frequently. Siegler *et al.* (1969) detected at least three 'models of madness' in Laing's 1960s work alone. Consequently, the schizophrenia described in *The Divided Self* (1959) is not the same as the schizophrenia described in *The Self and Others* (1961) or *Sanity, Madness and The Family* (Laing and Esterson, 1964). For in the last two works Laing turned directly towards an examination of interpersonal relations for an account of the genesis of insanity, whilst in the first he sought to base an understanding of schizophrenia in the language of 'schizophrenics' themselves. Nevertheless, the notion that schizophrenia was to be viewed as a property of group interrelations rather than as a disease of an isolated individual ran as a common thread throughout his work. Naturally, of all the relevant social groups which served to structure individual lives, the family was considered to be among the most important and it was there that Laing, Esterson and Cooper focused their attention. In so far as the anti-psychiatrists examined social processes rather than social structures, however, it was the operation of labelling procedures which caught their attention. So Cooper (1970), for example, not only argued that 'madness' was a property of systems of social relationships rather than of persons, (i.e. 'There are no schizophrenics' (1970: 43)), but also that schizophrenia was nothing more than a label which psychiatrists and others used to describe behaviour which they did not like. In that respect psychiatrists were viewed 'at best as the policemen of society' (Tantam, 1991: 341) – and psychiatric hospitals as gaols. Though in so far as anti-psychiatry expressed antipathy to the mental hospital as a therapeutic instrument it slotted in very snugly with those wider, mainstream pleas for deinstitutionalization which so characterized British and American social policy from the 1960s onward (referred to in Chapter 2). In that sense it was hardly oppositional at all.

The interest of the anti-psychiatrists in interpersonal relationships was not an isolated one. In fact, it was perfectly consistent with the ideas of a number of social theorists who were writing during the 1950s and 1960s and especially those of the labelling theorists proper. Most of the latter had developed their initial work in relation to criminal behaviour, and it was not really until the 1960s that the principles of labelling theory were applied to mental illness as such. The most direct application of the theory to psychiatric issues was to be found in the work of Scheff (1966). Scheff argued that what often passed for mental illness was no more than a form of residual deviance (that is, deviance which could not otherwise be categorized as criminal or, say, consciously subcultural). This residual rule-breaking could, stated Scheff, arise from all kinds of sources (the initial causes of bad behaviour could be organic, or social), and most of it was transitory. In some cases, however, persistent rule-breakers were encouraged by 'significant others' (Mead's term not Scheff's), to accept the suggestion that they were mentally ill; that is, to accept the label of madness. And once accepted, the career of the deviant was virtually sealed, for the stereotyped individual was left with no alternative but to act out the expectations which others had of him (or her), and to become mad. Consequently, among residual rule-breakers, argued Scheff, labelling was the most important cause of a career of residual deviance. (Interestingly, labelling theory seemed to have had a considerable impact on the education of the social workers and nurses who worked with members of the study group. And many of them therefore spoke of such things as 'the effects of negative labelling' on systems of self-perception, as well as of the 'stigmatizing' effects of being labelled mentally ill.)

Naturally, the theses of labelling theory did not go unchallenged within social science, Gove (1970) proving, in particular, to be a somewhat vociferous critic. Most of the criticisms, however, circled around the fact that the theory could not satisfactorily explain the causes of the initial episodes of deviance which supposedly led to the subsequent career. Yet what the critics could not negate was the fact that if labelling did have an effect on the self-images of individuals (even if it was only at the later stages of a career), then the process could prove to be very damaging indeed. And it was this last implication which provided the theoretical weaponry to those who argued that admission to a mental hospital or even the designation of being mentally ill, were damaging activities *per se.* For it now followed, that labelling and stereotyping were no longer minor inconveniences in the life of an individual, but processes which extended themselves right into the soul of the labelled individual. Goffman's publications on asylums (1961) and stigma (1963) in that sense represented but two halves of a single, yet powerful critique.

As has already been stated and as these references to Goffman's work imply, Scheff's notions were just one strand in a large web of theories which sought the origins of mental illness in patterns of social interaction. And taken collectively, those theories tended to advance one further significant claim – namely that the concept of mental illness was essentially a moral or social one rather than a medical one. The idea that mental illnesses were basically forms of social deviance rather than medical disorder had of course been present ever since Parsons (1951) had analysed the components of the sick role, and concluded that sickness was a form of social deviance. But during the 1960s this basic idea was advanced with a new force. And it was perhaps Szasz, more than anyone, who was to follow through the implications of the argument to its extremes (see Roth, 1976). Szasz (1970) sought to distinguish between 'diseases' – which could supposedly be defined in terms of histopathology or pathophysiology alone – and unacceptable forms of personal behaviour which were often interpreted as forms of sickness. The latter called forth, and even necessitated, social and moral evaluations, but had nothing to do with biochemical disease states. Yet according to Szasz, most of what was commonly referred to as mental illness belonged to this second, behavioural category. He consequently drew the conclusion that medical responses to such 'illnesses' were both superfluous and erroneous.

Szasz's arguments concerning the 'myth of mental illness' were widely applauded during the 1970s and 1980s, partly because they implied, among other things, that in so far as psychiatric disorder was nothing more than a form of social deviance, then professional psychiatry was little more than an agent of social control. Indeed, psychiatry was often represented as a (political) movement geared towards the repression of social deviants. And these political implications could be found not merely in the writings of the anti-psychiatrists such as Cooper (1967), but also in the writings of other critics. Thus, both those who adhered to the principles of what was loosely called 'critical psychiatry' (Ingleby, 1981), and those who supported the so called 'social control thesis' (Cohen and Scull, 1985) homed in on the political role of psychiatry in the wider social environment. These attacks on psychiatry as a profession were, however, far from being an unassociated and separate feature of the interactional theories which preceded them; indeed they were inextricably bound up with the broad claim – evident in the work of Goffman, Scheff, Cooper, Laing, Esterson and others – that asymmetric social relationships were essentially damaging to human personalities. And when combined with the late twentieth century tendency to see almost any kind of social asymmetry as an expression of violence, it becomes clear as to why the anti-psychiatrists, in particular, felt justified in describing psychiatry as a form of oppression.

One specific manifestation of the interest in asymmetric relationships within families was eventually to be combined with a wider concern with gender relations. The modern origins of the combination can of course be located as far back as 1949, when de Beauvoir (1953) had criticized the 'bourgeois family' for its crippling effects on the social development of women, but it was not truly until the 1970s that this line of analysis was developed specifically in relation to mental illness. In fact, Chesler (1972) must have been among the very first to argue that it was men who designated women as unstable and hysterical and that the origins of 'madness' were therefore to be found in forms of sexual oppression rather than in biology. In that sense the Freudian claim that 'Anatomy is destiny' (1957: 189) was thoroughly rejected, and with it so were almost all of the early twentieth century perceptions concerning the links which supposedly held between the female frame and its illnesses. Those earlier perceptions had of course been structured in terms of an hypothesized relationship between 'sex' and illness (rather than the socio-cultural category of 'gender' and illness). Though during the first half of the century data on sex-specific rates of mental illness were more commonly collected only as an offshoot of the study of prevalence rates in general rather than as a focus of study in their own right. So even when the Dohrenwends (1969) were able to list some 22 pre- and post-Second World War studies on sex-specific prevalence rates of psychiatric disorder, the fact remained that the majority of the original studies had been more truly concerned with other issues (such as community prevalence rates, or social class rates) rather than with variations in rates of disease among males and females. It is interesting to note, however, that of the 22 studies cited by the Dohrenwends, nine had concluded that rates of mental illness were higher for males than for females, and 11 had suggested the opposite. Yet it was really only after the inclusion of the 'neuroses' as identifiable forms of mental illness that women consistently appeared to have higher rates of first admission to mental hospitals, higher rates of readmission and higher rates of community prevalence than men. In other words it was only in the post 1945 era, that females began substantially to outnumber males in the population of the mentally ill. It is not surprising then, that by 1970, when the postwar sex-specific pattern of hospital admission had stabilized, Gove and Tudor (1973) were able to assert that it made little difference whether one analysed admissions to mental hospitals, treatment by general physicians or community surveys, 'All the data on mental illness indicate that more women than men are mentally ill' (1973: 827). And it is at this point that the feminist charges against a male dominated psychiatry began to appear.

As this last remark serves to suggest, the mapping of illness onto the sex of the subject did not result in a uniformity of understanding about the nature of the relationship which was consequently uncovered – to identify sex-specific patterns was one thing, to explain how they arose was another. Most of the post 1970 explanations which have been offered to account for such variations in mental illness have of course been reviewed elsewhere (see, for example Miles, 1988, 1991), and there is no need to repeat the exercise here. What is intriguing from our standpoint, however, is the fact that the majority of them tend to exhibit the same move away from a concern with biological determinants of illness and towards an interest in socio-cultural factors, as did explanations for the links between families and mental illness, and 'race' and mental illness before them. In other words, analyses of sex-specific rates of admission to mental hospital or sex-specific community prevalence rates were no longer taken as indications as to how female bodies might differ from male bodies, but rather as to how the different social circumstances of males and females manifested themselves in different types of psychiatric illness. One particular example of this kind of socio-culturally inclined analysis appeared in 1978 with the publication of Brown and Harris's *The Social Origins of Depression*. For by highlighting the importance of such things as long-term difficulties in housing, the differential impact of employment and the significance of 'intimate' and confiding relationships for mental stability, the researchers sought (and proved able) to locate manifestations of clinical depression in a social rather than a purely biological space. As a result, they were able to demonstrate how the expression of what were considered to be essentially biological features of mind were in fact mediated by social factors.

This relocation of psychiatric illness among women in a socio-cultural space (that is, a gender structured space), questioned yet again the extent to which a focus on the body of the mental patient alone could unlock the secrets of psychiatric disorder. And somewhat inevitably the new theoretical understanding of women's lives gave new vigour to the all important question which Merskey and Tonge (1965) had posed in their *Psychiatric Illness*, (previously mentioned in Chapter 3) – namely, 'Who is the real patient?' Indeed, by highlighting the significance of domestic interrelationships in the genesis of mental illness – even serious mental illness – psychiatrists from the mid-1950s onwards had both wittingly and unwittingly subscribed to the proposition that in family settings it was usually the whole group which was 'more or less disturbed' (Merskey and Tonge, 1965: 54), and not simply the individual within. In so doing they not only managed to reconstitute and re-present the family as a source of psychiatric disorder, but also to underline the ways in which, in the latter half of the twentieth century, mental illness was to be seen as something which was cemented into the very foundations of social life rather than just a peripheral and abnormal aspect of it. By implication the notion that one could contain such illness in an isolated asylum was necessarily redundant.

The Family as Haven

Among the professionals who worked with the study group it was mainly the Community Psychiatric Nurses (CPNs) and Social Workers who showed most interest in the family as a potential object for the exercise of professional skills. Indeed, the CPN service was in many respects as firmly anchored to the existence of the 'home visit' as the hospital nursing service had been to the psychiatric 'bed'. And in line with their interest in the family, the nurses in the study area had produced a handbook for relatives of people with serious mental illness. In the handbook 'high expressed emotion' (HEE) was cited as an important contributory factor to the onset and continuation of serious psychiatric illness. The latter was a concept which had been developed by Brown (see George Brown, 1985) in an attempt to account for the fact that schizophrenic patients 'were more likely to relapse if they returned to live with parents or wives than if they went to live in lodgings' (1985: 13). And in order to identify properly the new object, Brown developed a new instrument to assess it and to measure it, namely, the Camberwell Family Interview.

The significance of HEE from our standpoint is that its identification signifies the ways in which a newly emergent psychosocial space is seen to surround the modern mental patient. This space is not, however, simply restricted to the relationships which exist between the patient and his or her legally recognized kin, but is instead extended to the 'functional' psychosocial family, or the 'psychosocial network' in which the patient finds him- or herself in general (Pattison *et al.*, 1975). In other words, each and every patient can be seen as occupying the nodal point of a psychosocial system, and it is to this wider system that professional activity can be usefully directed. Naturally (and if the professionals who came in contact with the study group are anything to go by), in practice many nurses, psychiatrists, social workers and relatives continue to believe that, at base, serious psychiatric disorder is more than likely to be genetically programmed in some way, or at least biologically determined rather than socially induced. And, as we have already seen, many relatives of people exhibiting schizophrenic symptoms seem to prefer to call upon a lay understanding of genetics and biology as a source of explanation for serious psychiatric disorder in preference to what they see as the 'family blaming' theories of Bateson *et al.* (1956). Yet strangely, in the 1990s neither genetics nor psychiatric theories of socio-genesis tend to provide the key framework in terms of which 'the family' actually enters into the everyday practice of psychiatric workers. For instead, the family now enters into the professional environment mainly as a source of material support, or as a potential source of long-term care for the mentally ill. And far from being considered as 'the source of all our discontents', the family is instead viewed as a haven from stress and an important source of what is nowadays called informal care.

This reassessment of the family in the overall system of psychiatric care was of course presaged in many of the policy documents on 'care in the community' which were published during the 1980s. Thus both the Barclay Report (1982), and Griffiths's *Agenda for Action* (1988) extolled the virtues of the family as a site of emotional and social support. And Griffiths, for example, argued that, 'Families, friends, neighbours and other local people provide the majority of care in response to needs which they are uniquely well placed to identify and . . . [they] will continue to be the primary means by which people are enabled to live normal lives in community settings' (1988: 5). Furthermore, according to *People First* (DHSS Northern Ireland, 1990a) – the government policy document which directly related to the people in the study group – it was not only desirable for most people to be cared for in the bosom of their own families, but it was, apparently, what most people wanted.

Not surprisingly, in line with these demands for the domestication of psychiatric care has arisen a newly identified role and a newly identified system – the role is that of 'informal carer', and the system is that of informal welfare. And their invention has served to underline the ways in which the family in modern society (rather like disease states such as schizophrenia) has no immutable and timeless essence to be managed and organized for the benefit of its members, but rather is in large part, a product of the multiple discourses which routinely surround it. As such, the recognizable characteristics and properties of family life can be (and, in fact, are) constantly written and rewritten so as to better fit the perceived 'needs' of the age.

7

The Social Worlds of the Hospital

We are unable clearly to circumscribe the concepts we use; not because we don't know their real definition, but because there is no real 'definition' to them. To suppose that there *must* be would be like supposing that whenever children play with a ball they play a game according to strict rules.

Wittgenstein (1969: 25)

The Hospital as a Medical Institution

The hospital referred to in this study (and which henceforth shall be known as Ballybreen), is situated on the outskirts of the city which it primarily serves and is housed in what can only be described as very pleasant parkland. It was designed during the first decade of the present century and details of the design are recorded in the third, or 'Scottish and Irish' volume of the *Report of the Royal Commissioners on the Care and Control of the Feeble Minded* (1908). That Commission was the first official body in the UK to suggest that the term 'hospital' be used instead of asylum. And it is a change of terminology which, as we have already noted, signifies the official point at which the protective and segregative goals of asylum care began to be replaced by the goals of medical treatment. From 1908 onwards, one might say, the concept of asylum – understood as a place of retreat – was subordinated to the concept of hospital as a place for medical intervention.

The study hospital, as has been mentioned previously, was designed initially as a 'colony' with 'villas'. That is to say, designed with a vague notion of self-containment or self-sufficiency in mind (and many of the older patients continued to refer to the hospital as 'The Colony'). Originally it contained its own farmland and animals, its own laundry and cookhouses; its own administrative structure, churches, chapels, mortuary and workshops. Later on it incorporated its own surgical facilities, its own school of nursing and many other resources for both staff and patients. The patients, of course, were mainly housed in the villas, and these latter were designed in terms of an image of suburban domesticity which predominated in both Britain and Ireland at the turn of the century.

Even today they look like pleasant two to three storey red-brick houses which, were it not for their size, one might find in any leafy suburb of a large city. Naturally, during the intervening period (1910–90), many changes and alterations had been executed on both the villas and the grounds. And recently, as if to echo the moves from hospital to community care, the spatial expanse of the hospital has retracted and a number of wards and outbuildings have been closed. Despite that retraction however, Ballybreen continues to provide the major physical resource in terms of which people with chronic psychiatric disorders living in the Health Board Area are cared for and treated (in fact it provided some 25 per cent of all long-stay psychiatric places in the Region). As one might expect, however, given the outdated design and the absence of large scale investment, the buildings have generally failed to keep pace over the years with changes in psychiatric ideology. Most striking of all, perhaps, is the fact that the physical structure of the hospital continues to reflect the ideology of institutionalism in terms of which it was originally built – even down to the presence of railings and a gate house at the main entrance.

Once inside those gates and railings, however, the sociologically inclined visitor could find himself or herself directed to any one of about 27 different wards dotted across the hospital grounds, and during most of the study period (1989 and 1990) those wards contained some 743 patients (5 per cent of whom were legally detained and 95 per cent of whom were voluntary). Some wards, however, were closed during the period of the study (and a few reopened), and among the nursing staff talk of ward closures was a recurring conversational theme. In fact, it was clear even to a casual observer that the overall physical structure of the hospital was often dictated by the economics of retraction as much as by the logic of care and treatment (so, for example, patients were often moved around the villas for reasons of economy rather than for reasons of therapy), and it was certainly clear that 'cost-effectiveness' loomed large in the decisions of those who shaped the broad outlines of hospital policy. As a consequence, the hospital population exhibited a great deal of movement during the period of study and in that respect gave the lie to the image of the psychiatric hospital as a becalmed backwater where few things ever changed. Indeed, the continual movement of patients made it very difficult to get an accurate snapshot of the hospital population at any one time and to that extent the data contained in Tables 7.1 to 7.4, should be thought of as providing nothing more than 'freeze-frames' of dynamic social processes, rather than once-and-for-all assessments of inmate characteristics (and it is for this same reason that there are slight variations in the totals given for the different tables). Despite those limitations, however, the tabulated data do provide valuable insights into some significant and important features of hospital life and it is to those features that we must now turn.

It is immediately obvious, for example, that hospital in-patients were officially described and classified in a number of ways. And through Tables 7.1, 7.2 and 7.3, we can get some indication of the various interests which generated the diverse forms of description and classification which ordinarily operated in hospital life. Hence we can see, for example, how administrative and nursing interests, as well as those of clinical psychiatry, impinged on the classification and ordering of patients. And we can also begin to see that in routine practical terms, patients were allocated to wards as much on the basis of nursing interests (Table 7.3) as they were on the basis of diagnostic criteria. Indeed, in hospital, a clinical diagnosis was rarely the key or main determinant of patient fates and careers, and therefore the ward to which any one person was allocated depended as much (and probably more) on such things as their age, sex, degree of nursing difficulty and their links with the wider community, as on their perceived 'illness'. Naturally, the overwhelming majority of patients did have a principal psychiatric diagnosis. And in the language of the international (WHO) nosology (Table 7.1), the bulk of such diagnoses referred to psychotic states – though there was also a sizable number of people whose diagnosis referred to their intellectual capacities, and a large number of acute patients whose diagnosis was not established (at least for purposes of enumeration). In those terms we can see that the hospital mainly

Table 7.1 *Hospital in-patients by diagnostic category, age, sex and length of stay (n = 743)*

Diagnostic category*	% of patients	Age (Years) μ	δ	% Male	Median stay in months
Organic psychoses	34	78	12	31	24
Psychoses	38	62	17	52	144
Neuroses	6	65	19	37	36
Mental retardation	7	66	8	56	480
No diagnosis	14	58	21	38	(1 week)
Non-psychiatric diagnosis	1	55	22	50	24
All	100	67	18	42	48

* Coded according to World Health Organization (1977) codes

μ = mean

δ = standard deviation

provided a service for people with serious and chronic 'psychotic' illnesses rather than for those afflicted by relatively transient and neurotic illnesses. And one corollary of this is that patients categorized as 'neurotic' were organized mainly in terms of day hospitals, out-patient departments, day clinics in the community and small psychiatric departments in district general hospitals. (Some indication of the activity rates of the out- and in-patients systems in the overall region is reflected in the fact that there were some 16 treatment episodes in out-patient clinics for every in-patient 'bed' existing during 1989–90.) In a similar fashion, it is noticeable that the hospital service was one heavily tilted towards the care of older (and elderly) patients. In fact, the hospital had served as a long-term home for a significant proportion of patients – some of them having lived there for up to 60 years. And by implication, it is clear that Ballybreen contained very few adolescents, or people in their early 20s. This last feature is significant because it reflects strongly on hospitalization policies which are geared towards the rapid discharge of patients after short periods of 'stabilization' rather than towards long periods of stay. And it is these policies which generate the so called 'revolving door syndrome', the effects of which are so dramatically represented in Figure 2.2.

Table 7.2   *Hospital in-patients by administrative category, age, sex and length of stay (n = 743)*

Administrative category	% of patients	Age (Years) μ	δ	% Male	Median stay in months
Acute	13	49	19	42	(1 week)
Long-stay (18–64)	28	59	15	69	180
Long-stay elderly	20	75	10	26	132
Short-stay elderly	33	79	12	33	11
Rehabilitation	6	56	12	56	96

Of the 27 wards mentioned above, four were set aside as admission wards (two for males and two for females), and in the main they were organized so as to deal with acute psychiatric conditions (as might be found in the psychiatric units of district general hospitals). Consequently, their patient turnover was relatively rapid, and most of the residents left hospital well within 12 months of arrival. (In fact the definition of a long-stay patient used herein, is one who was hospitalized for 12 months or more – some 60 per cent of patients fell into this category.) A patient who remained in hospital for more than 12 months, however, was very likely to be transferred to one of the nine continuing care wards (for the 18–64 year old group), and it was from these latter wards that the patients referred to as 'the study group' were drawn. This was in part because the practical efforts to move people from hospital to community were (and are) essentially concentrated on this group, and partly because the assorted experiences of such patients provided a rich source of contrasts for research. Furthermore, policies for the care in the community of elderly patients with psychiatric symptoms had still not been finalized at the time of the study and very few of the older patients seemed likely to leave hospital. One route by means of which we can gain an understanding of the perceived nature and character of the problems which afflicted continuing care patients is outlined in Table 7.3. This table summarizes just a small amount of the detail which was collected from the nursing staff who were responsible for the long-stay patients. And it is possible to see therein, how the patient population has been divided into three broad groups according to various nursing and administrative interests. Thus we can see, for example, how for nursing purposes it was the 'disturbed' patients who were grouped together rather than say the schizophrenic

Table 7.3 *Nursing assessments of 209 long-stay (18–64 year old) patients*

| Perceived problem | Nursing category (by type of ward) | | |
	'Rehab' %	Continuing care %	'Disturbed' %
Serious/very serious psychological problems	18	35	88+
Serious/very serious behaviour problems	22	21	45*
Problems with social relationships	58	72*	48
Dangerous to others	—	—	11+
Inappropriate sexual behaviour	8	18	19
Moderate to serious self-neglect	80	88	82
Incontinence problems	18	18	22
Odd appearance	60	50	56
Absorbed in psychotic symptoms	73	47+	63
Potential for self-harm	16	9	30*
Numbers	45	137	27

+$p<0.01$, *$p<0.05$ compared to other two groups

patients; and the 'rehab' patients rather than just the psychologically stable. We can also see in Table 7.3 the kinds of issues which were routinely assessed in the consideration of psychiatric problems. So as well as assessments of psychological states, it is clear that considerations of social behaviour, social relationships, sexual behaviour, self-neglect and so on, also figure prominently. It is in this sense that the identification of a single illness or the provision of a one word 'diagnosis' is considered relatively unimportant in matters of practical hospital psychiatry. (Diagnostic terms such as schizophrenia or manic depression, rarely if ever appeared in nursing care notes – though such terms did appear in the medical 'charts'.) This should not, however, be taken to detract from the fact that there was a general consensus among medical and paramedical staff that the hospital existed first and foremost for the treatment of diseases and illnesses and that any other functions which it served were merely secondary. Indeed, mental illnesses lay at the heart of hospital life and, for the most part, such illnesses were treated and controlled by means of chemical medication (though some 5 per cent of these long-stay patients were not given any medication).

The wards for the non-elderly continuing care patients had, then, an internal logic of their own. Two of the wards, were devoted to the development of rehabilitation programmes and laid a heavy emphasis on social skills training and occupational therapy – in addition to medication. A further two were devoted to containment and control of 'disturbed' cases and the remainder adopted a more traditional orientation to both nursing care and to the outside world. The patients in the 'locked' or disturbed wards, of course, were patients who were regarded as difficult to cope with or who were 'actively psychotic' – (and who tended to be younger than the other patients). Here, as one might expect, there was little orientation to community care goals and the emphasis was essentially on 'stabilizing' the patient. The 'rehab' wards, on the other hand, generally adopted a more active policy towards release and life in the community generally, and movement into such wards was often viewed by patients anxious to return 'home' as the final step before discharge. In fact, 62 per cent of the long-term male patients and 50 per cent of female patients who were discharged from hospital between January 1987 and January 1990 came from these wards. In nursing parlance these wards contained the 'higher grade' patients, whilst the remaining five wards in the long-stay (18–64 year old) group tended to be viewed somewhat as back wards containing 'lower grade' patients. In terms of physical facilities, however, a casual visitor would have been hard pressed to differentiate between these wards and the rehabilitation wards. What the visitor would have noticed is that the inmates of the former were more often to be found sitting, standing or shuffling around the day-rooms, and this to a certain extent reflected the less active and less outwardly oriented nursing and medical philosophies which operated within them. Patients, of course, were constantly moving between these various categories: from continuing care into rehabilitation, from rehabilitation back into continuing care and sometimes into the locked wards. Patient progress was not always unilinear in that sense.

As is evident from Table 7.2 the majority of the patients in the hospital were actually to be found in the (14) wards for the elderly mentally infirm (EMI). In general, the patients in this group belonged to a world set apart and somewhat segregated from that of the acute and continuing care patients. This was true in both organizational and in informal terms. Thus the EMI patients were looked after in the main by a separate group of consultant psychiatrists, they lived in different wards, were rarely seen at any social functions or at any of the commonly held social and therapeutic sites within the hospital. Relationships between acute and continuing care patients, on the other hand, were far more flexible. This was perhaps because continuing care patients who had been discharged from hospital, often re-entered as acute patients, whilst the ranks of the continuing care group were always being renewed by patients from the acute wards. On an informal basis, both acute and continuing care patients could be found mingling in some of the social events at the hospital, or in the central meeting place for patients, which was a canteen/café known as the 'Singing Kettle'. And, overall, it was possible to examine the general movement of many of the older patients in terms of Goffman's (1961) concept of 'career'. Thus after entry as an acute patient, a mid-life career as a continuing care patient, followed by movement into the wards for the elderly infirm had been quite a common trajectory for many of those who had entered hospital in previous decades. In fact some 25 per cent of patients had lived in the hospital for 21 years or more and a few had moved through each one of the appropriate *rites de passage* to spend their final years in one or other of the psycho-geriatric wards.

Naturally, in so far as the hospital was viewed as an institution which dealt with diseases and illnesses, the major forms of therapy were medical – and especially chemical. Though, as we have already noted, other therapies such as occupational therapy and social skills training figured prominently in the treatment programmes of some patients. There was, however, virtually no mention of psychotherapy, family therapy or other forms of group based therapy for any of the long-term patients – though psychotherapy was used quite widely in both the Health Board Area and the Region (the latter providing one 'psychotherapy bed' for every 132 'mental illness beds' during the 1989–90 period – see, DHSS Northern Ireland, 1990b). This lack of emphasis on the social therapies resulted in large part from the tendency of medical staff to somatize nearly all of the problems which patients presented to them, and it mattered little whether those problems stemmed from social difficulties, behavioural awkwardness or cognitive abnormalities, the response tended to be similar – namely, to focus in on deficits within the individual. Indeed, the most common point of therapeutic focus was the patient's body and it was in order to stabilize or correct perceived deficits in the body that treatment programmes were designed and developed within a hospital regime. Over and above this, however, it was equally clear that the hospital served its population as something far more than a medical institution. For it also functioned as a shelter (asylum) for people who experienced 'problems with living'; and, in part, served as a mechanism of social control (though this was only strictly so for the small number of legally detained patients). Perhaps most important of all it functioned as a system of care for people who frequently exhibited abnormalities of thought, or who were just intangibly 'odd' in some way or another. Though all of these latter functions were seen by medical and nursing staff as secondary, peripheral and sometimes irrelevant to the main task. That task was the management (and potential alleviation) of serious mental illnesses.

Professional Representations of Psychiatric Disorder

Dramatis Personae: PSY = Psychiatrist, F = Freddie, a long-stay mental hospital in-patient.
Scene: A small office off a hospital ward. The psychiatrist is attempting to assess Freddie's 'mental state'.

325 PSY: Tell me Freddie, how do you feel in your nerves today?
328 F: I feel upset.
330 PSY: You feel upset Freddie? Why is that tell me?
333 F: Control of me. I feel like a thick sound from a plate. Dolphin been drove into the cooking room. There must be some kind of connection. [. . . inaudible].
339 PSY: A sound from a plate? What sort of sound is it Freddie?
342 F: Sound. Teacup. Rattle of a tea cup. Hold on my body. [. . . inaudible].
345 PSY: Tell me Freddie. How do you get on with the other patients?
348 F: Not too bad.

350 PSY: Do you ever feel that any of the other patients are ganging up against you Freddie? Trying to harm you?

354 F: Well I do Doctor. I do [. . . inaudible]

362 PSY: Can other people read your thoughts Freddie?

365 F: They do. They do doctor. Yes. Like when I'm smoking.

368 PSY: Do you ever feel that anyone is controlling you Freddie?

371 F: No.

373 PSY: Do you ever feel that you have any special gifts or powers Freddie?

376 F: With music Doctor. I seem to be annoyed by music. My brain, my mouth, my lips affected by music.

380 PSY: Do you ever feel that there's any external force controlling you Freddie?

383 F: I would speak of Germany doctor as a force toward me [. . . inaudible].

386 PSY: Do you ever go to any therapies Freddie?

388 F: I seem to arrive at Villa 11 Doctor. In a physical sort of way you know.

Freddie, as we can see, exhibited signs of what is referred to as thought disorder. His conversation often took bizarre turns, and he frequently made accusations about Germans. In addition, Freddie could often be found talking to himself in the corners of the ward, and he rarely bothered with any of the other patients and remained somewhat 'distant' in his relations with staff and inmates alike. Moreover, and unless he was prompted by the nursing staff, Freddie would not have been too fussed about such things as washing or wearing clean clothes. He had no effective contact with his relatives, no work, and apart from the hospital ward, nowhere to live. And all of these details together with other diverse facts about his current life and past history, were essentially taken to be symptomatic of a serious psychiatric disorder – namely schizophrenia. (The terms 'dementia praecox (simple)' appeared in Freddie's clinical notes and the term 'schizophrenia' in his nursing care notes.) Interestingly, however, despite the fact that all the signs of impairment were read from his social behaviour and psychological capacities, the real source of Freddie's disorder was assumed to lie elsewhere. In fact, the diverse social and psychological signs which have just been referred to were primarily regarded as pointing towards the presence of a further pathology, namely an unknown physical pathology – probably in the central nervous system. So it was essentially Freddie's central nervous system which served as the focus of his treatment programme – and at the core of that programme was a tranquillizer. In this respect it is interesting to note how both Freddie and the psychiatrist found common ground in their discussion of 'the nerves', and how for both men, 'the nerves' were seen to lie at the heart of the psychotic symptoms. Such a location of the patient's (multiple) problems in a single site (the nerves) was quite common in hospital.

Dramatis Personae: PSY = Psychiatrist, H = Harry, a long-stay mental hospital in-patient.

51 PSY: Do you have any friends here Harry?
53 H:· I don't know.
55 PSY: Do you have a friend?
57 H: Oh. I don't know.
60 PSY: Tell me. How do you feel in your nerves now?
63 H: I feel better in my nerves Mister.

[A series of other questions concerned to elicit whether Harry heard voices when there was no one else in the room, whether he got messages from the television and radio, and so on, followed. All were answered negatively by Harry.]

145 PSY: Hmm. I see.
147 H: I had a baby upstairs about a month ago Mister.
150 PSY: You had a baby Harry?
152 H: Yes. Upstairs. About a month ago Mister.
154 PSY: Don't you think that's a bit strange Harry. Men having babies. Men don't usually have babies do they?
158 H: They gave me a man child Mister . . .

Harry, as with Freddie, was also referred to as 'schizophrenic' though his psychological symptoms were quite different from those of Freddie. In both cases, however, their medication was similar since the disease referred to as schizophrenia is most commonly controlled by the use of one of a limited number of chemical therapies – Freddie, for example was the recipient of 100 ml of chlorpromazine (one of the most widely used of the neuroleptics), four times a day. Over the past decades, however, and as we have noted, there were numerous kinds of physical therapy used in the treatment of schizophrenia – such as, insulin coma therapy, electro-convulsive therapy and psycho-surgery. Both Freddie and Harry had experienced some of these and Freddie suffered from post-leucotomy epilepsy as a result of his previous operation. It should perhaps be noted that in addition to experiencing a thought disorder, Harry (like Freddie) was also homeless (in the sense of having no home outside of hospital), unemployed, relatively friendless and out of touch with his relatives. But in the framework of the psychiatrist's world, these latter features tended to be seen as a consequence of the illness, rather than a part of it. In fact, the disease process was viewed as the base problem (to be found probably in the brain), and the other problems were seen as being superstructural to it. What is more, whilst the problems of mental infrastructure were regarded as falling within the demesne of medical psychiatry, the problems of social superstructure (work, behaviour, social relations and even housing and personal finance) were regarded as belonging to the province of a variety of other professionals – nurses, occupational therapists, social workers and, to a lesser extent, psychologists and physiotherapists. Indeed, in the eyes of many psychiatrists (as we have previously noted) these latter roles are often regarded as facilitating roles which are necessary and essential, but ones which touch only on the surface of the basic problem – which is the disease/illness/disorder known as schizophrenia. In fact, this last belief forms *the* central tenet of psychiatric ideology and it is the one on which the existence of the psychiatric hospital is justified.

Hospital nurses, in general, seemed readily to accept the central assumptions of such medical ideology. To that extent they too believed that schizophrenia was a disease with a physical base, and they also tended to see the patient as the sole point of therapy. Patient problems, for example, were usually written up in the nursing notes as problems of individuals, and the nature of therapeutic programmes was concentrated on the patient alone. This is not to say that all forms of hospital nursing are or were disease oriented, or that the disease model of illness (as it is called in nursing texts), was the only model utilized. But it is to say that nurses believed in a deep seated physical illness as the hidden source and origin of the kinds of conversations, behaviours and attitudes which they routinely confronted. It is a belief which is neatly illustrated by the following extract which concerns a report on a conversation about the ninth readmission of a young 'schizophrenic' woman.

Dramatis Personae: R = Researcher, SI = Ward Sister, SN = Staff Nurse.
Scene: The ward manager's office.

R : So why is AM back here then? [i.e, hospital]
SI: Well AM has problems with her mother/ . . .

[At which point SN intervenes.]

SN: /Because she's mad. M.A.D. It's a scientific term. Ever heard of it?
SI: /mother, who has also been admitted to this hospital . . .

Just by chance the fate of this same patient cropped up in a discussion some months later in a day centre. This time, the researcher's question was addressed to the Community Psychiatric Nurse (CPN).

> *R:* Could you tell me something about AM?
> *CPN:* . . . AM is the most actively psychotic person I know/ . . .
>
> [And on this occasion it was a psychiatrist who intervened.]
>
> *PSY:* /She's *mad*. (Nodding his head).
> *CPN:* She lives with her mother and four . . .

Such an appeal to an inner and personal 'madness' was quite common in the hospital, though as the first of these two extracts indicates, some hospital nurses were concerned to point to other interpersonal (mainly family) factors in the creation and onset of symptoms. In fact, even though hospital nurses rarely (and probably never) worked in such fields as family or interpersonal relations, they often recognized that not everything could be explained by reference to a secret inner disorder. Thus, some nurses would routinely point towards non-somatic factors as sources of difficulty. Mothers came in for frequent mention as, for example, in statements such as: 'You only have to see his mother walk through that door to see what the problem [with John] is.' Despite this, however, the basic causes of psychiatric disorder were essentially viewed as forms of bodily disease – even though nurses came to know such 'disease' only through the external and outward features of behaviour, conversation and mannerism. Indeed, belief in disease held fast even when common sense ran counter to the disease hypothesis. Here, for example, is a report on a conversation in which one experienced staff nurse is puzzled about the absence of any schizophrenic symptoms in a specific in-patient. The conversation took place during a change over from a.m. to p.m. shifts when the outgoing nurses were expected to provide a detailed verbal report to the incoming ones.

> *SN1:* Does anyone know what's supposed to be wrong with G?
>
> [This question was met by blank looks all round and a momentary silence.]
>
> *SN2:* Schizophrenia I suppose.
> *SN1:* Hmm. (Pause). I've never seen any sign of it.
> *SN3:* Well, he's on chlorpromazine so he must be schizophrenic.

The fact that it is often possible to be considered schizophrenic without displaying any of the primary (or even secondary) symptoms would come as no surprise to hospital nurses, many of whose charges are considered to be 'burnt out', or more technically as cases of 'residual schizophrenia' – a state of schizophrenia in which symptoms are assumed to be virtually absent or blunted. (Indeed, the international nosology cites a further category of schizophrenia called Latent Schizophrenia in which there are symptoms 'which give the impression of schizophrenia though no definite and characteristic schizophrenic anomalies, present or past, have been manifest' (WHO, 1977: 185).) It is perhaps for that reason that the use of medication is itself taken as a symptom of disease. Whilst the fact that medication 'works' is frequently taken to be a conclusive argument for the presence of disease.

Medication, of course carries a heavy burden in hospital for it is seen as the primary and sometimes the only form of therapy available for psychiatric disorder. Nurses and psychiatrists are, for example, keen to relate stories as to how tiny alterations in tranquillizer dosage can either 'send people over the brink', or alternatively 'work wonders'. Thus it was said of one patient who had been administered chlorpromazine for years, that 'Lithium has been Alice's salvation'. In a similar way the recurrence of schizophrenic symptoms in ex-patients is often seen purely as a failure of medication. Thus, it was said of one of the younger patients who had been readmitted to hospital during the time of the study that his 'problem' was that he 'didn't take his medicine'. Whilst no reference was made about his (somewhat unusual) material and social circumstances. Given such faith in medicine it perhaps comes as no surprise to learn that to be treated for psychiatric disorder is often interpreted as a matter of being given the right medicine. The following extract (which does not concern a schizophrenic patient) illustrates the point. The question refers to a very mournful patient who had told the researcher many times that there was 'no point in life', and that she had 'lost interest in everything'. A lay person would probably have been tempted to describe her as being exceedingly depressed, but her nursing care notes contained no mention of this, and the ward manager was therefore asked to clarify the nature of her disorder.

> R: How would you describe L's problem then? I thought that she was suffering from depression?
> CN: No. It's not depression. We have treated her for depression and it's made no difference. No, LC has a personality disorder. . . .

Clearly, for this nurse it was quite possible to treat people's diseases by chemical means alone and without altering any aspects of their social or interpersonal conditions. Such a focus on the isolated patient may, in part, have been a reflection of the fact that most long-term hospital in-patients had very few social relationships to get involved with. Around one-third of the long-term in-patients under 65, for example, had no contact with relatives whatsoever, and patterns of in-patient friendship and social mixing were often unstable. Given such a lack of social interaction, one may feel that there was little else for hospital nurses to work on other than the inner disease process. What is fascinating about hospital nursing practice, however, is that alternative objects of therapy were routinely available and indeed used in ward life. Consider the following.

> *R:* Is E mentally ill, would you say?
> *SN:* Well. (Pause). I wouldn't say that.
> *R:* What's wrong with her then?
> *SN:* Nothing really. Her problems are behavioural rather than medical.
> These days she wouldn't even get inside a hospital. It's her behaviour
> which causes the problem.

And a similar reference to behaviour as an object of therapy is evident in the next statement.

> *SI:* Siobhan's problems are mainly behavioural you see. Her illness is
> under control. It's the behaviour which is the problem.

These comments were far from being isolated and sporadic and we can perhaps judge from the contents of Table 7.3 alone that the distinction between behaviour and illness was prominent in daily nursing and psychiatric practice, and tended to form the grounds on which much detailed discussion occurred. So marked changes in behaviour, for example, formed the occasion for reviews of medication and sometimes for subsequent alterations in such medication. More importantly it was patient behaviour which acted as the prime object of observation, discussion and analysis for most nurses. Thus, many schemes of patient assessment and description were designed in behavioural frameworks. (Usually it was commer- cially available assessment packages which were used in the wards, but during the period of study one of the clinical psychologists was attempting to devise a new behavioural rating instrument which would supposedly be more 'sensitive' to the known characteristics of the in-patient population.) In fact, behaviour was one of the few objects that the nursing staff had to work on and it is not surprising therefore that it served as a central point of attention and action. Yet despite that, it was still regarded as a mere symptom of a disease/illness/disorder which lay elsewhere. As if (in the language of Ryle (1949)), there was a 'second theatre' towards which the observable and common sense signs were merely pointing. Conse- quently, the *real* psychiatric problems were believed to reside in the patient's body, and it was truly speaking the somatic disorder which was regarded as the base and origin of the numerous other difficulties which patients commonly faced.

Table 7.4   *The social context of illness: some characteristics of long-stay patients in the two rehabilitation wards (n = 49)*

Age		Age1			Adm			Stay		Marstat
μ	δ	μ	δ	1o	μ	hi	1o	μ	hi	%
56	12	30	13	1	6	29	2	245	600	19

Employ	% Visit 1		% Visit 2		Socprob	Socmix
%	week	never	week	never	%	%
27	46	24	28	58	29	58

Age: Age in years; Age1: Age at first admission (years); Adm: Number of admissions; Stay: Continuous residence in hospital in months; Marstat: % ever married. Employ: % with any employment history; Visit 1: % who get a visit from any relative/friend; Visit 2: % who make any kind of visit to a relative/friend outside of hospital; Socmix: little or no interaction with other patients (nurse assessment); Socprob: Problems getting on with other residents (nurse assessment).

The extent and nature of some of those difficulties is outlined in Table 7.4. The table provides something of a summary concerning the social backgrounds of patients in the rehabilitation wards. Therein we can read of high rates of admission (and in many cases a very early age of first admission), low rates of marriage (or cohabitation), low rates of employment, the superficial nature of family contact and the high probability of patients experiencing difficulties in general social interaction. But of these numerous dimensions it is perhaps instructive to note that two of the most common sources of sustained and stable social contact – work and family – are almost entirely missing from the backgrounds of such patients. In that sense their lives circulated around a whole series of hollows and social vacuums. Naturally, even the most vigorous of somaticists would not deny the existence of a social and economic dimension to the various forms of psychiatric illnesses which he or she confronted, but in terms of daily and routine management of case loads, these latter problems were, for the most part, allocated to other professionals – housing, welfare and family relations to the social work department, employment and training to the occupational therapy department, the assessment of skills to the psychologist and the daily supervision of the medical regime to the nursing staff. All this, of course, was achieved under the banner of team work and interprofessional cooperation, but in reality the hospital was ultimately justified in terms of its being a place where diseases and illnesses were treated, and it was therefore a place where medical ideology reigned supreme. Yet at one and the same time, this site of medical knowledge and medical practice also served as a simple place of domicile. Indeed, it was home to a community of people who (as we have just discovered) had little in the way of social, cultural or material capital to call upon. They too had interpretations of hospital life – and among such interpretations those concerning the hospital as an instrument of medical therapy and those concerning the hospital as an instrument of legal oppression were rarely called upon. For most of the in-patients regarded the hospital first and foremost as a place of asylum.

The Patient's Image of the Hospital

I want to say here for ever and ever.

(Long-stay patient at the study hospital)

We have already noted how, from some point near to the mid-1950s, mental hospitals began to garner a bad reputation. This, despite the fact that such a reputation was far from being entirely justified in the light of the empirical evidence made available through sociological and anthropological studies of life in small and medium sized hospitals. Indeed the ambiguous nature of the evidence concerning the effects of hospitalization meant that, right up to the present day, it has been possible for different interest groups selectively to adopt and adapt different 'facts' so as either to condemn the continuation of long-stay hospitals, or to applaud their retention. Thus, in the UK, for example, we can find, on the one hand, the National Schizophrenia Fellowship (NSF) arguing for caution and prudence in the management of the hospital closure programme – on the grounds that there is need for asylum – and, on the other a pressure group such as MIND arguing for more rapid moves towards non-hospital care for the mentally ill – on the grounds that medical supervision should form only a small part of any service for those with psychiatric problems. Naturally, both groups claim to speak for the interests of people with serious psychiatric disorders, and in that respect both pressure groups see themselves as expressing the 'voice of the patient'.

The notion that there is some authentic and singular 'voice' of the patient is of course a mistaken one, if only because people with serious psychiatric disorders have interests and perspectives as varied and diverse as any other social group. In that respect it is clear that the representation of the 'inmate world' which Goffman (1961) portrayed in his discussions of hospital 'underlife', was no more and no less valid than the representation which was amplified in the work of Braginsky *et al.* (1969) – who argued that hospitals were among the few resources which patients could actually call upon and *use* in their attempts to cope with their social worlds. Indeed both Goffman and Braginsky *et al.* in their very different ways, emphasized how long-stay patients could actually manipulate elements of the hospital world for their own ends and in that sense they both gave the lie to the image of the patient as a passive recipient of medical (psychiatric) discipline. And it is essentially this vision of the psychiatric hospital as a resource for patients which I wish to draw upon here. For leaving aside the question as to whether the study hospital was a 'bad' or a 'good' place for patients to live, it was clear that many patients regarded it as an appropriate place for them to live – though not necessarily because they saw themselves as being ill, and still less because they saw themselves as having a disease.

Perhaps it is as a result of the stigma associated with mental illness that psychiatric patients rarely describe themselves as being mentally ill (even though they recognize other patients as being so). And they certainly do not regard reference to mental 'illness' as a convincing explanation for their present circumstances. Consequently, if patients are asked to give accounts of their psychiatric conditions they either deny that there is anything amiss or, instead choose to express their difficulties in vague and imprecise terms which have very little to do with the categories of professional psychiatry. For example, they rarely use professional diagnostic terms, and when they do, it is usually in a critical sense. Thus, when reference to an illness is actually made it is far more likely to be offered in terms of physical ailments than in terms of psychiatric ones. And perhaps it is because many people experience their personal woes in somatic terms (rather than, say, in terms of alteration of affect) that they frequently report their disorders through the language of physical (bodily) illness. So patients will readily say, for example, that they suffer with their 'nerves', that they come from a 'nervous family', that they are constantly bothered with nerves, that they feel unwell or just 'not themselves' or, more likely, refer to some general notion of dis-ease. Sometimes they point towards specific somatic conditions – excessive sweating, constipation, pains in the back, stomach aches, giddy spells and sometimes even specific (but imagined) organic conditions of the liver or heart, or kidney. Occasionally these explanations take a bizarre turn, so a patient might claim to have, say, a snake in their back which is eating away at them, or to have been made ill by dark spirits. And in line with an emphasis on somatic ailments, accounts of admission to hospital also turn on matters of bodily disorder. One patient claimed, for example, that immediately before his last admission his brain had 'exploded or something'; whilst another had claimed that a 'big black ball' had hit him in the middle of the forehead causing unconsciousness. A female patient who had been in hospital for many years, claimed that she had been admitted the day before for a very serious operation. Another claimed that when she was first admitted to hospital she thought that she was being taken to 'a physical hospital' and had she known where she was really bound for she would not have come, for it was not what she needed. Most patients, however, tended to shrug off all references to any illness in the first place. Thus one of the older male patients, for example, stated that he was 'King of Ireland' and had vast fortunes waiting for him in America. Only the conspiracy against him kept him in hospital. A female patient, regarded herself as healthy but argued that someone else was living in her house and therefore she had to stay in hospital because she had nowhere else to live. One of the younger patients claimed that the wrong people kept coming to collect her, but that when her real parents arrived she would go home. A male patient who admitted to being 'nervy' claimed that he was too busy to go home, another stated that he only worked at the hospital and was 'not like the rest of them'. However, a small number of patients did talk about themselves as being 'mental', or 'wired up' (local slang for being abnormal, bizarre, manic, or unsound). And a number of the female patients in particular accounted for their hospitalization by stating that they just could not 'cope outside'. One woman gave a detailed account of the onset of her depression – which had occurred at the time of her mother's death – and of her subsequent reactions, but such rationally constructed accounts were not easily acquired. Consequently, it was said by the nursing staff that patients, in general, tended to lack 'insight' into their psychiatric conditions. That is to say, they failed to draw upon even the vaguest principles of psychiatric medicine to account for their circumstances. And in a peculiar way it was only when patients came to accept a medical interpretation of their condition as one of 'being mentally ill' that staff felt able to talk of progress being made. Yet, as far as most patients were concerned, they were no more and no less 'ill' than was the population at large.

As has been previously pointed out, most of the hospital residents were voluntary patients and in the legal sense at least could leave hospital at any time (though very few could have achieved this without help). One of the paradoxes of hospital life, however, was that it was usually the patients who were legally detained that demanded immediate release – though the physical movements of such patients were not necessarily restricted in any way. In general, therefore, patients were quite content to remain in hospital. In conversation they would claim that they were 'not ready' to go home just yet, or just did not wish to leave, or sometimes that they had nowhere else to go. A few patients (with slightly odd physical characteristics, or very marked speech defects) claimed that people 'out there' often laughed at them and they therefore felt happier in the hospital grounds where everyone 'knows who we are'. One patient stated that he just had 'no time' for people 'in the town'. Another claimed that he wished 'to stay here [that is, in hospital] more than anywhere' but that he was 'realistic enough to know' that it could not be. And this was in addition to the comment of the patient cited at the opening of this subsection stating that he wished to live in the hospital 'for ever and ever'. When asked directly – through a series of structured interviews – whether they liked living in hospital, whether they wished to stay in hospital and whether they felt that their hospital lives were 'run too much by other people', the patients in the interview group answered positively to the first two kinds of questions (89 per cent and 61 per cent 'Yes') and negatively to the third kind (75 per cent 'No'). Indeed, by means of answers to these and other related questions (see Prior, 1991a), it was overwhelmingly clear that patients were quite content with their material and social environments in the hospital world. This in part was a reflection of the fact that most of the patients enjoyed freedom from the responsibility of looking after themselves (their clothes, their meals, their bedding and so on), and in part a reflection of the fact that most patients had very low expectations of the world. In the language of nursing and social work, the patients lacked 'motivation'. From the in-patient standpoint, however, the hospital buildings, the nurses, social workers and occupational therapists primarily served as a resource on which they could call in times of need – being aware of that need, few expressed a direct desire to leave for a home elsewhere.

Interestingly, these high rates of satisfaction and approval of hospital life were usually reinterpreted by psychiatric professionals in a manner which denied the veracity of patient responses. Thus a number of professionals argued that high rates of satisfaction with hospital life simply indicated the terrible state of 'institutionaliza- tion' into which the patients had drifted, and the awful extent to which patients had lost their independence. On occasion the researcher was told that one should not take patient responses to hospital life at face value, and that patients did not know 'any better'. It was frequently stated that patients were incapable of making rational choices, or that the patients had told the researcher only what they thought he wanted to hear. One social worker even went so far as to suggest that the patients were 'drugged' at the time of interview and that their responses were consequently of no use. And whatever the validity of these reinterpretations and dismissals, it was clear that a large number of professional psychiatric workers felt plainly uncomfortable when confronted with claims that people with psychiatric disorders might actually prefer institutional life to life 'in the community'.

This right to interpret and constantly reinterpret the responses of patients to their social worlds was, of course, seen as an essential and integral component of psychiatric work. Indeed, the tasks of the psychiatric professional were in large part seen as being to interpret correctly the various behavioural, cognitive and emotional signs and signals given off by the patient, in terms of prevailing psychiatric theory. And for the most part such acts of interpretation were ongoing throughout the working day. Thus, nurses, psychiatrists, social workers and occupational therapists constantly referred to aspects of patient mood, behaviour and talk in both their professional and casual conversational interchanges. Strangely, however, most contact between psychiatric professionals and their patients tended to occur only within tightly defined and formally structured settings. In other words, there were precise and exact times and circumstances under which patients and nurses, or patients and psychiatrists or patients and social workers met and interacted. Casual interchanges often existed, but by their very nature they were brief, fleeting and superficial. This closely managed apportioning of time was made possible, by and large, because the hospital was used as a canopy for two distinct social worlds – the world of the staff and the world of the in-patient – and these worlds were differentiated by all kinds of physical boundaries and symbolic structures. Thus there were, for example, many boundaries (both visible and invisible) over which the staff could step, but not the patients. Offices, cupboards, kitchens, dispensaries, workshops and entire buildings in that sense often served to mark out the geographical limits of the two worlds. And these physical divisions and markers were also integrated into a wider symbolic order of difference – evident in such features as the use of uniforms, language, behaviour and demeanour. In the staff world, for example, patients were discussed, analysed, and constantly examined through the medium of professional talk. On the other side of the symbolic division, however, stood the patients who would often have to wait or queue – for medicines, cigarettes, to ask questions, or simply to seek permission for interchange with the staff world. Unfortunately, most of these divisions were also apparent in the everyday lives of the ex-patients who had left to live in the community.

The in-patient world was not, of course, defined solely and simply in relation to the staff world. Indeed, in-patients proved able to construct and to participate in a social world of their own design. This latter could often be a world of friendship, social gatherings and constructive activity. Figure 7.1 for example, indicates something about the social worlds of patients in one of the rehabilitation wards. We can see within the sociogram the existence of social isolates and people with the flimsiest of social contacts, but it is also possible to use the diagram to locate the existence of many reciprocal social contacts and embryonic social networks. In fact,

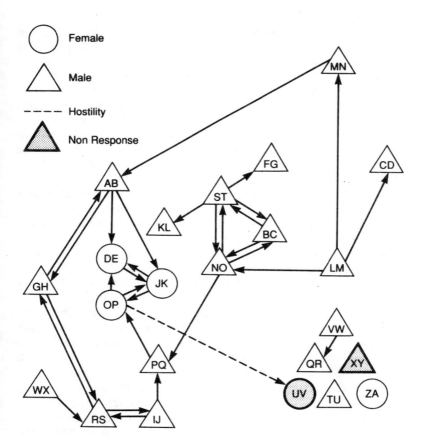

Figure 7.1 *Do you have a friend on this ward?*

the lines which interconnect the symbols indicate not just the presence of notional friendships but very often the existence of borrowing relationships, dependency relationships and sometimes even relationships of domination. Many of these affiliations were carried over into the numerous workshops and day centres which these patients attended, and in some cases they were even carried over into community life itself. As we shall see, however, being 'in the community' was no guarantee of being in a social network and in that sense institutional (hospital) life offered a social environment which was far broader than the one which patients could sometimes meet 'in the town'.

The Hospital as Asylum

It is evident from the data which we have just been discussing that mental illness (as a broad category of illness) is a polymorphic phenomenon, and in that sense there can never be any single 'definition' of it. Indeed, such polymorphism is above all evident in the fact that, at the level of personal detail, the patients in the study hospital had very little in common with each other save that their lives were organized by psychiatric professionals. So it was truly speaking treatment by a psychiatrist which defined their health status rather than any commonly held and clearly specified set of psychiatric signs and symptoms – and this statement holds true even when applied to patients within a single diagnostic group – such as, say, the schizophrenia group. It is for these kinds of reasons that it seems reasonable to suggest that mental illness is first and foremost a product of social practice rather than the expression of naturally occurring biological phenomena (though this is not in any way meant to deny or belittle the very serious personal problems with which psychiatric patients routinely grapple). And given this, it is inevitable that the specific objects of psychiatric focus tend to vary from person to person and from 'case' to case. So here it is behaviour which falls into the field of professional focus, there it is alterations of mood, and yet again, delusions or 'cognitive deficits', and very often signs of physical disorder. The routine activities of professionals in the study hospital certainly encompassed all those fields of focus and more. Yet the very presence of *illness* as such (and as distinct from, say, bad behaviour), only became visible in so far as its signs and symptoms were reflected through the specialized language, instruments and practices of professional psychiatric workers. For it was they, above all, who defined and shaped the characteristics of personal disorder as psychiatric phenomena, and it was they who created the patterns of *psychiatric* impairment which they routinely confronted with their physical, educational and social therapies.

Not surprisingly, and as in most psychiatric settings, the language and practices of the professionals in the study hospital awarded primacy of attention to the patient's body and in particular to the disease processes lurking within it – that is, with what the psychiatrists tended to refer to as 'the illness'. Consequently, the human frame was used as the central anchor point for both observation and treatment. And as a corollary of this it was clear that few, if any, of the professionals who worked within the study hospital felt able to confront the social and material circumstances in which patients found themselves as anything other than subsidiary or secondary conditions to the assumed inner bodily disorder. Perhaps it was inevitable, therefore, that members of the hospital staff sought to justify the presence of the hospital system almost entirely in terms of its being a site for medical therapy rather than as a place of welfare or care. Though in actual fact, the system fulfilled multiple functions – only some of which were manifestly 'medical'.

Most of the in-patients, of course, had a different understanding of the purposes and role of the hospital – an understanding which did not necessarily place the treatment of an illness at the core of the system. Indeed (and rather as Bott (1976) pointed out), there is a sense in which patients entered into hospital to seek a redefinition of the social relationships which they held with significant others rather than to seek 'treatment'. In that respect (as well as in many other respects) the hospital acted as an important resource for patients, their relatives and other close associates. It was, of course, a resource which they used and drew upon in different ways – partly as a place of domicile, partly as a retreat from the perceived pressures of the outside world and perhaps partly as a dumping ground. In terms of the multiple and competing systems of interpretation which circulated in the hospital, however, the patient view was normally awarded little weight, and this was to a large degree evident in the fact that patient perceptions and beliefs about daily existence were constantly subject to interpretation and reinterpretation by professional others. Naturally, this lack of attention to in-patient views ultimately reflected the fact that patients' lives and the complex human problems which emerged from those lives were forever subject to a medical discourse which saw in such things only signs of some other reality.

Nowadays, of course, the hegemony of medical ideology and medical practice is intended to be dissolved in the community solution – where the medical status of patients is supposed to be regarded as but one feature of their lives. This impending and consequent marginalization of medical psychiatry is in some respects to be represented in the fact that formal responsibility for the care of the long-term mentally ill is to be transferred from predominantly medical to predominantly welfare organizations. That, as we shall see, was indeed one of the consequences which flowed from the transfer of the study group patients from hospital to community life. That move did not, however, necessarily involve a transfer from institutional to mainstream life, and nor did it ultimately result in freedom from systems of professional dominance. Instead the most immediate consequence was a shift of the everyday responsibility for care and therapy away from the shoulders of highly trained professionals, and onto the shoulders of relatively untrained functionaries (care assistants), and very often onto the shoulders of people with little or no interest in psychiatric impairments whatsoever.

8
The Social Worlds of the Community

> The idea that in order to get clear about the meaning of a
> general term one had to find the common element in all its
> applications has shackled philosophical investigation; for it has
> not only led to no result, but also made the philosopher dismiss
> as irrelevant the concrete cases, which alone could have helped
> him to understand the usage of the general term.
>
> (Wittgenstein, 1969: 19)

From Disempowered Patient to Autonomous Consumer

Whilst 'mental hospitals' have had a markedly bad press during the
last 30 or so years there can be little doubt that 'community' has had
a comparatively good press. And we have already seen how the
social policy impetus for people suffering from psychiatric disorders
has long been located in community based rather than in hospital
based projects for care of the mentally ill. Indeed, this emphasis on
community has been underlined by the fact that almost every UK
government statement on the organization of psychiatric services
published since 1959 has argued against the expansion of long-term
hospital care and in favour of what it refers to as community care.
Though in practice, community care is taken simply to mean 'care
outside hospital' (DHSS Northern Ireland, 1990a: 11), or care
which is not in state institutions (Eastern Health and Social Services
Board (EHSSB), 1986). So Griffiths (1988), for example, describes
community care as care provided to people 'in their own homes,
group homes, residential care homes, hostels and nursing homes'
(1988: 3). In other words, community is ordinarily defined only in
terms of its opposition to any form of hospital based institutional
life.

Naturally, the advocates of community care argue variously about
the aims, benefits and purposes of the new order. So the mental
health association MIND, for example, in its *Report to Sir Roy
Griffiths* (1987) stated that community care was 'the best way to
enable those with a mental illness to achieve maximum autonomy
and self-determination' (1987: 2). Whilst the DHSS Community
Care Circular (1983) advocated such care in terms of the supposed

preferences of dependent individuals arguing that, 'Most people who need long-term care can and should be looked after in the community. That is what most of them want for themselves and what those responsible for their care believe to be best.' Griffiths himself on the other hand, placed the emphasis on the provision of choice and the exercise of responsibility, arguing that, 'if community care means anything it is that responsibility is placed as near to the individual' as possible (1988: viii). And the 1990 (DHSS Northern Ireland, 1990a) booklet, *People First*, argued that extending choice and helping people to live as independently as possible was the realistic way forward for structuring the 'delivery' of care. The detail is somewhat unfocused perhaps, but in broad terms it seems to be the case that most of the UK proponents of community care seek, in one way or another, to reconstruct the previously disempowered and institutionalized patient as an independent consumer in a free market society. And it is in that sense that the broad thrust of care in the community policies often appear to be driven by political rather than traditional psychiatric concerns. Perhaps because of this, there are some groups and individuals who have serious reservations about the suitability and efficacy of care in the community programmes. So the UK House of Commons Social Services Committee (House of Commons, 1985), for example, argued that there was still a need for 'asylum' for the mentally ill and that community care was not suitable for all. And the National Schizophrenia Fellowship (NSF) has been a particularly vociferous critic of community care policies. Thus, much of its literature talks about a 'silent tragedy' and a 'crisis' in which people are discharged from hospital into makeshift circumstances, so that ex-patients often end up in prison or homeless, or as suicides. And point seven of its '20 Point Plan' (NSF, 1989), argues for the retention of long-term hospital accommodation for those 'who just cannot cope outside'. These latter critiques do not, however, stem from any consistent political philosophy and so it is above all the language of choice, independence, personal responsibility and normalization which rules in discussions of care in the community policies, and this is predominantly the language which surfaces in the policy documents whose contents serve to shape the lives of the study group patients.

We shall examine the new lexicon of care in just a moment. First, however, it is important to point out that the opposition between hospital and community care is more often than not erroneously conflated with a second transition – namely one from institutional to non-institutional care. And this confusion between the two processes can be traced right back to the publications of the 1950s and

1960s (such as those of Barton, 1959; and Goffman, 1961) which attacked the idea of a mental hospital on the grounds of its capacity to institutionalize behaviour and corrupt the individuality of its inmates. As we shall see, this equation of community with non-institutional life is far from justified, and many of the aspects which Goffman saw as being defining characteristics of total institutions are fully present in community settings. Thus the tendency for almost any aspect of daily activity to be organized or directed by authority figures – for example the times at which people should wash, or sleep, or bath, or shop. The tendency for daily activities to be carried out in synchrony with a large group of others – for example, the times at which people have breakfast, or lunch, or the times at which people go shopping or indulge in leisure activities. And the tendency to view the directed and synchronized activities as fulfilling some kind of therapeutic or beneficial aim, can be found just as readily outside the hospital as within it. Needless to say, the people who live in such institutions often have a unique perspective on what such forms of organization are all about. And rather than interpreting 'institutions' as being oppressive to the expression of their individuality, often view them as suitable servants to their personal needs – so as one community resident approvingly defined it, an institution 'is where everything is done for you'.

Destinations

In a study of organizational constraints on psychiatric treatment, Byrd (1981) demonstrated that the key determinant of client fates often rested in what she called organizational needs (as opposed to client needs). Thus, she argued, although doctors, social workers and members of other relevant professional groupings, emphasized that client needs determine what is done to and for patients, in practice it is organizational demands which structure patient fates. For example, clients have to be (and can only be) matched to the number of openings available in the organizational structure itself. If therefore there are many facilities for the treatment of, say, substance abuse and few for depressive disorders then client fates will be more favourable for the 'addicts' than for others. Furthermore, and more importantly, she claimed that clients are likely to be classified and reclassified at various stages during their careers so as to 'better meet organizational requirements' (1981: 3).

Byrd's is an insightful study, and to some extent her findings have a ready application here, for in the hospital context it was clear that individual chances of entry into the rehabilitation wards and of subsequent discharge, depended not simply on the qualities of the person *qua* psychiatric patient, but also on the number of organizational 'openings' which were available at any one time. So the more openings there were available in a particular ward or a community the greater were the chances of moving into such an opening. To give one example, it was clear that the fates of some of the Catholic in-patients were shaped by the fact that, until recently, few hostel facilities were available in the Catholic or 'mixed' areas of Ballybreen, whilst there were numerous facilities in the Protestant areas. This difference is crucial in a sectarian society because it may well have been dangerous to discharge Catholics into Protestant areas. Entry into the community was not, therefore, simply a matter of some inner readiness on behalf of the patient, but was in part determined by the extent of the available organizational resources. And in line with these organizational constraints, the psychiatric characteristics of patients were frequently redefined so as to better 'fit' the openings available. Thus, the boundary which psychiatrists and hospital nurses drew between 'higher' and 'lower grade' patients constantly shifted as more community openings became available and the pressures to reduce in-patient numbers increased. Indeed, even in the relatively short span of time covered by the research process, the criteria for discharge from hospital changed markedly. Thus at one stage, it was said of Freddie (whose case was cited in Chapter 7) that his experiencing delusions should not in itself prove a bar to being discharged – despite the fact that his preoccupation with such delusions had constituted the *raison d'être* of his hospitalization since the 1950s.

It was evident during the period of the empirical study, then, that the fates of hospital in-patients were clearly being determined by shifts in ideology and social and medical policies, rather than by any inner change in the condition of the patients themselves. Indeed, and as we can guess from the information contained in Table 7.3, it is more than likely that the patients in the study group expressed their psychological, behavioural and social peculiarities just as forcefully in 1990 as they had done 10 or 20 or even 30 years previously. In that sense it is reasonable to suggest that their dehospitalization had little to do with advances in physical methods of treatment, spontaneous improvements in their psychiatric conditions, or even advances in non-somatic forms of psychiatric therapy. On the contrary, for their expulsion from the social world of the hospital into the world of the 'community' was more properly a product of extra-personal forces and circumstances which grew out of the changes in professional psychiatric practice which we have examined in the last seven or so chapters. One expression of their entry into the community was, of course, 'a transfer of care' (P. Brown, 1985). That is to say, a transfer of responsibility from the hospital to social service authorities. So at the point of discharge from hospital, the patients in the study group supposedly moved out of the domain of the medical authorities and into the domain of the social services. (In bureaucratic terms, however, their care was organized by a Health and Social Services Board which, in the jargon of the day, was supposed to deliver care in a seamless system.) This notional transfer of responsibility was not, however, a cause of the dehospitalization processes but merely a different expression of it. In the same way that the cost changes which were consequent on the move from hospital to community did not provide the rationale for the changes of patient life style (indeed it is still unclear as to what such cost changes might be), but followed necessarily from the ideological shifts and alterations of professional practice which we have discussed in previous chapters.

The term dehospitalization is, of course, a carefully chosen one. Chosen to indicate that the entry of in-patients into the community did not necessarily imply an escape from forms of institutional life.

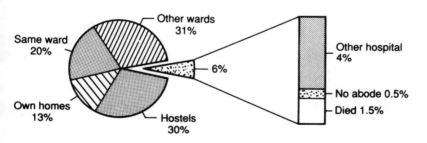

Figure 8.1 *First outcomes: destinations of 181 patients who entered the 'rehab' wards of the study hospital, 1986–90*

The destinations of people who lived in the 'rehab' wards between 1986 and 1990, for example, are summarized in Figure 8.1. And therein we can see that of the 181 patient episodes, just over 49 per cent resulted in patients being 'discharged' from hospital – and of those, 61 per cent resulted in entry to hostels, and just 30 per cent in a return to a family home. In fact, Figure 8.1 indicates quite clearly that the move from hospital to community is in fact a matter of institutional substitution rather than a move into an independent world of community life. Indeed, very few of the people with whom we are concerned could be said to have entered into any kind of independent existence whatsoever – and this was true even during the months (and years) which followed their discharge. Furthermore, and as has already been pointed out in Chapter 7, many in-patients have a history of multiple admissions, and so discharge from hospital did not necessarily mean that the world of the hospital was left behind for all time. Some insight into the second stage process of ex-patient life is provided by the information contained in Figure 8.2. This chart provides data on the destinations of the 54 people who first entered hostels between 1986 and 1990. In fact, most of the patients were admitted into one specific 'assessment hostel' at point of discharge from hospital and were consequently relatively easy to trace. The tracking of these second moves, again displays a transfer of people between institutions rather than entry into a mainstream world. And as we shall see, it is the 'group homes' (which, despite the title, exhibit numerous institutional features) that turn out to be the true community equivalent of the hospital ward.

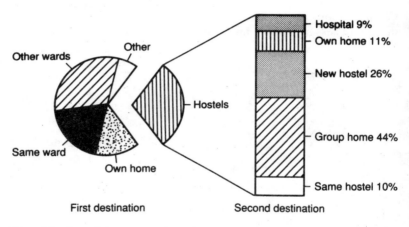

Figure 8.2   *Second destinations of people originally discharged to hostels*

As one might expect, there were small numbers of people who left for 'no fixed abode'. That is to say, people who left hospital for the street, for night shelters and for doss houses – though it is only fair to point out that entry into this nether-world was chosen by individuals themselves rather than a consequence of (poor) organizational planning. Naturally, the existence of these kinds of outcomes make it impossible to equate care in the community with universal improvements in material circumstances or 'quality of life'. That is, unless one redrafts the discourse of care so as to consider the expression of choice, individuality and 'personal responsibility' as advances in themselves. Naturally, the politicization of discourses on health, health care, and health promotion in the UK during the 1980s and 1990s (and which is evidenced in such publications as, *Community Care: Agenda for Action* (Griffiths, 1988), and *The Health of the Nation* (Department of Health, 1992)) has made such a redrafting possible.

Ideologies of Community Care

As far as professional care workers are concerned, the two most important watchwords of community services are those of independence and normalization. And the main aim of social services personnel in general, as well as of many of the care workers who worked in statutory and voluntary sector hostels and homes, was to give practical expression to these features above all others. Along with these big objectives, however, documents drawn up in community settings also cited a series of related and subsidiary aims – such as, for example, the provision of opportunities for choice, or the development of respect for the individual, or the reduction of stigma. And in most of the Health and Social Services Board hostels, training and educational goals were incorporated into both the mission statements and the routine procedures which occurred within them. So in each specific setting there was always a mix of aims and intentions – and an even greater mix of practices. The brief extracts which follow (gathered from the mission statements of a number of different hostels) illustrate the breadth of concern.

- To provide 'real opportunities for reintegration into the community'.
- To 'improve the quality of life of the individual'.
- To 'maximize potential and foster independence'.
- To work on the 'principle of normalization'.
- To 'establish potential for independent and semi-independent living'.
- To 'promote dignity, personal choice, integration and participation'.
- To 'provide a better quality of life and to prevent institutionalization'.

Few of the homes and hostels in the private sector, however, gave any such indication of their aims.

The concept of normalization, of course, has its theoretical beginnings in the work of Wolfensberger (1972), though he in turn traces its origins to the practices of the Danish Mental Retardation Service in the late 1960s. In his own explication of the principles of normalization, Wolfensberger lays emphasis on the physical and social integration of disabled people into mainstream social life. In the study setting, however, those who talked of normalization usually had far more limited aims than this in mind. The practices of the Danish Service, of course, were probably just the earliest documented expression of a much wider trend which is now evident in all advanced industrial societies. And that trend is in large part linked to a series of economic, technological and social processes whereby the significance of the body as a major source of physical and therefore of occupational capital has been diminished. (The concept of 'physical capital' is Bourdieu's (1986).) Thus, as the economic significance of human physical capacities has been reduced in modern economies, so claims for equality of opportunity and equality of treatment for disabled individuals have increased. And, more pertinently, the arguments which have been used to advance the economic and social demands of people with physical disabilities have been further extended so as to apply to the lives of the mentally handicapped, and from there, to the fates of the mentally ill.

This changing role of physical (bodily) capital in modern economies can also be linked to a second set of changes. These latter concern the extent to which people with 'abnormal bodies' have challenged the systems of medical hegemony which once defined their social status. So whereas during the earlier part of the century the medical profession was able to define people with mental and physical disabilities almost solely in terms of medical discourse, it is clear that in the latter part of the century such definitional strategies are no longer regarded as acceptable. In that sense chronic 'illness' and disability are now viewed as merely one source of difficulty among others, and the significance of such disability in everyday human activity is consequently marginalized. In some cases (as with mental handicap), the perceived abnormality is redefined in such a way as to remove it almost entirely from the scope of medical discourse (so the mentally handicapped become 'people with learning difficulties'). And given these trends it is easy to see that the movement of the mentally ill from hospital to community settings signals much more than a simple physical movement of patients from one site to another. For whereas in the psychiatric hospital 'illness' dominates both patient identity and everyday life (as was in fact seen in Chapter 7), in the community a person's 'illness' is regarded as just one aspect of existence. One specific organizational correlate of this shift of emphasis is evident in the fact that ex-hospital patients are more than likely to be integrated first and foremost into the primary health care system rather than into any specialized psychiatric service. Though there was some evidence to suggest that people with serious psychiatric illnesses had some difficulty in being accepted by General Practitioners. And together with this transfer of medical management from a specialized service to a primary health care service goes a transfer of responsibility from health to welfare organizations. Contact with nurses, especially Community Psychiatric Nurses (CPNs), Social Workers and Psychiatrists is of course maintained, but such professionals no longer dictate the circumstances of everyday life. (Circumstances which are now more likely to be in the hands of private sector entrepreneurs, voluntary care workers, social services care assistants and so on.) Indeed, the structuring of care for the mentally ill in terms of community based sites has even given rise to demands for the creation of a new occupational role – that of the 'community carer'. It is a role which was first identified by the Audit Commission (1986), and thereafter given favour by Griffiths (1988: 2) himself.

As with normalization, the concept of independence is usually given a somewhat restrictive and limited meaning in practical empirical circumstances (to do with freedom from institutional restraint). Yet in the wider and broader discourse on community care the term is in fact related to fundamental processes at work in the social, economic and political fabric at large. Some of these forces have been previously identified by Williams (1988), who points towards the free-market ideologies associated with the independence movement. And there can be little doubt that in broad ideological terms, the move towards independence is not simply concerned with the relaxation of petty institutional restraints on disabled people, but more frequently with a broader attempt to reconstruct the members of socially dependent groups as autonomous 'consumers'. Consumers are, of course, more commonly referred to as clients (rather than patients), and many of the official documents on community care seek to represent such clients in the image of the rational purchaser of goods and services so beloved of classical utilitarian theory. Thus *Community Care: Agenda for Action* (Griffiths, 1988) speaks of the need for innovation, competition and the mixed economy of care which supposedly maximizes the options available to consumers, and in like manner the DHSS (Northern Ireland) document *People First* (1990a), echoes this market oriented discourse. Of course, the purchaser of care and the consumer of care are not necessarily identical entities (the first is more likely to be an organization and the second an individual), and in that sense the language of free-market economics does not always apply directly to the mentally ill as persons.

But the general thrust of the independence movement is neverthe-less to conceive of the person with serious and chronic psychiatric impairments in the role of a consumer rather than in the role of a dependent patient. In this respect the ex-patient is encouraged to reconstruct his or her social identity in terms of a symbolic order other than that related to the order of illness, disability and dependency which so characterizes routine hospital life. That is to say, other than that in terms of which the 'sick role' is ordinarily structured.

This new symbolic order is, above all, one built around the notion of consumer 'needs', the consumption of objects and the creation of life styles. The fulfilment of such needs and the formation of such life styles, of course, forms the characteristic mode of social activity in all post-industrial societies and serves as an integral component of the system of production (Kellner, 1989). But modern systems of consumption are also aimed at the differentiation and atomization of individuals, and as such result in the endless formation and reformation of social distinctions. And therein lies a problem for people with psychiatric disorders. For as we have seen, one significant aspect of serious mental illness as it is assessed in the late twentieth century, is the perceived inability of mentally ill persons to manipulate a symbolic order successfully, or at least, with any rational plan. And this observation alone should generate suspi-cions about the potential of people who are mentally ill to integrate themselves as consumers into mainstream social life. This apart from the fact that the majority of people with serious psychiatric disorders simply do not have material resources sufficient to locate themselves as active economic agents in the wider society – the modal disposable income for members of the study group after the deduction of subsistence costs, for example, was just £10 per week. Hence, rather than entering into the social worlds of the economi-cally active, ex-patients in the community tend to live in a subworld of the disabled and the handicapped and the sick – a subworld in which contacts with mainstream life are, at best, fleeting and superficial.

Social Worlds of the Ex-patient

Imagined Communities
We have already noted something about destinations and spoken of the reality of institutional substitution. It is a common enough result, and one which is, for example, replicated in both the Darenth Park Hospital study (Korman and Glennerster, 1990), and

the Claybury and Friern study (Tomlinson, 1991). And although most of the places in which the Ballybreen ex-patients found themselves bore little physical resemblance to the old psychiatric hospital, they nevertheless remained institutions in almost every other sense of the word. (One private sector home, for example, was even listed in the phone book as a 'Psychiatric Hospital'.) Institutions in the community, of course, took various titles – Nursing Home, Salvation Army Hostel, Private Retirement Home, Residential Home, Group Home or just a simple mailing address. Many of them were sited in poorer parts of the city, and sometimes in lawless and violent parts of the city where residents were subject to acts of petty theft and/or personal attack from people in the neighbourhood (though not necessarily because they were ex-hospital patients). Predictably, some institutions were located in large converted middle class mansions (built in areas of the city which had once seen better days), so in general it was only the smaller group homes which were likely to be found in the outer suburbs – and they were usually located on working class housing estates. In fact, with the exception of the group homes (which we shall come to in a few moments), the buildings into which ex-hospital patients were discharged usually presented a clearly identifiable institutional facade to the world – albeit on a much smaller scale than the hospital. Though more important perhaps than the exterior of such buildings, was the fact that the interior structure almost always evidenced features of institutional life and design. It was therefore usually easy enough to find such things as rooms with locks and door catches deliberately removed (by officials), upper storey windows modified so as to open only partially, and areas of a building reserved for the use of staff alone (and outside of which residents had to wait, or queue, or make requests to enter). Indeed, as in the hospital, such areas invariably served to form the material boundaries in terms of which staff and inmates organized their social worlds. In addition to aspects of building design, of course, many of the sites in which ex-patients found themselves retained a significant number of the organizational and interactional features which had been evident in the hospital world. Thus daily events (breakfasts, dinners, bath times) were time-tabled and often strictly governed, and the scope for the assertion of individuality was suppressed in numerous other ways. Some homes and hostels, for example, had plans of the daily seating arrangements (which residents were supposed to adhere to at meal times) pinned on the walls – a feature which was not even present in hospital wards – and the protection of personal privacy was no more evident in the community than it had been in hospital. Thus,

Officers-In-Charge of homes and hostels and the members of their staffs (note the terminology here), usually controlled all manner of financial, medical and personal details of client lives – details which were freely open to inspection by almost any 'insider'. More importantly, the routine relationships between staff and residents often adopted a highly directive nature and residents invariably deferred to the 'staff' as a source of instruction and assistance. And in this respect, at least, the social world of the in-patient and the world of the ex-patient ran in parallel.

Group homes (which were much favoured by advocates of care in the community programmes), were naturally enough well positioned for structuring a 'normal' lifestyle – by the very fact of their domestic design and suburban location. In terms of interpersonal relations and everyday living, however, group homes still managed to retain many features of institutional life. So routine daily existence, for example, was frequently overdirected in both its broad and in its narrow features. Group home residents were often told what to do, how to dress and what to eat. Their daily lives often took on similar patterns to those which had been left behind in the psychiatric hospital – they attended the same day centres, went to the same leisure centres, met the self same individuals (and very often attended social evenings in the old hospital). In addition, the overall nature and structure of staff–patient relationships (as in the hostels and 'homes' referred to above) tended to replicate those which could be found in the hospital. So very often, tiny details of everyday interaction and routine activities were carefully monitored and controlled by care assistants (such as what time residents got out of bed, what they kept in their lockers and what they did during the day). Not surprisingly, perhaps, some residents complained about being told what to do 'all of the time', and some objected to the frequent invasions of privacy. (Though given the nature of psychiatric disorders, some of these complaints were invariably expressed in terms of paranoid delusions.) Many of the ex-patients claimed that their lives in group homes were 'no different' from their lives in hospital, or that life in the community was 'just the same' as it was in hospital. Whilst others, though not objecting to the various directives to which they were subject, claimed that they 'needed' to be told what to do. Indeed, the percentage of residents in the study group who agreed with the proposition that their lives were 'run too much by other people' was no less than that found among hospital patients (roughly 19 per cent).

Some of the ex-patients lived at home and they were not directly subject to the kinds of restrictions which institutional residents faced. Indeed being discharged from hospital to 'home' was viewed by the political advocates of care in the community as the ideal outcome. Thus the government booklet *People First* argued that the aim of a community mental health service should be to 'bring individually tailored packages of service to people's homes' (DHSS Northern Ireland, 1990a: 16), because home was where most people who needed professional care wished to be. The homes into which patients were discharged were, as one would expect, certainly domestic in scale and appearance, and sometimes contained relatives or other familiar individuals. But in some cases the ex-patient's 'home' was a home only in the physical sense of the word. It did not always house other individuals, or it perhaps contained people whom the ex-patient disliked or was suspicious of. Nor did being at home necessarily result in an escape from relationships of domination and subordination. And some homes clearly fell outside of a socio-cultural concept of 'home' which is occasionally encountered in many modern discussions of community care. Segal and Baumohl, for example, conceptualize home as a place where there exists a 'matrix of desirable and highly valued attachments' (1988: 249). This lack of affiliative bonds was in fact characteristic of the circumstances of many of the ex-hospital patients and served to underline the ways in which their being *in* the community was far from being a guarantee of their *belonging* to a community.

Table 8.1   *Some aspects of in-patient and ex-patient lives*

	In-patients In the 'rehab' wards	Ex-patients In hostels/ group homes	In own homes
Diagnosed schizophrenic (%)	87	73	50*
Adm (μ)	6	5	10*
Marstat (%)	81	88	46*
Visit 1 (%)	46	32	69*
Visit 2 (%)	28	46	56
Network Size (μ)	5	7	8
Activity (μ)	3.5	2.5	1.5*
Numbers	49	48	16

Adm: Average number of hospital admissions; Marstat: % of people never married; Visit 1: % who get a visit from any relative/friend; Visit 2: % who make any kind of visit to a relative/friend outside of place of residence; Network size: Average size of social network; Activity: Average number of days per week spent in OT or other directed activity.

* $p < 0.05$ compared with the other two groups.

Naturally, the social worlds of ex-hospital patients (like the worlds of in-patients) can be partially mapped and traced in terms of the number and extent of social contacts which individuals report. And Table 8.1 gives some indication of the comparative size of the social networks of the different groups. (The definition of a network is provided in the Appendix, see page 198.) As the table indicates the overall size of network for ex-patients was much the same as it was for in-patients and in that sense being in the community did not result in any major alterations of lifestyle. Nor was the substance of social relationships any different. A diagrammatic representation of social relations in one of the group homes is, for example, provided in Figure 8.3, and as we can see, the patterns are similar to those which one might find in a hospital ward – containing both reciprocated and unreciprocated relationships combined with ele-

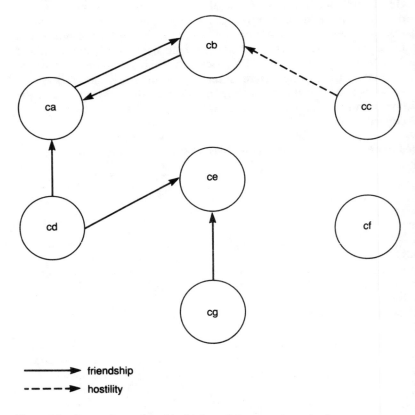

Figure 8.3   *Do you have a friend in this house? Patterns of perceived friendship in a small group home*

ments of social isolation. (And these conclusions are not inconsistent with those from other UK studies – see, for example, Tomlinson, 1991.) Indeed, the major determinant of network size was age rather than location, so that whilst many of the younger patients had friends and relatives to call upon (irrespective of their living circumstances), the older patients did not. What is most interesting of all, however, is the fact that in the community the nature of these social relationships and interrelationships tended to take on a new significance in the discourse of professional psychiatric workers.

Images of Disorder

It was stated in Chapter 7 that one of the prime features of hospital life was that, as far as professionals were concerned, *treatment* dominated care. And one might say the same about life in community settings, but with one major difference – namely that in the latter, the concept of treatment is broadened to cover phenomena which would normally be regarded as peripheral in a hospital context. Thus, in the community such things as personal relationships, 'emotional atmosphere' and mundane material conditions were all regarded as constituting an essential part of the therapeutic mesh within which patients lived. Consequently, professional assessments of life outside of hospital were based on a much wider vision of an individual and his or her needs and capacities than was life in hospital. Naturally enough, notions of disease and illness still figured in understandings of serious mental disorder, and CPNs and Social Workers were just as prepared to cite a disease (commonly referred to as 'the illness') as the ultimate source and origin of client problems as were the hospital staff before them. Equally, nurses and psychiatrists in the community relied just as readily on the chemical control of symptoms as did their hospital based counterparts – though the actual chemicals used and the ways in which they were administered tended to differ in the two settings. And community based nurses, social workers and psychologists continued to observe, describe and analyse their patients in terms of the same behavioural discourse which was utilized in Ballybreen hospital. To that extent the presence and nature of psychiatric disorder (on a day to day basis) was primarily encountered in terms of its behavioural manifestations. Furthermore, it was clear that the concepts of psyche and mind were as marginal to a professional understanding of patients in the community as it was to an understanding of hospital in-patients. Psychotherapy as a mode of treatment was used, but in the region as a whole there was only one out-patient psychotherapy session for every 18.5 'psychiatric' sessions during 1989–90, and none involved the patients in the study group. Indeed, the dominant and all pervasive vision of mental illness as (at base) nothing more than a form of physical illness, was firmly underpinned at a wider organizational level through the provision and use of psychiatric units in general hospitals. These latter were in large part provided so as to represent mental illness in an entirely different light from that which had filtered through the old psychiatric hospital system. In actual fact, however, their focus on body and nerves replicated the exact same somatology which was present in the old 'asylum', and to that extent they merely fostered the continuation of a physicalist discourse under a different organizational guise. As far as the members of the study group were concerned, however, only a tiny number of people had actually been admitted to a psychiatric unit – most readmissions continuing to take place at the specialized psychiatric hospital.

Despite these similarities in outlook of hospital based and community based professionals, however, it was clear that (with the CPNs especially) new and different considerations in the description and explanation of serious psychiatric disorders routinely emerged in community settings. And of these the most significant was consideration of family and other social relationships in 'stabilizing' or 'exciting' the patient. Indeed, this consideration of social relationships as a major element in the therapeutic tincture was sometimes used as a base from which to question the appropriateness of psychiatric units in general hospitals as suitable sites for treatment. (Doubts about the suitability of units in general hospitals for the treatment of psychiatric illness have, of course, been expressed throughout the decades – see, for example, Baruch and Treacher 1978; Martin *et al.*, 1961; WHO, 1953.) Thus the relevance of providing 'bed space' in the manner of a medical ward, was questioned by some CPNs who believed that the therapeutic emphasis ought to be placed on social, occupational and counselling activities and contexts rather than on chemical treatments. Needless to say such occupational activities and social contexts were not easily catered for in a general hospital setting. What is more, for the CPN, it was the 'home visit' which acted as the cornerstone of the psychiatric system rather than the hospital bed, and in many ways the altered ideological outlook of the CPN (as compared with the ward nurse) was underpinned by the fact that the former was usually located in a radically different site from that of their hospital counterparts, namely, a Community Health Centre rather than a ward.

This concern with the interpersonal milieu in which patients lived as a key factor in the therapeutic process was evidenced most clearly in discussions of and conversations about specific patients on the CPN register. And it is an emphasis which is rather nicely brought out, for example, in the following conversational extract which arose out of a discussion between the researcher and two Community Psychiatric Nurses (CPNs) about what was 'wrong with Jon' (one of the study group patients).

> *CPN1:* Jon's problems are part of a family syndrome. His mother suffers with her nerves. His sister is schizophrenic. His brother has been in hospital. [. . .]
> *CPN2:* Yes. You see. The CPN has to treat the whole family and not just the person on the list. And our workload ought to be treated in terms of families rather than individuals. . . . We have to look at the family dynamics.

This reference to the family as a source of psychiatric therapy would never have appeared in the context of the hospital ward, and this was not simply because of the contingencies of the case at hand. Instead, the reason for the contrast is to be found in the fact that a concentration on the family or social relationships as a field of therapy ran directly counter to the hospital emphasis on the individual patient as the source and origin of psychiatric problems. In hospital the illness was 'in' the patient and had to be 'treated' as such. In community settings, whilst the seat of the illness might be considered to be in the patient, its day to day manifestations were very clearly linked to the emotional and practical nature of family and other interpersonal relationships. Naturally enough, references to family relationships took many different forms – sometimes they were casual, such as the reference to mothers having 'long apron strings' which supposedly stifled and retarded what CPNs considered to be normal psychiatric functioning. At other times it was in terms of references to families who tended to 'pressurise' their members, and sometimes by reference to nothing more concrete than 'home circumstances'. Thus, stated one CPN, 'if home circumstances break down, that ensures that the person breaks down'. Though naturally enough, elementary references to what we might call material circumstances (as well as emotional and interpersonal contexts) also figured in accounts and explanations of mental stability and relapse. Thus poor housing, and especially overcrowding, as well as lack of employment, were things which were frequently cited as contributing factors to psychiatric instability.

As was previously mentioned in Chapter 6, in the city in which this study was carried out, the CPN service had produced booklets directly aimed at relatives and families of people categorized as schizophrenic which outlined the role of family members in creating or upsetting the conditions for mental stability (EHSSB, 1989). The booklet indicated how the activities and attitudes of relatives were crucial to the development of the illness. Relatives were encouraged to reduce the amount of 'pressure' they placed on schizophrenic affines and to be constructive in their approaches to the latter. This focus on the family and social relationships was, however, seen by some CPNs as a source of potential conflict with social workers, who were working within the same field. It was sometimes said of social workers that they were 'doing our job' – that is to say, overlapping their interests with what were regarded as techniques of nursing. In the hospital, of course, such conflicts never arose because the professional terrain of family and family interrelationships were part of a 'negotiated order' (Strauss, 1963) in which family life was allocated to social work rather than to nursing. In this respect it seemed as if the (relatively) new field of nursing focus was also being carved out as a new area of professional practice, and this inevitably conflicted with the interests of those who were already established on the disputed territory. Such interprofessional competitiveness was, of course, more likely to overflow in relation to the treatment of minor rather than serious psychiatric disorder – and especially where Social Workers and CPNs turned to the use of counselling techniques as a means of managing distress related to such things as eating disorders, cases of minor depression, post traumatic stress disorder, or alcoholism. (The existence of interprofessional conflict between CPNs and Social Workers has, of course, been noted in other community contexts as well as this one – see, for example, Woof and Goldberg, 1988.)

This contest over sites for therapeutic practice in many ways helped to emphasize the wider focus of the community gaze which was evident in much professional practice – namely, a gaze directed towards social relations rather than biological characteristics. Interestingly, however, it was also a gaze which contrasted strongly with that of the lay assistants and residential staff who worked in the hostels and group homes to which ex-patients were dispatched. The latter tended to hold to ideas and images of therapy and illness which were more in line with those found within the old hospital than those which were prevalent in the staff rooms of the community based health centres. Thus lay assistants, for example, were usually inclined to see a hostel or home primarily as a place for living, whilst treatment was regarded as something that went on elsewhere. In consequence, therapy was seen solely as a function of the CPN, the staff at the day centres, or the General Practitioner. And there was little recognition of the CPN belief that nearly all aspects of daily life could be structured so as to be of some therapeutic value. In the homes and hostels of the statutory and voluntary sectors such physicalist images of psychiatric impairment were liable to be 'corrected' by professionally trained staff, but in the private sector homes there were few alternatives to such visions, and so it was there above all that the older biological and genetic images of mental illness persisted.

Overall, then, it is clear that the influence of family and other social relationships were considered much more closely (and in a somewhat different light) by community based professionals, than they were by hospital based professionals. In part this may simply have been a reflection of the differing social circumstances in which long-term hospital patients and community based patients found themselves (the long-stay patients had, after all, few contacts with relatives of any kind). Or it may have been related to the fact that the psychiatric hospital dealt mainly with cases of serious psychiatric disorder – whilst in the community the CPN encountered a large number of cases of relatively minor disorder. But given that both hospital nurses and CPNs were effectively dealing with the same patients, this altered focus can also be seen as reflecting a radically different understanding about what mental illness was and what the appropriate objects of therapy might be. For in the community those objects were far broader and much larger than could be encompassed in the body of the isolated and individualized patient alone.

Patterns of Activity

In addition to a focus on family and social relationships, CPNs also gave emphasis to the role of purposeful and structured activities in the therapeutic order. Idleness and poorly organized plans of action were, for example, regarded as things to be avoided, whilst the introduction of activities and hobbies into people's daily lives was seen to be essential for 'good mental health'. Thus, argued the author of the advice booklet, 'the sooner a programme of care is begun all the better because it helps prevent the sufferer falling into a routine of bad habits' (EHSSB, 1989). Even when patients refused to enter into day centres, therefore, CPNs would do their best to devise some kind of elementary 'programme' for their community clients, and this interest in activity was part of that broader therapeutic vision which seemed to be so characteristic of community life. Though, in many cases, the programme might include nothing more elaborate than encouraging the patient to get out of bed at a set time each day, tidying a room, or watching television. In that sense the CPN tended to do little more than elevate the mundane and ordinary aspects of everyday life into the sphere of the therapeutic. This professionalization of the mundane was especially evident in the work of Occupational Therapists who, in line with the precepts of the age, also undertook 'home visits'. In general, however, the provision of therapeutic activities usually involved entry into formally organized day centres, day hospitals and industrial therapy units rather than activities in ordinary domestic settings (see Table 8.1).

As with the residential facilities, day centres and day hospitals came in a variety of shapes and sizes, and sported a wide range of objectives. And in the same way that the mission statements of residential homes provided a mix of aims, so too did the statements of day centres and related facilities. Thus words and phrases pertaining to normalization, quality of life, the integration of 'clients' into everyday activities and the like, were as readily visible in the documents of the day centres as they were in the documents of the social services hostels and group homes. In addition, and in at least two cases, the role of structured activities in preventing the onset of morbid symptoms was mentioned and in one case their role in reducing the impact of stigma figured in the policy document. As well as variations in policy, there were also variations in the types and kinds of activities which were offered. Some centres concentrated on relaxation and creative activities such as art work, sewing and stitching, photography and gardening. Others concentrated on 'Activities of Daily Living', such as elements of personal hygiene, cosmetic and domestic tasks, or training in 'life skills' and interpersonal skills in general. Occasionally there was an emphasis on industrial therapy rather than recreation therapy and an attempt to redirect the patient (or ex-patient) towards the world of employment (none of the people in the study group, however, obtained any kind of full-time employment). But as well as offering activities to clients, the day centres also fulfilled an important role within the overall system of psychiatric care, and especially in so far as they formed part of the observational web within which patients/clients were ordinarily enmeshed. Thus, most if not all of the statutory sector centres sought to formally monitor and assess their clients, and they also formed part of a periodic review system in which social workers, psychiatrists, day centre staff and community psychiatric nurses all had a role. Indeed, it was in the process of 'review' that the centrality of such phenomena as client behaviour – which was most commonly assessed by means of commercial instruments – and features of client social interaction were made manifest.

As well as variations in ideas about the aims and activities of day centres, there was also ambiguity about the therapeutic role which could be played by these centres. In large part this confusion emanated from a failure to distinguish between professionally organized therapy (of different kinds) and things and activities which had therapeutic value. Thus, after explaining what the work of his centre was about, the Officer-in-Charge of one of the larger units summed up by saying 'it's all therapy', adding that therapy was not simply something which came 'out of a bottle'. In using this phrase he presumably sought to indicate that the entire milieu and structure of the unit was regarded as serving some therapeutic purpose or other, and that even the smallest detail of daily life could be used so as to fulfil a therapeutic function – including the act of 'clocking on' in the mornings. (The latter, he said, helped to 'structure the day'.) Despite this, no formal counselling or other therapeutic sessions were held within the centre. And perhaps it was whilst thinking of therapy in this formal structured sense that an OIC of a voluntary sector centre – which provided a large range of well organized activities – could claim that 'there [was] no therapy at the centre' (though there were many activities). In like manner some Officers-in-Charge argued that treatment and therapy were preserves of the day hospitals and that the centres had only a minor role to play in the prevention of illness and the stabilization of mental health. In that sense therapy was seen as the function of the nursing or psychiatric rather than of the day centre staff. And these kinds of attitudes quite naturally found a loud echo in the conversations of the hospital based staff who recognized the virtues of occupational therapy but saw it as being of a lesser order than the major therapy of chemical control. Nevertheless, and despite such differences of opinion and divergencies in the assessment of what was and what was not therapeutic, we can perhaps begin to see how the increased provision of day centre facilities and occupational therapy programmes is not just one more administrative adjunct of care in the community programmes, but in part a fundamental reassessment of what illnesses such as schizophrenia might be, and of what the 'schizophrenic patient' actually needs.

Whatever their therapeutic function and whatever their role in the overall pattern of the psychiatric service it was clear that most of the day care locations were far from being monopolized by people with psychiatric problems or by mentally handicapped individuals. In actual fact these two client groups tended to be provided with quite separate facilities – a situation which in a sense paralleled the old hospital divide. Instead each centre contained a mixed clientele composed of ex-hospital patients, members of physically handicapped groups and sometimes other impaired individuals. Very often they contained people who had psychiatric problems but who had never been hospitalized. But be that as it may, it was clear that the world of the ex-patient group was a very narrow one and – as had been the case in many of the homes and hostels – the daily world of ex-patients was filled with people who had either been in the old psychiatric hospital as patients themselves, or people who had worked there in some professional capacity or other. During the evenings many of the day care facilities were turned over to voluntary groups and ex-patient clubs. These too (as Bierer had pointed out in the 1940s) could be seen as part of a wider therapeutic web, and consequently a large proportion of the ex-patient group were encouraged to attend such clubs. It was noticeable, however, that the membership of the clubs did not differ significantly from the membership of the day centres – one of the clubs was actually centred on the old hospital and had exactly the same mix of ex-patients and in-patients as previously. And so once again, it was possible to see that the social horizons of the mentally ill were truly speaking limited to those of a subworld composed of psychiatric in-patients, ex-patients, members of handicapped groups and professional and voluntary psychiatric workers. To that extent the daytime world of ex-patients and the evening world of pastimes and recreation were essentially one and the same. Indeed, the ex-hospital patients' contacts with mainstream life were always transitory and fleeting, and most of the ex-patients' patterns of daily contact did little more than emulate features of their hospital life. Consequently it was clear to many of those who had lived in the old hospital that the move from hospital to community did not entail any radical transformation in lifestyle. In other words ex-patients seemed destined to form a community within a community where links between their world and the mainstream world were always peripheral to everyday life and never central. In addition there was a small number of ex-patients who attended no centres, who participated in no activities, who lived in relative isolation and whose only point of contact with the psychiatric system was the fortnightly visit from the CPN (who administered the so called 'depot' or slow release injection). And in their cases one could begin to see the emergence of a social situation and an overall context reminiscent of that which was once referred to as 'back ward' culture.

From Personal Crisis to Social Crisis

In a discussion on the future of the mental hospital, Martin and his colleagues at Claybury Hospital (Essex), stated that we 'delude ourselves' if we believe that 'mental and physical illnesses are essentially the same' (Martin *et al.*, 1961: 55). And since mental illnesses were not as one with organic illnesses they required a different organizational response. Martin *et al.* sought to comprehend that response within the conceptual canopy of social psychiatry, regarding plans for the development of psychiatric units within general hospitals as essentially misguided. But in retrospect it is easy to see where Martin *et al.*'s own analysis fell short – for they assumed that the future for psychiatric services lay in the development of medically supervised therapeutic communities, whereas it was actually to lie in the large scale resettlement of patients into various kinds of non-medical settings (only some of which would ever lay claim to any therapeutic functions).

The new patterns of resettlement quite naturally came to reflect a new range of beliefs about the nature of mental illness. And the activities and personnel which were to be found in the new sites served to provide new images of mental illness and the mentally ill – ones which were very different from those which had been generated by the activities which were found in the old asylums. Above all, perhaps, the new settings underlined the fact that mental illnesses (or forms of psychiatric impairment, as they were increasingly referred to), were no longer to be regarded as conditions which required segregation in specialized buildings and isolated institutions, but instead were things to be integrated into the very heart of everyday life and thus 'normalized'. And that, of course, is why the day centres, the therapeutic clubs and the group homes in which members of the study group found themselves, were firmly located in the midst of the mundane, the suburban and the familiar. Whilst the fact that the new sites were (operationally speaking, at least) under the tutelage of the social rather than the medical services emphasized the ways in which psychiatric impairment was seen as something far broader and far more complex than could be encapsulated under the old pathological concept of 'organic lesions'. Indeed, and as we have seen, the significance of medical treatment in general was in a sense marginalized through integration of psychiatric patients into the primary health care system rather than into any specialized and segregated psychiatric system. Whereas the complexity of the phenomena referred to as 'psychiatric' was in large part mirrored through the numerous kinds of assessment to which patients were routinely subjected (namely, behavioural, psychological and physical assessments), and the diverse kinds of therapy to which they were exposed (namely, chemical, social, and occupational).

Redrafting the lexicon of psychiatric discourse, however, did not necessarily mean that the everyday experiences of psychiatric patients had been radically changed. On the contrary, for as we have seen, psychiatric patients did not automatically enter into new social worlds because they lived in new or different buildings. Nor were they accepted more openly and readily by the community at large simply because they had a new mailing address. In fact, one of the ex-hospital patients even had considerable difficulty in finding a General Practitioner to accept her as part of the practice. This aside from the fact that the overwhelming majority of ex-hospital patients' social contacts were with other psychiatric patients and psychiatric care workers, rather than with people whose main source of contacts were with mainstream society. And perhaps that was why a number of people in the study group failed to see 'any difference' in their community lives as compared with their hospital lives. For when all was said and done, they attended the same day centres as previously, they saw the same social workers, spoke to the same nurses (albeit wearing everyday clothes rather than uniforms), and usually lived with exactly the same individuals as they had done in hospital. For most people it was only the dwellings that were different.

9

Epilogue: Representations of Mental Illness

> Collective representations are the result of an immense
> co-operation, which stretches out not only into space but into
> time as well.
>
> (Durkheim, 1915: 16)

In its original Durkheimian context the concept of social representations was used so as to underline the significance of extra-personal phenomena for the structuring of social life. And perhaps it was because the word became confused with notions of group mind and then tangled up – by Durkheim (1965) himself – with a metaphysics of the social, that both the term and the concept fell into disfavour and disuse. That is until they were resurrected in French social psychology – mainly by Moscovici during the early 1960s (see Moscovici, 1984, 1988), and then extended into the fields of health and illness during the following decades (see, Herzlich, 1973; Jodelet, 1989, 1991). The emphasis of this later work was directed mainly towards the analysis of everyday thinking and lay representations of what had previously been considered as essentially technical concepts (such as, illness and disease, mental handicap, and the notion of causation). And the general research focus was thereafter extended to almost any field of 'common sense' thinking or 'naive psychology', irrespective of its substantive context. Thus, in English social psychology Hewstone (1983) and his associates put the term to use in an examination of naive scientific reasoning, and their lines of investigation have been further extended in recent social psychological work to topics involving representations of childhood and the like (see, for example, Duveen and Lloyd, 1990). The emphasis on lay representations and common sense is a novel and interesting one, but in so far as representations are regarded as a component of the belief, attitudinal or cognitive systems of individual subjects, the social psychologists have tended to throw the sociological connotations of the term overboard – with Durkheim. For it is plainly clear that the latter did not believe it possible to reduce the world of the social to aspects of personal cognition. Indeed, for him there were 'two worlds and two sciences' (1965: 2) – the individual and the social – each of which existed in its own right. And it was for the sociologist to concentrate on the second realm, whilst leaving the first realm to those who wished to study the psychological properties of the individual subject.

Ultimately, social representations, even in the Durkheimian sense, are nothing but the products of individuals in interaction (or cooperation as Durkheim referred to it). For it is human activity which both creates the social world and which holds the various elements of social life together as a coherent whole. In that respect we might say that the social world is primarily constituted in and through human praxis and it is certainly as a result of such praxis that social representations arise. This means for example, that representations of mental illness are a direct product of those who have been concerned to describe and explain the nature of such illness, as well as those who have sought to manage it and to treat it (and even to 'cure' it). For in pursuing such aims and interests, psychiatric professionals have inevitably produced materials and things and ideas which serve to define the shape and nature of the objects to which they have attended. Thus special kinds of buildings have been produced to house and to treat the mentally ill; particular laws have been enacted to cope with regulation of illness behaviour; nosologies have been produced so as to classify the relevant ailments; roles have arisen and specific occupations have been invented so as to assist in the management of psychiatric disorder. What is more, texts and handbooks have been written to clarify the perceived nature of the various disorders which go to make up what is these days referred to as psychiatric impairment, and specific social policies have been designed to cope with the organizational consequences of the ever changing forms of treatment to which such disorder has been subject. (And it is, of course, these same representations which we have been examining throughout the length of this text.) Rarely, however, can we trace the origin or design of these various products to known and identifiable subjects. Naturally, buildings have architects and laws have draughtsmen and textbooks and nosologies have authors (though in the medical world, at least, authors are rarely singular individuals), but the images which are defined by means of such social representations are not to be found in the conscious minds of their producers. On the contrary they are to be found only in the products themselves. So it is by means of the actual buildings, legal documents, texts, the pattern of the division of labour, the practical professional activities of nurses, social workers, psychiatrists, and so on, that the nature of social (and in our case medical) objects is revealed. What is more, such representations often tend to gel as coherent systems in such a way that each component is 'held fast by what lies around it'

(Wittgenstein, 1974: para. 144). So belief in certain kinds of mental illnesses as 'organic diseases', for example, is in part held fast by the fact that they are 'treated' in hospitals or medical units, by medically trained personnel, and controlled by the use of chemicals and so on. And so it is therefore the entire organizational mesh which goes towards defining what the objects of everyday practical human concern might be.

This is not to claim that there is absolutely no need to interrogate real live human beings in empirical settings about what they believe or what they think or what they do in relation to, say, mental illness or psychiatric disorder. Indeed what people *do*, how they behave, what instruments and concepts they use are absolutely central to social investigation. But in most cases, active subjects are so deeply enmeshed in the system of representations of which we speak that their behaviour and conversation can only emit weak reflections of the more general principles and categories which make up the overall system. Thus, to take just one example, the occupational mesh in terms of which modern psychiatric disorder is managed and organized, and which serves to define the objects of professional psychiatric practice cannot be found in specific and isolated subjects – though the fact that an individual might refer to himself as a nurse, or a social worker, or an occupational therapist naturally provides clues to the presence of the much wider system of the division of labour in terms of which such roles are structured.

In this book we have focused almost solely on professional representations of mental illness. It is, however, necessary to recognize that there are numerous other sources and other genres of representation – such as might, for example, be produced by mentally ill people themselves (who carry the personal symptoms of such illness), or the lay public who continue in large measure to speak in terms of lunacy, nervous breakdowns, and of madness 'being in the family'. Naturally, the analysis of such representations would involve separate studies in themselves and all that we can do here is to note that these untapped sources are as important for defining the concept of a mental illness as are the medical and other professional representations which have been dealt with herein.

In so far as representations are fixed within a matrix, however, we can say that they constitute an ideology. Ideology is in that sense contained in representations – in texts, spaces, the social organization of human relationships, in human behaviour and human practices. (In the words of Althusser, 'The lived relations between [human beings] and the world . . . is ideology itself' (1977: 232).) As such, a new ideology of mental illness is represented in new texts, new spaces, new treatments, new occupational roles, new laws and new social policies. And we have seen throughout this book how these representations have altered during the twentieth century. Thus the old isolated asylum which kept its charges behind high walls and railings, and which had its entrance guarded by a gate house, is now being replaced by new structures – the group home, the community based hostel and the day centre. And therein lies a clear change in the representation of serious mental disorder in the twentieth century. There is no need to search 'behind' these buildings for hidden social and economic interests, or to argue that there is some hidden intelligence at the source of the change. Rather the relocation of the patients is the change itself; it is, in its own right, a key component of the new ideological system in terms of which mental illness is to be understood. This is not to deny the possibility that specific human interest groups often seek to exploit such changes for their own political or economic ends, but it is to deny that social representations are mere shadows of what is real and concrete.

Whilst it would be wrong to see changes in the psychiatric system as being imposed by 'outsiders' and members of extra-discursive interest groups, however, it would also be a mistake to consider that the organizational consequences of reconceptualizing mental disorder had been entirely foreseen or fully understood by psychiatric professionals themselves. Ideologies and their effects on social life are rarely planned in detail and the history of human activity is littered with the unintended consequences of human actions. Indeed, Merton (1967) even suggested at one stage that the study of such unintended consequences should form the core of social scientific investigations. But unintended consequences or not, the implication of the position adopted in this book has been that changes in the organization of psychiatric services and facilities can only be fully comprehended from within the system. In that sense the claims forwarded in this book stand in some contrast to the assertions of those who persistently argue that the rationales and origins of organizational change are to be found in the motives of reformers and lawmakers and politicians, and who consequently write their histories as if psychiatry did not exist – or as if it served merely as a pliable tool of policy makers.

Perhaps it is also worth underlining one other implication of our analysis at this stage. It is that the study of disease is no more immune to sociological analysis than is the study of illness and sickness. For as Fleck (1979) showed, disease is as much a social construction as is any lay interpretation of sickness. And 'disease' no more presents itself to the pathologist as a natural kind than does witchcraft to the anthropologist. In that respect the much favoured distinction (see, Feinstein, 1967; Freidson, 1970; Kleinman, 1973) between biologically determined disease entities (which fall within the realm of medicine), and the socially variable illness responses of the afflicted (which fall within the proper realm of social science) is not a valid one. For it is always professional practice (that is, a *social* process) which defines disease and disorder, and this is no less so in somatic medicine than it is in psychiatry. So, in relation to the latter speciality, what defines a psychiatric disorder is not some fundamental feature of a 'natural kind', but its inclusion in the psychiatric system for all practical purposes. And the validity of this proposition is perhaps most clearly evidenced by the history of those disorders which have been moved out of the realm of psychiatry and into, say, neurology. The history of both epilepsy and Parkinson's disease fit into this pattern, and the study and treatment of Alzheimer's disease may well follow the same route. In consequence, then, there is a need to develop a truly sociological perspective on (mental) diseases and (mental) illness which takes into account the fact that such phenomena belong as much to social and cultural contexts as they do to persons. And that is why it is only through the study of the ways in which such things as psychiatric services are organized and the ways in which psychiatric issues are presented and re-presented through diverse forms of professional practice that we can arrive at a sound understanding of what psychiatric disorders are. Similarly, we can perhaps begin to see that whatever the biological basis of what we call psychiatric disorder might be, biology – or 'anatomy' as Freud (1957: 189) would have it – does not determine 'destiny'. For the biological traits of human beings have to be both evaluated and responded to by others. And it is only through the *socially organized* processes of evaluation and response that disorders of soma and psyche are made visible.

Appendix: A Brief Note on the Empirical Research

The empirical work on which the book was based centred on the patients and ex-patients of a hospital which provided about 25 per cent of long-term in-patient psychiatric beds in a Region of one and half million people. The relevant fieldwork was carried out in three main phases – the first was executed during the summer of 1988, the second during the spring/summer of 1989 and the third during the calendar year of 1990.

The focus of the hospital based fieldwork was the 18–64 year old long-stay patient group, and especially those who lived in the rehabilitation wards. The focus of the community based fieldwork was on the ex-patients and the hostels, homes and institutions to which they had been discharged between 1986 and 1990. In addition, study visits were made to day centres, day hospitals and industrial therapy centres which contained any ex-patients from the 'rehab' wards. During the times at which patients were interviewed, the long-stay patients in the hospital numbered 209, and of those 49 were to be found in the 'rehab' wards. Seventy-nine ex-hospital patients had moved into the community from those wards between 1986 and 1990.

The substantive issues on which the research process concentrated were four in number, namely: professional ideologies of care and treatment; patient routines and activities; social networks of patients; and the community destinations of patients and their current locations. As well as directing observational and informal interview techniques to these four issues, a number of formal instruments were used. These were the *Community Placement Questionnaire* (Clifford, 1986) – used in relation to 209 in-patients – and the *Resident's Interview* (PSSRU, 1990) which was adopted for use with 128 rehabilitation and ex-rehabilitation patients. Questions on social networks were designed according to principles outlined by McCallister and Fischer (1978), and these questions were added to the *Resident's Interview*. For the purposes of this study, networks were defined primarily in relation to friendship measures. Thus the pattern of ego's network was determined by acquiring information about (i) the number of friends whom ego claimed to have in his/her place of residence, (ii) the number of named individuals whom ego claimed to speak to 'most of all' in the residence, (iii) the number of named individuals from whom ego 'could borrow small things or ask small favours', (iv) the number of friends cited in the occupational therapy (OT) or comparable location, (v) the number of named individuals whom ego spoke with 'most of all' in the OT location, (vi) the number of people who normally came to visit ego on a weekly basis (excluding professionals), plus (vii) the number of people who were visited by ego during either the week of the interview or the previous week. Wherever possible, the answers given were then checked against information provided by hospital and community psychiatric nursing staff. The non-response rate of hospital in-patients was low – only two patients – whilst in the community 18 patients were lost to the study through one cause or another. Other sources of data for the empirical study included the hospital census; the nursing care notes of the 'rehab' patients; documents and files held in the 'assessment' hostel; and policy documents, mission statements and review statements of day centres and places of residence. Somewhat ironically, permission to access documents relating to the study hospital during the earlier part of the century was refused, and for the purposes of the book I have therefore called upon data relating to a second hospital – which was also situated in the study Region. (Details of the appropriate files are cited in Prior (1991b).)

For 'theoretical comparison' two neighbouring hospitals were visited, and so was one hospital in Dublin. During the course of the study the author was also able to visit psychiatric hospitals and psychiatric units in Germany, Belgium and the USA (Ohio). Further details concerning the empirical work and the instruments which were used may be found in Prior (1991a).

References

Books and Articles

Ackerman, N. (1966) 'Family Therapy', in S. Arieti (ed.), *American Handbook of Psychiatry*. Vol 3, 2nd edn. New York: Basic Books.

Ackner, B. (ed.) (1963) *Handbook for Psychiatric Nurses*, 9th edn. London: Baillière.

Alaszewski, A. (1986) *Institutional Care and the Mentally Handicapped*. London: Croom Helm.

Allderidge, P. (1991) 'The Foundation of the Maudsley Hospital', in G. Berrios and H. Freeman (eds), *150 Years of British Psychiatry: 1841–1991*. London: Gaskell. pp. 79–88.

Allport, G. (1938) *Personality: a Psychological Interpretation*. London: Constable.

Althusser, L. (1977) *For Marx*. London: New Left Books.

American Psychiatric Association (1952) *Diagnostic and Statistical Manual: Mental Disorders*. Washington DC.

American Psychiatric Association (1987) *Diagnostic and Statistical Manual: Mental Disorders*, 3rd revised edn. (DSM-III-R). Washington DC.

Andersson, O. (1962) *Studies in the Prehistory of Psychoanalysis*. Svenska Bokförlaget.

Armstrong, D. (1983) *Political Anatomy of the Body: Medical Knowledge in Britain in the Twentieth Century*. Cambridge: Cambridge University Press.

Armstrong, P. (1947) 'Aspects of Psychiatric Social Work in Mental Health', *British Journal of Psychiatric Social Work*, 1047: 36–44.

Audit Commission (1986) *Making a Reality of Community Care*. London: HMSO.

Ayllon, T. and Michael, J. (1959) 'The Psychiatric Nurse as a Behavioral Engineer', *Journal of the Experiential Analysis of Behavior*, 2 (2): 323–34.

Bachelard, G. (1984) *The New Scientific Spirit*. Boston: Beacon Press. (First published 1934.)

Baker, A., Davies, R.L. and Sivadon, P. (1959) *Psychiatric Services and Architecture*. Public Health Papers No. 1. Geneva: World Health Organization.

Barclay Committee Working Party Report (1982) *Social Workers, Their Roles and Tasks*. London: Bedford Square Press.

Barnes, J.A. (1954) 'Class and Committees in a Norwegian Island Parish', *Human Relations*, 3: 307–12.

Barton, R. (1959) *Institutional Neurosis*. Bristol: J. Wright.

Baruch, G. and Treacher, A. (1978) *Psychiatry Observed*. London: Routledge and Kegan Paul.

Bateson, G., Jackson, D.D., Haley, J. and Weakland, J. (1956) 'Toward a theory of schizophrenia', *Behavioral Science*, 1: 251–64.

Bateson, W. (1906) 'An address on Mendelian heredity and its application to man', *Brain*, 24 (2): 157–79.

Bateson, W. (1909) *Mendel's Principles of Heredity*. Cambridge: Cambridge University Press.

Belknap, I. (1956) *Human Problems of a State Mental Hospital*. New York: McGraw-Hill.

Bentall, P. (ed.) (1990) *Reconstructing Schizophrenia*. London: Routledge.

Benveniste, E. (1971) *Problems in General Linguistics*. Coral Gables: University of Miami Press.

Berger, P.L. and Luckman, T. (1967) *The Social Construction of Reality: a Treatise in the Sociology of Knowledge*. Harmondsworth: Penguin.

Bernheim, H. (1891) *Hypnotisme, suggestion, psychothèrapie: Etudes nouvelles*. Paris: Doin.

Bertillon, J. (1903) *Nomenclature des Maladies*. Paris: Montevrain.

Bhaskar, R. (1975) *A Realist Theory of Science*. Leeds: Leeds Books Ltd.

Bhaskar, R. (1989) *Reclaiming Reality*. London: Verso.

Biegel, D.E., McCardle, E. and Mendelson, S. (1985) *Social Networks and Mental Health: An Annotated Bibliography*. Beverly Hills: Sage.

Bierer, J. (1948) *Therapeutic Social Clubs*. London: Institute of Social Psychiatry and H.K. Lewis.

Bierer, J. (1952) *The Day Hospital*. London: H.K. Lewis.

Bleuler, E. (1950) *Dementia Praecox or the Group of Schizophrenias*. New York: International Universities Press.

Bloor, D. (1991) *Knowledge and Social Imagery*. London: University of Chicago Press.

Bloor, M., McKeganey, N. and Fonkert, D. (1988) *One Foot in Eden: a Sociological Study of the Range of Therapeutic Community Practice*. London: Routledge.

Bott, E. (1957) *Family and Social Networks*. London: Tavistock.

Bott, E. (1976) 'Hospital and Society', *British Journal of Medical Psychology*, 49: 97–140.

Bourdieu, P. (1986) 'The forms of capital', in J. Richardson (ed.), *Handbook of Theory and Research for the Sociology of Education*. New York: Greenwood Press.

Bowling, A. (1991) *Measuring Health: a Review of Quality of Life Measurement Scales*. Milton Keynes: Open University Press.

Boyle, M. (1990) *Schizophrenia – a scientific delusion?* London: Routledge.

Braginsky, B.M., Braginsky, D.D. and Ring, K. (1969) *Methods of Madness: the Mental Hospital as a Last Resort*. New York: Holt, Reinhart and Winston.

Brain, W.R. (1933) *Diseases of the Nervous System*, 1st edn. London: Oxford University Press.

Brain, W.R. (1940) *Diseases of the Nervous System*, 2nd edn. London: Oxford University Press.

Breuer, J. and Freud, S. (1955) 'Studies on Hysteria', in *Standard Edition of the Complete Psychological Works of Sigmund Freud*. Vol. 2. London: Hogarth Press. (First published 1895.) pp. 1–307.

Briggs, A.K. and Agrin, A.R. (1981) *Crossroads: A Reader for Psychosocial Occupational Therapy*. The American Occupational Therapy Association.

Brill, H. and Patton, R.E. (1957) 'Analysis of 1955–56 Population Fall in New York State Mental Hospitals in First Year of Large Scale use of Tranquillizing Drugs', *American Journal of Psychiatry*, 114: 509–17.

Brill, H. and Patton, R.E. (1959) 'Analysis of Population Reduction in New York State Mental Hospitals During the First Four Years of Large Scale Therapy with

Psychotropic Drugs', *American Journal of Insanity*, 116: 495–508.

Brill, H. and Patton, R.E. (1962) 'Clinical Statistical Analysis of Population Changes in New York State Mental Hospitals since the Introduction of Psychotropic Drugs', *American Journal of Psychiatry*, 119: 20–35.

Brooker, C. (1990) 'Schizophrenia: All in the Family?', *Nursing Times*, 86 (2): 26–9.

Brown, G.W. and Birley, J.L.T. (1968) 'Crises and Life Changes and the Onset of Schizophrenia', *Journal of Health and Social Behaviour*, 9: 203–14.

Brown, G.W. and Harris, T. (1978) *The Social Origins of Depression. A Study of Psychiatric Disorder in Women*. London: Tavistock.

Brown, George (1985) 'The Discovery of Expressed Emotion: Induction or Deduction?', in J. Leff and C. Vaughn (eds), *Expressed Emotion in Families*: its Significance for Mental Illness. New York: Guilford Press.

Brown, P. (1985) *The Transfer of Care: Psychiatric Deinstitutionalization and its Aftermath*. London: Routledge and Kegan Paul.

Bruce, L.C. (1906) *Studies in Clinical Psychiatry*. London: Methuen.

Brugger, C. (1931) 'Versuch einer Geisteskrankanzählung in Thuringen', *Zeitschrift fur die gesamte Neurologie und Psychiatrie*, 133: 352–90.

Bry, I. and Rifkin, A.H. (1962) 'Freud and the History of Ideas: Primary Sources, 1886–1910', *Science and Psychoanalysis*, 6–36.

Buckley, A.C. (1927) *Nursing Mental and Nervous Diseases*. London: Lippincott.

Burgess, E.W. (1926) 'The Family as a Unity of Interacting Personalities', *The Family*, 7 (1): 3–9.

Burr, J. and Budge, U.V. (1976) *Nursing the Psychiatric Patient*, 3rd edn. London: Baillière, Tindall and Cox.

Burt, C. (1925) *The Young Delinquent*. London: University of London Press.

Burt, C. (1937) *The Backward Child*. London: University of London Press.

Butler, A. and Pritchard, C. (1983) *Social Work and Mental Illness*. London: Macmillan.

Byrd, D.E. (1981) *Organizational Constraints on Psychiatric Treatment: the Outpatient Clinic*. Greenwich: JAI Press.

Cannon, A. and Hayes, E.D.T. (1932) *The Principles and Practice of Psychiatry*. London: Heinemann.

Castel, R., Castel, F. and Lovell, A. (1982) *The Psychiatric Society*. New York: Columbia University Press.

Cattell, J.M. (1890) 'Mental Tests and Measurements', *Mind*, 15: 373–81.

Cattell, R.B. (1965) *The Scientific Analysis of Personality*. Harmondsworth: Penguin.

Caudhill, W. (1958) *The Psychiatric Hospital as a Small Society*. Cambridge, Mass: Harvard University Press.

Chase, R.H. (1914) *Mental Medicine and Nursing*. London: J.P. Lippincott.

Chesler, P. (1972) *Women and Madness*. New York: Doubleday.

Clark, D. (1965) 'The Therapeutic Community: Concept, Practice and Future', *British Journal of Psychiatry*, 11: 947–54.

Clark, D. (1977) 'The Therapeutic Community', *British Journal of Psychiatry*, 131: 553–64.

Clausen, J.A. and Kohn, M.L. (1959) 'Relation of Schizophrenia to the Social Structure of a Small City', in B. Pasamanick (ed.), *Epidemiology of Mental Disorder*. Washington, DC: American Association for the Advancement of Science. pp. 69–94.

Clifford, P.I. (1986) *The Community Placement Questionnaire*. London: National

Unit for Psychiatric Research and Development, Lewisham Hospital.

Cohen, S. and Scull, A.T. (eds) (1985) *Social Control and The State*. Oxford: Blackwell.

Cole, R.H. (1913) *Mental Diseases*, 1st edn. London: London University Press.

Commonwealth of Australia Bureau of Census and Statistics (1907) *The Nomenclature of Diseases and Causes of Death as Revised and Adopted in 1900 by the International Commission*. Melbourne.

Cooper, D. (1967) *Psychiatry and Anti-Psychiatry*. London: Tavistock.

Cooper, D. (1970) *The Death of the Family*. Harmondsworth: Penguin.

Copeland, J. (1981) 'What is a "Case"? a Case for What?', in J.K. Wing, P. Bebbington and L.N. Robins (eds), *What is A Case?* London: Grant McIntyre. pp. 9–12.

Cullum, S. (1905) 'Sedatives and Narcotics in the Treatment of the Insane', *The Dublin Journal of Medical Science*, 120: 161–81.

Cumming, E. and Cumming, J. (1957) *Closed Ranks: An Experiment in Mental Health Education*. Cambridge, Mass.: Harvard University Press.

Curran, D. and Guttman, E. (1943) *Psychological Medicine: a Short Introduction to Psychiatry*, 1st edn. Edinburgh: E. and S. Livingstone.

Davies, T.S. (1954) 'Chlorpromazine in Mental Deficiency', *Lancet*, I: 819.

Day, K. and Jancar, J. (1991) 'Mental Handicap and the Royal Medico-Psychological Association', in G. Berrios and H. Freeman (eds), *150 Years of British Psychiatry: 1841–1991*. London: Gaskell. pp. 268–78.

Dear, M.J. and Wolch, J.R. (1987) *Landscapes of Despair: From Deinstitutionalization to Homelessness*. Cambridge: Polity Press.

de Beauvoir, S. (1953) *The Second Sex*. London: Hamish Hamilton.

Decker, H.S. (1971) 'The Medical Reception of Psychoanalysis in Germany, 1894–1907: Three Brief Studies', *Bulletin of the History of Medicine*, 45: 475–9.

Delaporte, F. (1986) *Disease and Civilization: The Cholera in Paris, 1832*. Cambridge, Mass.: The MIT Press.

Delay, J., Deniker, P. and Tardieu, Y. (1953) 'Hibernotherapie et cure de sommeil en thérapeutique psychiatrique et psychosomatique', *La Presse medicale*, 61 (ii): 1165–6.

Diethelm, O. (1936) *Treatment in Psychiatry*. New York: Macmillan.

Dohrenwend, B.P. and Dohrenwend, B.S. (1969) *Social Status and Psychological Disorder: A Causal Inquiry*. New York: John Wiley.

Dugdale, R.L. (1910) *The Jukes. A Study in Crime, Pauperism, Disease and Heredity*. New York: Putnam.

Dunham, H.W. and Weinberg, S.K. (1960) *The Culture of the State Mental Hospital*. Detroit: Wayne State University Press.

Dunton, W.R. and Licht, S. (eds) (1950) *Occupational Therapy: Principles and Practice*. Springfield: Charles C. Thomas.

Durkheim, E. (1915) *The Elementary Forms of the Religious Life*. London: George Allen and Unwin.

Durkheim, E. (1952) *Suicide: a Study in Sociology*. London: Routledge and Kegan Paul. (First published 1897.)

Durkheim, E. (1964) *The Rules of Sociological Method*. New York: The Free Press. (First published 1901.)

Durkheim, E. (1965) *Sociology and Philosophy*. London: Cohen and West.

Durkheim, E. and Mauss, M. (1963) *Primitive Classification*. London: Cohen and West. (First published 1903.)

Duveen, G. and Lloyd, B. (eds) (1990) *Social Representations and the Development of Knowledge*. Cambridge: Cambridge University Press.

Eastern Health and Social Services Board (EHSSB) (1986) *Strategic Planning for the Health and Personal Social Services 1987–1992*. Belfast: EHSSB.

Eastern Health and Social Services Board (EHSSB) (1989) *Schizophrenia: What Relatives Should Know*. Belfast: EHSSB.

Ellenberger, H.F. (1970) *The Discovery of the Unconscious. The History and Evolution of Dynamic Psychiatry*. New York: Basic Books.

Ellenberger, H.F. (1972) 'The story of "Anna O": A critical review with new data', *Journal of the History of the Behavioral Sciences*, 8: 267–79.

Evans-Pritchard, E.E. (1937) *Witchcraft Oracles and Magic among the Azande*. London: Oxford University Press.

Eysenck, H.J. (1953) *Uses and Abuses of Psychology*. Harmondsworth: Penguin.

Eysenck, H.J. (1959) 'Learning theory and behaviour therapy', *Journal of Mental Science*, 105: 61–75.

Eysenck, H.J. (1965) *Fact and Fiction in Psychology*. Harmondsworth: Penguin.

Fagin, C.M. (1970) *Community Psychiatry. Treatment in the Home*. Philadelphia: F.A. Davis.

Faris, R.E. and Dunham, H.W. (1939) *Mental Disorder in Urban Areas: An Ecological Study of Schizophrenia and Other Psychoses*. Chicago: University of Chicago Press.

Feinstein, A.R. (1967) *Clinical Judgement*. Huntingdon: Robert E. Krieger.

Feyerabend, P. (1975) *Against Method*. London: New Left Books.

Fidler, G.S. and Fidler, J.W. (1954) *Introduction to Psychiatric Occupational Therapy*. New York: Macmillan.

Finnane, M. (1981) *Insanity and the Insane in Post-Famine Ireland*. London: Croom Helm.

Fleck, L. (1979) *Genesis and Development of a Scientific Fact*. Chicago. University of Chicago Press. (First published 1935.)

Flugel, J.C. (1921) *The Psycho-Analytic Study of the Family*. London: Hogarth Press.

Frankenberg, R. (1966) *Communities in Britain: Social Life in Town and Country*. Harmondsworth: Penguin.

Freeman, H.L., Fryers, T. and Henderson, J.H. (1985) *Mental Health Services in Europe: 10 Years on*. Copenhagen: World Health Organization.

Freeman, W. and Watts, J.W. (1942) *Psychosurgery*. Springfield: Charles Thomas.

Freidson, E. (1970) *Profession of Medicine: A Study of the Sociology of Applied Knowledge*. New York: Dodd, Mead and Co.

French, L.M. (1940) *Psychiatric Social Work*. New York: The Commonwealth Fund.

Freud, S. (1953) *The Interpretation of Dreams. Standard Edition of the Complete Psychological Works of Sigmund Freud*, Vol. 5. London: Hogarth Press. (First published 1900.)

Freud, S. (1957) 'On the Universal Tendency to Debasement in the Sphere of Love', *Standard Edition of the Complete Psychological Works of Sigmund Freud*, Vol. 11. London: Hogarth Press. (First published 1910.) pp. 179–90.

Freud, S. (1966a) 'Preface and Footnotes to Charcot's Tuesday Lectures', *Standard Edition of the Complete Psychological Works of Sigmund Freud*, Vol. 1. London: Hogarth Press. (First published 1892–4.) pp. 131–7.

Freud, S. (1966b) 'Charcot', in *Standard Edition of the Complete Psychological Works of Sigmund Freud*, Vol. 3. London: Hogarth Press. pp. 11–23.

Freud, S. (1977) *Case Histories I: 'Dora' and 'Little Hans'. The Pelican Freud Library*, Vol. 8. Harmondsworth: Penguin.

Gall, J.F. and Spurzheim, G. (1809) *Recherches sur le système nerveux en general, et sur celui du cerveau en particulier*. Paris.

Gamarnikow, E. (1978) 'Sexual Division of Labour: the Case of Nursing', in A. Kuhn and A. Wolpe (eds), *Feminism and Materialism: Women and Modes of Production*. London: Routledge and Kegan Paul. pp. 96–123.

Garrett, A. (1949) 'Historical Survey of the Evolution of Casework', *Journal of Social Casework*, 214–29.

Gay, P. (1988) *Freud: A Life for Our Time*. London: J.M. Dent.

Gedo, J.E. and Pollock, G.H. (1976) 'Freud: The Fusion of Science and Humanism. The Intellectual History of Psychoanalysis', *Psychological Issues Monograph 34/35*, 9 (2–3): 1–449.

Gelder, M. (1991) 'Adolf Meyer and his Influence on British Psychiatry', in G. Berrios and H. Freeman (eds), *150 Years of British Psychiatry: 1841–1991*. London: Gaskell. pp. 419–35.

Gelder, M., Gath, D. and Mayou, R. (1988) *Oxford Textbook of Psychiatry*. Oxford: Oxford University Press.

Goddard, H.H. (1912) *The Kallikak Family: A Study in the Heredity of Feeble-Mindedness*. New York: Macmillan.

Goffman, E. (1961) *Asylums: Essays on the Social Situation of Mental Patients and Other Inmates*. New York: Anchor Books.

Goffman, E. (1963) *Stigma: Notes on the Management of a Spoiled Identity*. New Jersey: Prentice Hall.

Goldberg, D. and Huxley, P. (1980) *Mental Illness in the Community: The Pathway to Psychiatric Care*. London: Tavistock.

Goldberg, E.M. (1957) 'The Psychiatric Social Worker in the Community', *British Journal of Psychiatric Social Work*, 4 (2): 4–15.

Goldberg, E.M. and Morrison, S.L. (1963) 'Schizophrenia and social class', *British Journal of Psychiatry*, 109: 785–802.

Goshen, C.F. and Keenan, E.A. (1959) *Psychiatric Architecture*. Washington DC: American Psychiatric Association.

Gould, S.J. (1984) *The Mismeasure of Man*. Harmondsworth: Penguin.

Gove, W.R. (1970) 'Societal Reaction as an Explanation of Mental Illness: an Evaluation', *American Sociological Review*, 35: 873–84.

Gove, W.R. and Tudor, J.F. (1973) 'Adult Sex roles and Mental Illness', *American Journal of Sociology*, 78: 812–35.

Greenblatt, M., Levinson, D.J. and Williams, R.H. (eds) (1957) *The Patient and the Mental Hospital*. Glencoe: The Free Press.

Greenblatt, M., York, R.H. and Brown, E.L. (eds) (1955) *From Custodial to Therapeutic Patient Care in Mental Hospitals*. New York: Russell Sage Foundation.

Griffiths, R. (1988) *Community Care: Agenda for Action*. London: HMSO.

Grob, G. (1973) *Mental Institutions in America: Social Policy to 1875*. New York: Free Press.

Hare, E.H. (1956) 'Mental Illness and Social Conditions in Bristol', *Journal of Mental Science*, 102: 349–57.

Haworth, N. (1933) 'Occupational Therapy', *The Lancet*, I: 171.

Haworth, N.A. and Macdonald, E.M. (1940) *The Theory of Occupational Therapy*, 1st edn. London. Baillière, Tindall and Cox.

Healy, D. (1990) 'A New Science of Insanity', *New Scientist*, 6 Oct.: 34–7.

Hemingway, B.J. (1988) *Mental Health Assessment in Occupational Therapy*. New Jersey: Slack Inc.

Henderson, D.K. and Gillespie, R.D. (1927) *A Textbook of Psychiatry*, 1st edn. London: Oxford University Press.

Henderson, D.K. and Gillespie, R.D. (1940) *A Textbook of Psychiatry*, 5th edn. London: Oxford University Press.

Herzlich, C. (1973) *Health and Illness: A Social-Psychological Analysis*. London: Academic Press.

Hewstone, M. (ed.) (1983) *Attribution Theory: Social and Functional Extensions*. Oxford: Basil Blackwell.

Hill, M. (1978) 'Relations with Other Agencies', in DHSS, *Social Service Teams: The Practitioner's View*. London: HMSO.

Hillery, G.A. (1955) 'Definitions of Community: Areas of Agreement', *Rural Sociology*, 80 (2): 111–23.

Hirschhorn, K. and Cooper, H.L. (1961) 'Chromosomal Aberrations in Human Disease: a Review of the Status of Cytogenetics in Medicine', in M.F.A. Montagu (ed.), *Genetic Mechanisms in Human Disease*. Springfield: Charles C. Thomas. pp. 3–55.

Hollingshead, A.B. and Redlich, F.C. (1958) *Social Class and Mental Illness: A Community Study*. New York: John Wiley.

Horney, K. (1937) *The Neurotic Personality of Our Time*. London: Kegan Paul.

House of Commons (1985) *Second Report of the Social Services Committee: Community Care*, H.C.13. London: HMSO.

Hudson, B.L. (1982) *Social Work with Psychiatric Patients*. London: Macmillan.

Hunter, R. and Macalpine, I. (1974) *Psychiatry for the Poor: 1851 Colney Hatch Asylum; Friern Hospital 1973: A Medical and Social History*. London: Dawsons.

Huxley, P. (1985) *Social Work Practice in Mental Health*. Aldershot: Gower.

Ingleby, D. (ed.) (1981) *Critical Psychiatry. The Politics of Mental Health*. Harmondsworth: Penguin.

Janosik, E.H. and Davies, J.L. (1989) *Psychiatric Mental Health Nursing*, 2nd edn. Boston: Jones and Bartlett.

Jodelet, D. (ed.) (1989) *Les Représentations Sociales*. Paris: Presses Universitaires de France.

Jodelet, D. (1991) *Madness and Social Representations*. Hemel Hempstead: Harvester Wheatsheaf.

John, A.L., Leite-Ribeiro, M.O. and Buckle, D. (1963) *The Nurse in Mental Health Practice*. Geneva: World Health Organization.

Joint Commission on Mental Illness and Health (1961) *Action for Mental Health*. New York: Basic Books.

Jones, Ernest (1959) *Free Associations*. London: The Hogarth Press.

Jones, Ernest (1964) *The Life and Work of Sigmund Freud*, edited and abridged L. Trilling and S. Marcus. Harmondsworth: Penguin.

Jones, Kathleen (1972) *A History of the Mental Health Services*. London: Routledge and Kegan Paul.

Jones, Kathleen (1988) *Experience in Mental Health. Community Care and Social Policy*. London: Sage.

Jones, Kathleen (1991a) 'The Culture of the Mental Hospital', in G. Berrios and H. Freeman (eds), *150 Years of British Psychiatry: 1841–1991*. London: Gaskell. pp. 17–28.

Jones, Kathleen (1991b) 'Law and Mental Health', in G. Berrios and H. Freeman (eds), *150 Years of British Psychiatry: 1841–1991*. London: Gaskell. pp. 89–102.

Jones, Kathleen and Sidebottom, R. (1962) *Mental Hospitals at Work*. London: Routledge and Kegan Paul.

Jones, Maxwell. O. (1968) *Social Psychiatry in Practice*. Harmondsworth: Penguin.

Kalinowsky, L.B. and Hoch, P.H. (1946) *Shock Treatments and Other Somatic Treatments in Psychiatry*. London: Heinemann.

Kallman, F.J. (1938) *The Genetics of Schizophrenia*. New York: J.J. Augustin.

Kellner, D. (1989) *Jean Baudrillard: From Marxism to Postmodernism and Beyond*. Cambridge: Polity Press.

Kendell, R.E. (1975) *The Role of Diagnosis in Psychiatry*. Oxford: Blackwell.

Kevles, D.J. (1985) *In the Name of Eugenics: Genetics and the Uses of Human Heredity*. New York: Alfred Knopf.

Kirk, S. and Therrien, M. (1975) 'Community Mental Health Myths and the Fate of Formerly Hospitalized Mental Patients', *Psychiatry* 38: 209–17.

Kleinman, A. (1973) 'Medicine's Symbolic Reality: On a Central Problem in the Philosophy of medicine', *Inquiry*, 16: 206–13.

Klerman, G.L. (1961) 'Historical Baselines for the Evaluation of Maintenance Drug Therapy and Discharged Psychiatric Patients', in M. Greenblatt, D.J. Levinson, G.L. Klerman (eds.), *Mental Patients in Transition*. Springfield: Charles C. Thomas. pp. 287–302.

Korman, N. and Glennerster, H. (1990) *Hospital Closure*. Milton Keynes: Open University Press.

Kraepelin, E. (1902) *Clinical Psychiatry. A Text-Book for Students and Physicians*, edited by A.R. Defendorf. London: Macmillan.

Kraepelin, E. (1904) *Lectures on Clinical Psychiatry*. London: Bailliére, Tindall and Cox.

Kretschmer, E. (1925) *Physique and Character*. London: Kegan Paul.

Kuhn, T.S. (1970) *The Structure of Scientific Revolutions*, 2nd edn. Chicago: Chicago University Press.

Laing, R.D. (1959) *The Divided Self: An Existential Study in Sanity and Madness*. London: Tavistock.

Laing, R.D. (1961) *The Self and Others*. London: Tavistock.

Laing, R.D. and Esterson, A. (1964) *Sanity, Madness and the Family*. London: Tavistock.

Leach, E. (1967) *A Runaway World?*. London: BBC Publications.

Leighton, A.H. (1959) *My Name is Legion*, Vol. 1 of the Stirling County Study. New York: Basic Books.

Lemkau, P., Tietze, C. and Cooper, M. (1941) 'Mental-Hygiene Problems in an Urban District', *Mental Hygiene*, 25: 624–46.

Lévy-Bruhl, L. (1985) *How Natives Think*. Princeton: Princeton University Press. (First published 1910.)

Lewis, E.O. (1929) 'An Investigation into the Incidence of Mental Deficiency', in Board of Control, *Report of the Mental Deficiency Committee*. London: HMSO.

Lewontin, R. (1992) 'The Dream of the Human Genome', *New York Review of Books*, 39 (10): 31–40.

Lidz, T., Cornelison, A.R., Fleck, S. and Terry, D. (1957) 'The Intrafamilial Environment of Schizophrenic Patients: II. Marital Schism and Marital Skew', *American Journal of Psychiatry*, 64: 241–8.

Linton, R. (1936) *The Study of Man*. New York: Appleton-Century.

208   *References*

Lord, J.R. (1929) 'The Evolution of the Nerve Hospital as a Factor in the Progress of Psychiatry', *Journal of Mental Science*, 75: 307–15.

Lukes, S. (1973) *Émile Durkheim. His Life and Work: A Historical and Critical Study*. London: Allen Lane the Penguin Press.

McCallister, L. and Fischer, C.S. (1978) 'A procedure for surveying personal networks', *Sociological Methods and Research*, 7 (2): 131–48.

McGuffin, P. and Murray, R. (eds) (1991) *The New Genetics of Mental Illness*. London: The Mental Health Foundation.

Mackenzie, W.J.M. (Chairman) (1955) *The Work of the Mental Nurse*. Joint Committee of the Manchester Regional Hospital Board: Manchester University Press.

Maddison, D., Day, D. and Leadbetter, B. (1963) *Psychiatric Nursing*. Edinburgh: Churchill Livingstone.

Maddison, D., Day, D. and Leadbetter B. (1970) *Psychiatric Nursing*, 3rd edn. Edinburgh: Churchill Livingstone.

Maddison, D., Day, D. and Leadbetter, B. (1975) *Psychiatric Nursing*, 4th edn. Edinburgh: Churchill Livingstone.

Main, T.F. (1946) 'The hospital as a therapeutic institution', *Bulletin of the Menninger Clinic*, 10: 66–70.

Mangen, S.P. (ed.) (1985) *Mental Health Care in the European Community*. Beckenham: Croom Helm.

Martin, D.V. (1955) 'In the Mental Hospital', *The Lancet*, 3 Dec.: 1188–90.

Martin, D.V., Pippard, J., Shoenberg, E., Kelsey, D. and Watson, A. (1961) 'The Future of Psychiatric Hospitals', *Mental Health Bulletin*, 20: 55–8.

Martin, J.P. (1984) *Hospitals in Trouble*. Oxford: Blackwell.

Maudsley, H. (1908) *Heredity, Variation and Genius*. London: John Bale.

May, A.R. and Gregory, E. (1963) 'An Experiment in District Psychiatry', *Public Health*, 78: 19–25.

Mayer-Gross, W. (1948) 'Mental Health Survey in a Rural Area', *Eugenics Review*, 40: 140–8.

Mayer-Gross, W., Slater, E. and Roth, M. (1954) *Clinical Psychiatry*. London: Cassell.

Mead, G.H. (1934) *Mind, Self and Society. From the Standpoint of a Social Behaviorist*. Chicago: University of Chicago Press.

Meagher, E.T. (1929) *General Paralysis and Its Treatment by Induced Malaria*. Board of Control, London: HMSO.

Medical Research Council (1987) *Research into Schizophrenia: Report of the Schizophrenia and Allied Conditions Committee to the Neurosciences Board*. London: Medical Research Council.

Medico-Psychological Association (1923) *Handbook for Mental Nurses*, 7th edn. London: Baillière, Tindall and Cox.

Menninger, K. (1948) 'Changing Concepts of Disease', *Annals of Internal Medicine*, 29: 318–25.

Mereness, D.A. and Taylor, C.M. (1974) *Essentials of Psychiatric Nursing*, 9th edn. St Louis: C.V. Mosby.

Merskey, H. and Tonge, W.L. (1965) *Psychiatric Illness*. London: Baillière, Tindall and Cox.

Merton, R.K. (1967) 'Manifest and Latent Functions', in *On Theoretical Sociology*. New York: The Free Press. pp. 73–138.

Miles, A. (1988) *Women and Mental Illness: The Social Context of Female Neurosis*.

Brighton: Wheatsheaf.

Miles, A. (1991) *Women, Health and Medicine*. Milton Keynes: Open University Press.

Miles, A.P. (1954) *American Social Work Theory*. New York: Harper.

Mills, C.K. (1915) *Nursing and Care of the Nervous and the Insane*. London: Lippincott.

Mills, C.W. (1970) *The Sociological Imagination*. Harmondsworth: Penguin.

MIND (1987) *Report to Sir Roy Griffiths*. London: MIND.

Mitchell, J.C. (ed.) (1969) *Social Networks in Urban Situations*. Manchester: Manchester University Press.

Moniz, E. (1936) 'Les premiers operatoires dans le traitement de certaines psychoses', *L'Encephale*, 31 (2): 1–29.

Moore, S. (1961) 'A Psychiatric Out-Patient Nursing Service', *Mental Health Bulletin*, 20: 51–4.

Mora, G. (1959) 'Recent American Psychiatric Developments', in S. Arieti (ed.), *American Handbook of Psychiatry*, Vol. 1. New York: Basic Books.

Morgan, C.D. and Murray, H.A. (1935) 'A Method for Investigating Fantasies: the Thematic Apperception Test', *Archives Neurology and Psychiatry*, 34 (2): 289–306.

Morris, P. (1969) *Put Away: A Sociological Study of Institutions for the Mentally Retarded*. London: Routledge and Kegan Paul.

Moscovici, S. (1984) 'The Phenomena of Social Representations', in S. Farr and S. Moscovici (eds), *Social Representations*. Cambridge: Cambridge University Press. pp. 3–70.

Moscovici, S. (1988) 'Notes Toward a Description of Social Representations', *European Journal of Social Psychology*, 18: 211–50.

Mulzer, P. (1910) *The Therapy of Syphilis: Its Development and Present Position*. London: Riebman.

Murray, H.A. (1938) *Explorations in Personality*. New York: Oxford University Press.

Myers, J.K. and Bean, L.L. (1968) *A Decade Later: A Follow-up of Social Class and Mental Illness*. New York: John Wiley.

Myerson, A. (1940) 'Mental Disorders in Urban Areas', *American Journal of Psychiatry*, 96: 995–7.

National Schizophrenia Fellowship (NSF) (1989) *The NSF 20 Point Plan*. Surbiton, Surrey: National Schizophrenia Fellowship.

Nisbet, R.A. (1966) *The Sociological Tradition*. New York: Basic Books.

Noguchi, H. and Moore, J.W. (1913) 'A Demonstration of Treponema Pallidum in the Brain in Cases of General Paralysis', *Journal of Experimental Medicine*, 17: 232–8.

Oakeshott, M. (1962) *Rationalism in Politics and Other Essays*. London: Methuen.

Odencrantz, L. (1929) *The Social Worker in Family, Medical and Psychiatric Social Work*. New York: Harper.

Offe, C. (1984) *Contradictions of the Welfare State*. London: Hutchinson.

Painter, T.S. (1923) 'Studies in Mammalian Spermatogenesis. II. The Spermatogenesis of Man', *Journal of Experimental Zoology*, 37 (3): 291–321.

Parsons, T. (1951) *The Social System*. London: Routledge and Kegan Paul.

Parsons, T., Bales, R.F. and Shils, E.A. (1953) *Working Papers in the Theory of Action*. New York: Free Press.

Pattison, E.M., Defrancisco, D., Wood, P., Frazier, H. and Crowder, J. (1975). 'A

Psychosocial Kinship Model for Family Therapy', *American Journal of Psychiatry*, 132 (12): 1246–51.

Pearson, K. (1930) *The Life, Letters and Labours of Francis Galton*, Vol. IIIA. Cambridge: Cambridge University Press.

Penrose, L.S. (1938) *A Clinical and Genetic Study of 1280 Cases of Mental Defect*. Medical Research Council, London: HMSO.

Penrose, L.S. (1949) *The Biology of Mental Defect*. London: Sidgwick and Jackson.

Personal Social Services Research Unit (PSSRU) (1989) *Care in the Community: Final Report. Discussion Paper 615*. Canterbury: University of Kent at Canterbury.

Personal Social Services Research Unit (PSSRU) (1990) *Resident's Interview*. Canterbury: University of Kent at Canterbury.

Pilgrim, D. (1990) 'Competing Histories of Madness', in P. Bentall (ed.), *Reconstructing Schizophrenia*. London: Routledge. pp. 211–33.

Prior, L. (1991a) *The Social Worlds of Psychiatric and Ex-Psychiatric Patients in Belfast*. Belfast: Health and Health Care Research Unit, Queen's University of Belfast.

Prior, L. (1991b) 'Mind, Body and Behaviour: Theorizations of Madness and the Organization of Therapy', *Sociology* 25 (3): 403–21.

Prior, L. (1992) 'The Local Space of Medical Discourse: Disease, Illness and Hospital Architecture', in J. Lachmund and G. Stollberg (eds), pp. 67–84. *The Social Construction of Illness*. Stuttgart: Franz Steiner.

Ramon, S. (1985) *Psychiatry in Britain: Meaning and Policy*. London: Croom Helm.

Rapoport, R.N. (1960) *Community as Doctor*. London: Tavistock.

Raush, H.L. and Raush, C.L. (1968) *The Halfway House Movement: A Search for Sanity*. New York: Appleton Century Crofts.

Reynolds, W. and Cormack, D. (1990) *Psychiatric and Mental Health Nursing: Theory and Practice*. London: Chapman and Hall.

Reznek, L. (1987) *The Nature of Disease*. London: Routledge and Kegan Paul.

Rice, D. (1955) 'The use of lithium salts in the treatment of manic states', *Journal of Mental Science*, 102: 604–11.

Roberts, J.F. (1940) *Medical Genetics*, 1st edn. London: Oxford University Press.

Roberts, J.F. (1959) *Medical Genetics*, 2nd edn. London: Oxford University Press.

Roberts, J.F. (1970) *Medical Genetics*, 5th edn. London: Oxford University Press.

Robinson, P. (1930) *A Changing Psychology in Social Case Work*. Chapel Hill: University of North Carolina Press.

Rooney, P. and Mathews, R. (1982) *Worcester Development Project Psychiatric Provision – Where Do We Go From Here?* Mental Health Buildings Evaluation Pamphlet No. 3., London: DHSS Works Group.

Rorschach, H. (1942) *Psychodiagnostics*, 3rd edn. Berne: Hans Huber.

Rosanoff, A.J. (1917) 'Survey of Mental Disorders in Nassau County, New York', *Psychiatric Bulletin*, 2 (2): 109–231.

Roth, M. (1976) 'Schizophrenia and the Work of T. Szasz', *British Journal of Psychiatry*, 129: 317–26.

Roth, W.F. and Luton, F.H. (1943) 'The Mental Health Program in Tennessee: 1. Description of the Original Study Program; 2. Statistical Report of a Psychiatric Survey in a Rural County', *American Journal of Psychiatry*, 99: 662–75.

Rothman, D. (1971) *The Discovery of the Asylum*. Boston: Little, Brown.

Rothman, D. (1980) *Conscience and Convenience: The Asylum and its Alternatives in Progressive America*. Boston: Little, Brown.

Rothman, D. (1985) 'Social Control: the Uses and Abuses of the Concept in the History of Incarceration', in S. Cohen and A.T. Scull (eds), *Social Control and The State*. Oxford: Blackwell. pp. 106–17.

Rowitz, L. and Levy, L. (1968) 'An Ecological Analysis of Treated Mental Disorders in Chicago', *Archives of General Psychiatry*, 19: 571–9.

Rowland, H. (1939) 'Friendship Patterns in the State Mental Hospital', *Psychiatry*, 2 (3): 363–73.

Rudolf, G. de M. (1927) *Therapeutic Malaria*. London: Oxford University Press.

Rushing, W.A. (1964) *The Psychiatric Profession: Power, Conflict and Adaptation in a Psychiatric Hospital Staff*. Chapel Hill: University of North Carolina Press.

Ryle, G. (1949) *The Concept of Mind*. London: Hutchinson.

Sadler, W.S. (1937) *Psychiatric Nursing*. St Louis: C.V. Mosby.

St Leger, F. and Gillespie, N. (1991) *Informal Welfare in Belfast: Caring Communities?* Aldershot: Avebury.

Sakel, M. (1938) *The Pharmacological Shock Treatment of Schizophrenia*. New York: Nervous and Mental Disease Publishing.

Sands, I.J. (1928) *Nervous and Mental Diseases for Nurses*. London: W.B. Saunders.

Sargant, W. and Slater, E. (1944) *An Introduction to Physical Methods of Treatment in Psychiatry*, 1st edn. Edinburgh: E. and S. Livingstone.

Sargant, W. and Slater, E. (1963) *An Introduction to Physical Methods of Treatment in Psychiatry*, 4th edn. Edinburgh: E. and S. Livingstone.

Schafer, R. (1948) *The Clinical Application of Psychological Tests*. New York: International Universities Press.

Scharfetter, C. (1983) 'Schizophrenia', in M. Shepherd and O.L. Zangwill (eds), *Handbook of Psychiatry*, Vol 1. Cambridge: Cambridge University Press. pp. 39–40.

Scheff, T.J. (1966) *Being Mentally Ill: A Sociological Theory*. Chicago: Aldine.

Schwab, J.J. and Schwab, M.E. (1978) *Sociocultural Roots of Mental Illness: An Epidemiologic Survey*. New York: Plenum Medical Books.

Scott, J. (1988) 'Social Network Analysis', *Sociology*, 22 (1): 109–26.

Scull, A.T. (1984) *Decarceration: Community Treatment and the Deviant – A Radical View*, 2nd edn. Cambridge: Polity Press.

Scull, A.T. (1989) *Social Order/Mental Disorder: Anglo-American Psychiatry in Historical Perspective*. London: Routledge.

Sedgwick, P. (1982) *PsychoPolitics*. London: Pluto.

Segal, S.P. and Baumohl, J. (1988) 'No Place Like Home: Reflections on Sheltering a Diverse Population', in C. Smith and J.A. Giggs (eds), *Location and Stigma*. Boston: Unwin Hyman. pp. 249–63.

Shepherd, M. (1966) *Psychiatric Illness in General Practice*. London: Oxford University Press.

Siegler, M., Osmond, H. and Mann, H. (1969) 'Laing's Models of Madness', *British Journal of Psychiatry*, 115: 947–59.

Slade, P.D. (1990) 'The Behavioural and Cognitive Treatment of Psychotic Symptoms', in R.P. Bentall (ed.), *Reconstructing Schizophrenia*. London: Routledge. pp. 234–53.

Slater, E. and Roth, M. (1969) *Clinical Psychiatry*, 3rd edn. London: Ballière, Tindall and Cassell.

Southard, E.E. (1917) 'Alienists and Psychiatrists', *Mental Hygiene*, 1: 567–71.

Southard, E.E. and Jarrett, M.C. (1922) *The Kingdom of Evils*. London: George Allen and Unwin.

Srole, L., Langner, T.S., Michael, S.T., Kirkpatrick, P., Opler, M.K. and Rennie, T.A.C. (1962) *Mental Health in the Metropolis: The Midtown Manhattan Study*. New York: McGraw-Hill.

Srole, L., Langner, T.S., Michael, S.T., Kirkpatrick, P., Opler, M.K. and Rennie, T.A.C. (1977) *Mental Health in the Metropolis: The Midtown Manhattan Study*, revised and enlarged edn. New York: Harper Torch Books.

Stagner, R. (1936) *Psychology of Personality*. New York: McGraw-Hill.

Stanton, A.H. and Schwartz, M.S. (1954) *The Mental Hospital*. New York: Basic Books.

Stewart, J.P. (1908) *The Diagnosis of Nervous Diseases*, 2nd edn. London: Edward Arnold.

Stewart, W.A. (1969) *Psychoanalysis: The First Ten Years, 1888–1898*. London: George Allen and Unwin.

Stoddart, W.H.B. (1908) *Mind and Its Disorders*, 1st edn. London: H.K. Lewis.

Stoddart, W.H.B. (1919) *Mind and Its Disorders*, 3rd edn. London: H.K. Lewis.

Stoddart, W.H.B. (1921) *Mind and Its Disorders*, 4th edn. London: H.K. Lewis.

Strauss, A., Schatzman, L., Ehrlich, D., Bucher, R. and Sabshin, M. (1963) 'The Hospital and its Negotiated Order', in E. Freidson (ed.), *The Hospital in Modern Society*. New York: Free Press. pp. 147–69.

Strauss, A., Schatzman, L., Bucher, R., Ehrlich, D. and Sabshin, M. (1981) *Psychiatric Ideologies and Institutions*. London: Transaction Books.

Strömgren, E. (1950) 'Statistical and Genetical Population Studies Within Psychiatry: Methods and Principal Results', *Congres Internationale de Psychiatrie Paris VI, Psychiatrie Sociale*, Paris: Hermann. pp. 155–88.

Sullivan, H.S. (1962) *Schizophrenia as a Human Process*. New York: W.W. Norton.

Sulloway, F.J. (1979) *Freud, Biologist of the Mind: Beyond the Psychoanalytic Legend*. New York: Basic Books.

Szasz, T. (1960) 'The myth of mental illness', *American Psychologist*, 15 Feb. 113–18.

Szasz, T. (1970) *The Manufacture of Madness*. New York: Harper and Row.

Tantam, D. (1991) 'The Anti-Psychiatry Movement', in G. Berrios and H. Freeman (eds), *150 Years of British Psychiatry: 1841–1991*. London: Gaskell. pp. 333–50.

Thompson, C. (1988) *The Instruments of Psychiatric Research*. Chichester: John Wiley.

Timms, N. (1960) 'Theorizing about Social Casework', *British Journal of Psychiatric Social Work*, 5: 70–4 and 137–41.

Timms, N. (1964) *Psychiatric Social Work in Great Britain (1939–62)*. London: Routledge and Kegan Paul.

Timms, N. and Timms, R. (1977) *Perspectives in Social Work*. London: Routledge and Kegan Paul.

Titmuss, R.M. (1963) 'Community Care – Fact or Fiction?', in H. Freeman and J. Farndale (eds), *Trends in Mental Health Services*. Oxford: Pergamon.

Toennies, F. (1971) *On Sociology: Pure, Applied and Empirical*, ed. W.J. Cahnman and R. Heberle. Chicago: University of Chicago Press.

Tomlinson, D.R. (1991) *Utopia, Community Care and the Retreat from the Asylum*. Milton Keynes: Open University Press.

Tredgold, A.F. (1922) *Mental Deficiency (Amentia)*, 4th edn. London: Baillière, Tindall and Cox.

Vogel, E.F. and Bell, N.W. (1968) 'The Emotionally Disturbed Child as the Family Scapegoat', in N.W. Bell and E.F. Vogel (eds), *A Modern Introduction to the*

Family. New York: Free Press. pp. 412–27.
Wagner-Jauregg, J. (1922) 'The Treatment of Paresis by Inoculation of Malaria', *Journal of Nervous and Mental Diseases*, 55 (5): 369–75.
Warner, R. (1985) *Recovery from Schizophrenia: Psychiatry and Political Economy*. London: Routledge and Kegan Paul.
Watson, G. (1953) 'Introduction', in M. Jones *et al*. *The Therapeutic Community. A New Treatment Method in Psychiatry*. New York: Basic Books.
Watson, J.B. (1925) *Behaviorism*. London: Kegan Paul.
Watson, J.B. and Reynor, R. (1919) 'Conditioned Emotional Reaction', *Journal of Experimental Psychology*, 3: 1–4.
Watson, R.I. (1977) *Selected Papers on the History of Psychology*, ed. J. Brodzek and R.B. Evans. Hanover: University of New Hampshire Press.
Weissert, W.G., Cready, C.M. and Pawelak, J.E. (1988) 'The Past and Future of Home and Community Based Long-Term Care', *The Milbank Quarterly*, 66 (2): 309–87.
Whipple, G.M. (1910) *Manual of Mental and Physical Tests*. Baltimore: Warwick and York.
Willard, H.S. and Spackman, C.S. (1947) *Principles of Occupational Therapy*. London: J.P. Lippincott.
Williams, G. (1988) 'The Movement for Independent Living: An Evaluation and Critique', *Social Science and Medicine*, 17 (15): 1003–10.
Willson, M. (1983) *Occupational Therapy in Long-Term Psychiatry*. Edinburgh: Churchill Livingstone.
Willson, M. (1984) *Occupational Therapy in Short-Term Psychiatry*. Edinburgh: Churchill Livingstone.
Winch, P. (1958) *The Idea of a Social Science and its Relation to Philosophy*. London: Routledge and Kegan Paul.
Wing, J.K. and Brown, B.W. (1970) *Institutionalism and Schizophrenia*. Cambridge: Cambridge University Press.
Wing, J.K., Bebbington, P. and Robins, L.N. (eds) (1981) *What is a Case? Problem of Definition in Psychiatric Community Surveys*. London: Grant McIntyre.
Winters, E.E. (ed.) (1952) *The Collected Papers of Adolf Meyer*, Vol. IV. Baltimore: Johns Hopkins Press.
Wittgenstein, L. (1967) *Philosophical Investigations*. Oxford: Blackwell.
Wittgenstein, L. (1969) *The Blue and Brown Books*. Oxford: Blackwell.
Wittgenstein, L. (1974) *On Certainty*. Oxford: Blackwell.
Wittgenstein, L. (1979) *Wittgenstein and the Vienna Circle*. Oxford: Blackwell.
Wolfensberger, W. (1972) *The Principle of Normalization in Human Services*. Toronto: National Institute on Mental Retardation.
Wolff, H., Bateman, A. and Sturgeon, D. (1990) *UCH Textbook of Psychiatry: An integrated approach*. London: Duckworth.
Wollheim, R. (1971) *Freud*. London: Fontana.
Woodworth, R.S. (1917) *Personal Data Sheet*. Chicago: C.H. Stoelting.
Woof, K. and Goldberg, D.P. (1988) 'Further Observations on the Practice of Community Care in Salford. Differences Between Community Psychiatric Nurses and Mental Health Social Workers', *British Journal of Psychiatry*, 153: 30–7.
Wootton, B. (1959) *Social Science and Social Pathology*. London: Allen and Unwin.
World Health Organization (1948) *Manual of the International Statistical Classification of Diseases, Injuries and Causes of Death*, 2 Vols, 6th revision. Geneva: World Health Organization.

World Health Organization (1953) *Expert Committee on Mental Health: Third Report*, No. 73. Geneva: World Health Organization.

World Health Organization (1957) *The Psychiatric Hospital as a Centre for Preventive Work in Mental Health: Expert Committee on Mental Health, Fifth Report*, No. 134. Geneva: World Health Organization.

World Health Organization (1961) *Teaching of Psychiatry and Mental Health:* Public Health Papers No. 9. Geneva: World Health Organization.

World Health Organization (1977) *Manual of the International Statistical Classification of Diseases, Injuries and Causes of Death*, 2 Vols, 9th revision. Geneva: World Health Organization.

Wynne, L.C., Ryckoff, I.M., Day, J. and Hirsch, S.I. (1958) 'Pseudo-Mutuality in the Family Relations of Schizophrenics'. Reprinted in N.W. Bell and E.F. Vogel (eds) (1968), *A Modern Introduction to the Family*. New York: Free Press.

Zorbaugh, H.W. (1929) *The Gold Coast and the Slum*. Chicago: Chicago University Press.

Official UK (Government) Publications

Board of Control:

(1929) *General Paralysis and Its Treatment by Induced Malaria*. London: HMSO.

(1931a) *Colonies for Mental Defectives: Report of the Departmental Committee on the Construction of Colonies*. London: HMSO.

(1931b) *The 17th Annual Report of the Board of Control 1930*. London: HMSO

(1933) *Memorandum on Occupational Therapy for Mental Patients*. London: HMSO.

(1940) *Suggestions and Instructions for the Arrangement, Planning and Construction of Mental Hospitals*. London: HMSO.

Board of Education and Board of Control:

(1929) *Report of the Mental Deficiency Committee* (Wood Committee). London: HMSO.

Department of Health:

(1990) *On the State of the Public Health: the Annual Report of the Chief Medical Officer*. London: HMSO.

(1992) *The Health of the Nation: A Strategy for Health in England*. London: HMSO.

Department of Health and Social Security:

(1975) *Better Services for the Mentally Ill*, Cmnd 6233. London: HMSO.

(1977a) *The Role of Psychologists in the Health Services* (Trethowan Committee). London: HMSO.

(1977b) *In-patient Statistics from the Mental Health Enquiry for England: 1974*. London: HMSO.

(1983) *Care in the Community*, HC(83)6 and LAC(83)5. London: HMSO.

(1984a) *In-patient Statistics from the Mental Health Enquiry for England: 1979*. London: HMSO.

(1984b) *In-patient Statistics from the Mental Health Enquiry for England: 1981*. London: HMSO.

(1985) *In-patient Statistics from the Mental Health Enquiry for England: 1982.* London: HMSO.

(1986) *Neighbourhood Nursing: A Focus for Care* (Cumberlege Report). London: HMSO.

Department of Health and Social Security Northern Ireland:

(1990a) *People First: Community Care in Northern Ireland for the 1990s.* Belfast: DHSS.

(1990b) *Health and Personal Social Services Statistics 1989–1990.* Belfast: DHSS.

Department of Social Services:

(1988) *Community Care: Agenda for Action. Report to the Secretary of State for Social Services by Sir Roy Griffiths.* London: HMSO.

Ministry of Health:

(1959) *Report of the Ministry of Health. Part II. On the State of the Public Health.* London: HMSO.

(1961) *Ministry Circular HM 61(25),* 28 March. London: HMSO.

(1963) *Health and Welfare: the Development of Community Care,* Cmnd 1973. London: HMSO.

(1966) *Central Health Services Council. The Post-Certificate Training and Education of Nurses. A Report by a Sub-Committee of the Standard Nursing Advisory Committee.* London: HMSO.

(1968) *Central Health Services Council. Psychiatric Nursing: Today and Tomorrow.* London: HMSO.

Inter-Departmental Committee (Ministries of Health, Labour, Pensions):

(1968) *Report of the Committee on Local Authority and Allied Personal Services,* Cmnd 3703 (Seebohm Report). London: HMSO.

Royal Commissions and Reports:

(1908) *Report of the Royal Commissioners on the Care and Control of the Feeble Minded.* (Radnor Report). London: HMSO.

(1926) *Report of the Royal Commissioners on Lunacy and Mental Deficiency* (Macmillan Commission). London: HMSO.

Miscellaneous:

(1901) *The Census of Ireland 1901: General Report.* Dublin: HMSO.

Index

abreaction, 68
  see also therapy
admissions
  to mental hospital, 38–40
  to wards in the study hospital, 148–9
after-care, *see* psychiatric social worker
age
  and mental illness, 111–12
  and social contact, 183
  in the study hospital, 147, 151
Alaszewski, A., 35
alcoholism, *see* categories of illness
Allport, G., 62
Althusser, L., 195
Alzheimer's disease, *see* categories of illness
amentia, *see* categories of illness
anti-institutionalism, 35, 39
anti-psychiatry movement, 137–8, 140
architecture
  of asylums and hospitals, 9, 11, 25–30
  of community facilities, 44–6, 179–80
  as a form of representation, 8–11, 25, 28
assessment of patients
  in the study hospital, 149
asylum
  as a community, 104, 120
  demise of word, 26, 29
  design of, 25
  logic of, 26, 31
  as a refuge, 152, 160
  see also mental hospital; nerve hospital; psychiatric hospital; psychiatric unit; psychopathic hospital
attendants of the insane
  in contrast to nurses, 29, 80
  as linchpins of a hospital, 35–6

Bachelard, Gaston, 16
back wards
  in the community, 190

back wards, *cont.*
  in the hospital, 150–1
Barclay, Sir Peter
  report on *Social Workers, Their Roles and Tasks*, 91, 93, 123, 144
Barnes, J.A.
  a new theorization of community, 122
Barton, R., 36
Bateson, G., 137
Bateson, W., 129
behaviour
  concept of, 100–1
  in the community, 183
  as a new object of study, 66
  in the study hospital, 101, 158
behaviourism, 100–1
Belknap, I., 35
Berger, Peter, 78, 102
Bertillon, J., 76
Bhaskar, R., 15
Bierer, J., 44–5
Binet, Alfred
  and psychometric tests, 98
biography
  as an object of sociological analysis, 2–3
  as an object of psychiatric study, 55, 64–5, 88, 118
Bleuler, Eugene, 78, 122
Board of Control, 24
  defines mental defect, 99
  and design of colonies, 26–7
  and evaluation of therapy, 52–3
  and occupational therapy, 94, 96
body
  as repository of illness, 50–61, 66, 161–2, 167
  as a target for therapy, 70–5, 152, 184, 187
  and the visibility of illness, 11–12, 36, 61
Bott, Elizabeth,
  and community, 122